50% OFF
Online GED Prep Course!

By Mometrix

Dear Customer,

We consider it an honor and a privilege that you chose our GED Study Guide. As a way of showing our appreciation and to help us better serve you, we are offering **50% off our online GED Prep Course.** Many GED courses cost hundreds of dollars and don't deliver enough value. With our course, you get access to the best GED prep material, and **you only pay half price**.

We have structured our online course to perfectly complement your printed study guide. Our GED Prep Course contains **over 140 lessons** that cover all the most important topics, **180+ video reviews** that explain difficult concepts, over **700 practice questions** to ensure you feel prepared, and over **400 digital flashcards**, so you can fit in some studying while you're on the go.

Online GED Prep Course

Topics Covered:
- Reasoning Through Language Arts
    - Reading Comprehension
    - Critical Thinking
    - Writing
- Mathematical Reasoning
    - Number Operations
    - Algebra, Functions, and Patterns
    - Measurement and Geometry
- Science
    - Physical Science
    - Earth and Space Science
- Social Studies
    - History and Government
    - Economics

Course Features:
- GED Study Guide
    - Get content that complements our best-selling study guide.
- 3 Full-Length Practice Tests
    - With over 700 practice questions, you can test yourself again and again.
- Mobile Friendly
    - If you need to study on the go, the course is easily accessible from your mobile device.
- GED Flashcards
    - Our course includes a flashcard mode consisting of over 400 content cards to help you study.

To receive this discount, visit us at mometrix.com/university/ged/ or simply scan this QR code with your smartphone. Enter code **ged50off** at checkout.

If you have any questions or concerns, please contact us at support@mometrix.com.

Sincerely,

FREE Study Skills Videos/DVD Offer

Dear Customer,

Thank you for your purchase from Mometrix! We consider it an honor and a privilege that you have purchased our product and we want to ensure your satisfaction.

As part of our ongoing effort to meet the needs of test takers, we have developed a set of Study Skills Videos that we would like to give you for FREE. These videos cover our *best practices* for getting ready for your exam, from how to use our study materials to how to best prepare for the day of the test.

All that we ask is that you email us with feedback that would describe your experience so far with our product. Good, bad, or indifferent, we want to know what you think!

To get your FREE Study Skills Videos, you can use the **QR code** below, or send us an **email** at studyvideos@mometrix.com with *FREE VIDEOS* in the subject line and the following information in the body of the email:

- The name of the product you purchased.
- Your product rating on a scale of 1-5, with 5 being the highest rating.
- Your feedback. It can be long, short, or anything in between. We just want to know your impressions and experience so far with our product. (Good feedback might include how our study material met your needs and ways we might be able to make it even better. You could highlight features that you found helpful or features that you think we should add.)

If you have any questions or concerns, please don't hesitate to contact me directly.

Thanks again!

Sincerely,

Jay Willis
Vice President
jay.willis@mometrix.com
1-800-673-8175

GED® Math
Preparation Book 2023-2024

3 Full-Length Practice Tests

GED Secrets Study Guide, Step-by-Step Video Tutorials

Certified Content Alignment

Copyright © 2022 by Mometrix Media LLC

All rights reserved. This product, or parts thereof, may not be reproduced, stored in a retrieval system, or transmitted in any form or by any means—electronic, mechanical, photocopy, recording, scanning, or other—except for brief quotations in critical reviews or articles, without the prior written permission of the publisher.

Written and edited by Mometrix

Printed in the United States of America

This paper meets the requirements of ANSI/NISO Z39.48-1992 (Permanence of Paper).

Mometrix offers volume discount pricing to institutions. For more information or a price quote, please contact our sales department at sales@mometrix.com or 888-248-1219.

Mometrix Media LLC is not affiliated with or endorsed by any official testing organization. All organizational and test names are trademarks of their respective owners.

Paperback
ISBN 13: 978-1-5167-2223-5
ISBN 10: 1-5167-2223-X

DEAR FUTURE EXAM SUCCESS STORY

First of all, **THANK YOU** for purchasing Mometrix study materials!

Second, congratulations! You are one of the few determined test-takers who are committed to doing whatever it takes to excel on your exam. **You have come to the right place.** We developed these study materials with one goal in mind: to deliver you the information you need in a format that's concise and easy to use.

In addition to optimizing your guide for the content of the test, we've outlined our recommended steps for breaking down the preparation process into small, attainable goals so you can make sure you stay on track.

We've also analyzed the entire test-taking process, identifying the most common pitfalls and showing how you can overcome them and be ready for any curveball the test throws you.

Standardized testing is one of the biggest obstacles on your road to success, which only increases the importance of doing well in the high-pressure, high-stakes environment of test day. Your results on this test could have a significant impact on your future, and this guide provides the information and practical advice to help you achieve your full potential on test day.

Your success is our success

We would love to hear from you! If you would like to share the story of your exam success or if you have any questions or comments in regard to our products, please contact us at **800-673-8175** or **support@mometrix.com**.

Thanks again for your business and we wish you continued success!

Sincerely,
The Mometrix Test Preparation Team

Need more help? Check out our flashcards at:
http://mometrixflashcards.com/GED

Table of Contents

Introduction	1
Secret Key #1 – Plan Big, Study Small	2
Secret Key #2 – Make Your Studying Count	3
Secret Key #3 – Practice the Right Way	4
Secret Key #4 – Pace Yourself	6
Secret Key #5 – Have a Plan for Guessing	7
Test-Taking Strategies	10
Mathematical Reasoning	15
Basic Math	15
Geometry	39
Statistics and Probability	62
Algebra	76
GED Math Practice Test #1	119
Answer Key and Explanations for Test #1	132
GED Math Practice Test #2	141
Answer Key and Explanations for Test #2	150
GED Math Practice Test #3	155
Answer Key and Explanations for Test #3	163
How to Overcome Test Anxiety	168
Causes of Test Anxiety	168
Elements of Test Anxiety	169
Effects of Test Anxiety	169
Physical Steps for Beating Test Anxiety	170
Mental Steps for Beating Test Anxiety	171
Study Strategy	172
Test Tips	174
Important Qualification	175
How to Overcome Your Fear of Math	176
What Is Math Anxiety?	176
Debunking Math Myths	179
Tips and Strategies for Overcoming Math Anxiety	180
Remember, You Can Do This!	182
Tell Us Your Story	183

Introduction

Thank you for purchasing this resource! You have made the choice to prepare yourself for a test that could have a huge impact on your future, and this guide is designed to help you be fully ready for test day. Obviously, it's important to have a solid understanding of the test material, but you also need to be prepared for the unique environment and stressors of the test, so that you can perform to the best of your abilities.

For this purpose, the first section that appears in this guide is the **Secret Keys**. We've devoted countless hours to meticulously researching what works and what doesn't, and we've boiled down our findings to the five most impactful steps you can take to improve your performance on the test. We start at the beginning with study planning and move through the preparation process, all the way to the testing strategies that will help you get the most out of what you know when you're finally sitting in front of the test.

We recommend that you start preparing for your test as far in advance as possible. However, if you've bought this guide as a last-minute study resource and only have a few days before your test, we recommend that you skip over the first two Secret Keys since they address a long-term study plan.

If you struggle with **test anxiety**, we strongly encourage you to check out our recommendations for how you can overcome it. Test anxiety is a formidable foe, but it can be beaten, and we want to make sure you have the tools you need to defeat it.

Secret Key #1 – Plan Big, Study Small

There's a lot riding on your performance. If you want to ace this test, you're going to need to keep your skills sharp and the material fresh in your mind. You need a plan that lets you review everything you need to know while still fitting in your schedule. We'll break this strategy down into three categories.

Information Organization

Start with the information you already have: the official test outline. From this, you can make a complete list of all the concepts you need to cover before the test. Organize these concepts into groups that can be studied together, and create a list of any related vocabulary you need to learn so you can brush up on any difficult terms. You'll want to keep this vocabulary list handy once you actually start studying since you may need to add to it along the way.

Time Management

Once you have your set of study concepts, decide how to spread them out over the time you have left before the test. Break your study plan into small, clear goals so you have a manageable task for each day and know exactly what you're doing. Then just focus on one small step at a time. When you manage your time this way, you don't need to spend hours at a time studying. Studying a small block of content for a short period each day helps you retain information better and avoid stressing over how much you have left to do. You can relax knowing that you have a plan to cover everything in time. In order for this strategy to be effective though, you have to start studying early and stick to your schedule. Avoid the exhaustion and futility that comes from last-minute cramming!

Study Environment

The environment you study in has a big impact on your learning. Studying in a coffee shop, while probably more enjoyable, is not likely to be as fruitful as studying in a quiet room. It's important to keep distractions to a minimum. You're only planning to study for a short block of time, so make the most of it. Don't pause to check your phone or get up to find a snack. It's also important to **avoid multitasking**. Research has consistently shown that multitasking will make your studying dramatically less effective. Your study area should also be comfortable and well-lit so you don't have the distraction of straining your eyes or sitting on an uncomfortable chair.

The time of day you study is also important. You want to be rested and alert. Don't wait until just before bedtime. Study when you'll be most likely to comprehend and remember. Even better, if you know what time of day your test will be, set that time aside for study. That way your brain will be used to working on that subject at that specific time and you'll have a better chance of recalling information.

Finally, it can be helpful to team up with others who are studying for the same test. Your actual studying should be done in as isolated an environment as possible, but the work of organizing the information and setting up the study plan can be divided up. In between study sessions, you can discuss with your teammates the concepts that you're all studying and quiz each other on the details. Just be sure that your teammates are as serious about the test as you are. If you find that your study time is being replaced with social time, you might need to find a new team.

Secret Key #2 – Make Your Studying Count

You're devoting a lot of time and effort to preparing for this test, so you want to be absolutely certain it will pay off. This means doing more than just reading the content and hoping you can remember it on test day. It's important to make every minute of study count. There are two main areas you can focus on to make your studying count.

Retention

It doesn't matter how much time you study if you can't remember the material. You need to make sure you are retaining the concepts. To check your retention of the information you're learning, try recalling it at later times with minimal prompting. Try carrying around flashcards and glance at one or two from time to time or ask a friend who's also studying for the test to quiz you.

To enhance your retention, look for ways to put the information into practice so that you can apply it rather than simply recalling it. If you're using the information in practical ways, it will be much easier to remember. Similarly, it helps to solidify a concept in your mind if you're not only reading it to yourself but also explaining it to someone else. Ask a friend to let you teach them about a concept you're a little shaky on (or speak aloud to an imaginary audience if necessary). As you try to summarize, define, give examples, and answer your friend's questions, you'll understand the concepts better and they will stay with you longer. Finally, step back for a big picture view and ask yourself how each piece of information fits with the whole subject. When you link the different concepts together and see them working together as a whole, it's easier to remember the individual components.

Finally, practice showing your work on any multi-step problems, even if you're just studying. Writing out each step you take to solve a problem will help solidify the process in your mind, and you'll be more likely to remember it during the test.

Modality

Modality simply refers to the means or method by which you study. Choosing a study modality that fits your own individual learning style is crucial. No two people learn best in exactly the same way, so it's important to know your strengths and use them to your advantage.

For example, if you learn best by visualization, focus on visualizing a concept in your mind and draw an image or a diagram. Try color-coding your notes, illustrating them, or creating symbols that will trigger your mind to recall a learned concept. If you learn best by hearing or discussing information, find a study partner who learns the same way or read aloud to yourself. Think about how to put the information in your own words. Imagine that you are giving a lecture on the topic and record yourself so you can listen to it later.

For any learning style, flashcards can be helpful. Organize the information so you can take advantage of spare moments to review. Underline key words or phrases. Use different colors for different categories. Mnemonic devices (such as creating a short list in which every item starts with the same letter) can also help with retention. Find what works best for you and use it to store the information in your mind most effectively and easily.

Secret Key #3 – Practice the Right Way

Your success on test day depends not only on how many hours you put into preparing, but also on whether you prepared the right way. It's good to check along the way to see if your studying is paying off. One of the most effective ways to do this is by taking practice tests to evaluate your progress. Practice tests are useful because they show exactly where you need to improve. Every time you take a practice test, pay special attention to these three groups of questions:

- The questions you got wrong
- The questions you had to guess on, even if you guessed right
- The questions you found difficult or slow to work through

This will show you exactly what your weak areas are, and where you need to devote more study time. Ask yourself why each of these questions gave you trouble. Was it because you didn't understand the material? Was it because you didn't remember the vocabulary? Do you need more repetitions on this type of question to build speed and confidence? Dig into those questions and figure out how you can strengthen your weak areas as you go back to review the material.

Additionally, many practice tests have a section explaining the answer choices. It can be tempting to read the explanation and think that you now have a good understanding of the concept. However, an explanation likely only covers part of the question's broader context. Even if the explanation makes perfect sense, **go back and investigate** every concept related to the question until you're positive you have a thorough understanding.

As you go along, keep in mind that the practice test is just that: practice. Memorizing these questions and answers will not be very helpful on the actual test because it is unlikely to have any of the same exact questions. If you only know the right answers to the sample questions, you won't be prepared for the real thing. **Study the concepts** until you understand them fully, and then you'll be able to answer any question that shows up on the test.

It's important to wait on the practice tests until you're ready. If you take a test on your first day of study, you may be overwhelmed by the amount of material covered and how much you need to learn. Work up to it gradually.

On test day, you'll need to be prepared for answering questions, managing your time, and using the test-taking strategies you've learned. It's a lot to balance, like a mental marathon that will have a big impact on your future. Like training for a marathon, you'll need to start slowly and work your way up. When test day arrives, you'll be ready.

Start with the strategies you've read in the first two Secret Keys—plan your course and study in the way that works best for you. If you have time, consider using multiple study resources to get different approaches to the same concepts. It can be helpful to see difficult concepts from more than one angle. Then find a good source for practice tests. Many times, the test website will suggest potential study resources or provide sample tests.

Practice Test Strategy

If you're able to find at least three practice tests, we recommend this strategy:

UNTIMED AND OPEN-BOOK PRACTICE

Take the first test with no time constraints and with your notes and study guide handy. Take your time and focus on applying the strategies you've learned.

TIMED AND OPEN-BOOK PRACTICE

Take the second practice test open-book as well, but set a timer and practice pacing yourself to finish in time.

TIMED AND CLOSED-BOOK PRACTICE

Take any other practice tests as if it were test day. Set a timer and put away your study materials. Sit at a table or desk in a quiet room, imagine yourself at the testing center, and answer questions as quickly and accurately as possible.

Keep repeating timed and closed-book tests on a regular basis until you run out of practice tests or it's time for the actual test. Your mind will be ready for the schedule and stress of test day, and you'll be able to focus on recalling the material you've learned.

Secret Key #4 – Pace Yourself

Once you're fully prepared for the material on the test, your biggest challenge on test day will be managing your time. Just knowing that the clock is ticking can make you panic even if you have plenty of time left. Work on pacing yourself so you can build confidence against the time constraints of the exam. Pacing is a difficult skill to master, especially in a high-pressure environment, so **practice is vital**.

Set time expectations for your pace based on how much time is available. For example, if a section has 60 questions and the time limit is 30 minutes, you know you have to average 30 seconds or less per question in order to answer them all. Although 30 seconds is the hard limit, set 25 seconds per question as your goal, so you reserve extra time to spend on harder questions. When you budget extra time for the harder questions, you no longer have any reason to stress when those questions take longer to answer.

Don't let this time expectation distract you from working through the test at a calm, steady pace, but keep it in mind so you don't spend too much time on any one question. Recognize that taking extra time on one question you don't understand may keep you from answering two that you do understand later in the test. If your time limit for a question is up and you're still not sure of the answer, mark it and move on, and come back to it later if the time and the test format allow. If the testing format doesn't allow you to return to earlier questions, just make an educated guess; then put it out of your mind and move on.

On the easier questions, be careful not to rush. It may seem wise to hurry through them so you have more time for the challenging ones, but it's not worth missing one if you know the concept and just didn't take the time to read the question fully. Work efficiently but make sure you understand the question and have looked at all of the answer choices, since more than one may seem right at first.

Even if you're paying attention to the time, you may find yourself a little behind at some point. You should speed up to get back on track, but do so wisely. Don't panic; just take a few seconds less on each question until you're caught up. Don't guess without thinking, but do look through the answer choices and eliminate any you know are wrong. If you can get down to two choices, it is often worthwhile to guess from those. Once you've chosen an answer, move on and don't dwell on any that you skipped or had to hurry through. If a question was taking too long, chances are it was one of the harder ones, so you weren't as likely to get it right anyway.

On the other hand, if you find yourself getting ahead of schedule, it may be beneficial to slow down a little. The more quickly you work, the more likely you are to make a careless mistake that will affect your score. You've budgeted time for each question, so don't be afraid to spend that time. Practice an efficient but careful pace to get the most out of the time you have.

Secret Key #5 – Have a Plan for Guessing

When you're taking the test, you may find yourself stuck on a question. Some of the answer choices seem better than others, but you don't see the one answer choice that is obviously correct. What do you do?

The scenario described above is very common, yet most test takers have not effectively prepared for it. Developing and practicing a plan for guessing may be one of the single most effective uses of your time as you get ready for the exam.

In developing your plan for guessing, there are three questions to address:

- When should you start the guessing process?
- How should you narrow down the choices?
- Which answer should you choose?

When to Start the Guessing Process

Unless your plan for guessing is to select C every time (which, despite its merits, is not what we recommend), you need to leave yourself enough time to apply your answer elimination strategies. Since you have a limited amount of time for each question, that means that if you're going to give yourself the best shot at guessing correctly, you have to decide quickly whether or not you will guess.

Of course, the best-case scenario is that you don't have to guess at all, so first, see if you can answer the question based on your knowledge of the subject and basic reasoning skills. Focus on the key words in the question and try to jog your memory of related topics. Give yourself a chance to bring the knowledge to mind, but once you realize that you don't have (or you can't access) the knowledge you need to answer the question, it's time to start the guessing process.

It's almost always better to start the guessing process too early than too late. It only takes a few seconds to remember something and answer the question from knowledge. Carefully eliminating wrong answer choices takes longer. Plus, going through the process of eliminating answer choices can actually help jog your memory.

Summary: Start the guessing process as soon as you decide that you can't answer the question based on your knowledge.

How to Narrow Down the Choices

The next chapter in this book (**Test-Taking Strategies**) includes a wide range of strategies for how to approach questions and how to look for answer choices to eliminate. You will definitely want to read those carefully, practice them, and figure out which ones work best for you. Here though, we're going to address a mindset rather than a particular strategy.

Your odds of guessing an answer correctly depend on how many options you are choosing from.

Number of options left	5	4	3	2	1
Odds of guessing correctly	20%	25%	33%	50%	100%

You can see from this chart just how valuable it is to be able to eliminate incorrect answers and make an educated guess, but there are two things that many test takers do that cause them to miss out on the benefits of guessing:

- Accidentally eliminating the correct answer
- Selecting an answer based on an impression

We'll look at the first one here, and the second one in the next section.

To avoid accidentally eliminating the correct answer, we recommend a thought exercise called **the $5 challenge**. In this challenge, you only eliminate an answer choice from contention if you are willing to bet $5 on it being wrong. Why $5? Five dollars is a small but not insignificant amount of money. It's an amount you could afford to lose but wouldn't want to throw away. And while losing

$5 once might not hurt too much, doing it twenty times will set you back $100. In the same way, each small decision you make—eliminating a choice here, guessing on a question there—won't by itself impact your score very much, but when you put them all together, they can make a big difference. By holding each answer choice elimination decision to a higher standard, you can reduce the risk of accidentally eliminating the correct answer.

The $5 challenge can also be applied in a positive sense: If you are willing to bet $5 that an answer choice *is* correct, go ahead and mark it as correct.

Summary: Only eliminate an answer choice if you are willing to bet $5 that it is wrong.

Which Answer to Choose

You're taking the test. You've run into a hard question and decided you'll have to guess. You've eliminated all the answer choices you're willing to bet $5 on. Now you have to pick an answer. Why do we even need to talk about this? Why can't you just pick whichever one you feel like when the time comes?

The answer to these questions is that if you don't come into the test with a plan, you'll rely on your impression to select an answer choice, and if you do that, you risk falling into a trap. The test writers know that everyone who takes their test will be guessing on some of the questions, so they intentionally write wrong answer choices to seem plausible. You still have to pick an answer though, and if the wrong answer choices are designed to look right, how can you ever be sure that you're not falling for their trap? The best solution we've found to this dilemma is to take the decision out of your hands entirely. Here is the process we recommend:

Once you've eliminated any choices that you are confident (willing to bet $5) are wrong, select the first remaining choice as your answer.

Whether you choose to select the first remaining choice, the second, or the last, the important thing is that you use some preselected standard. Using this approach guarantees that you will not be enticed into selecting an answer choice that looks right, because you are not basing your decision on how the answer choices look.

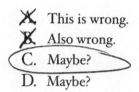

This is not meant to make you question your knowledge. Instead, it is to help you recognize the difference between your knowledge and your impressions. There's a huge difference between thinking an answer is right because of what you know, and thinking an answer is right because it looks or sounds like it should be right.

Summary: To ensure that your selection is appropriately random, make a predetermined selection from among all answer choices you have not eliminated.

Test-Taking Strategies

This section contains a list of test-taking strategies that you may find helpful as you work through the test. By taking what you know and applying logical thought, you can maximize your chances of answering any question correctly!

It is very important to realize that every question is different and every person is different: no single strategy will work on every question, and no single strategy will work for every person. That's why we've included all of them here, so you can try them out and determine which ones work best for different types of questions and which ones work best for you.

Question Strategies

⊘ READ CAREFULLY

Read the question and the answer choices carefully. Don't miss the question because you misread the terms. You have plenty of time to read each question thoroughly and make sure you understand what is being asked. Yet a happy medium must be attained, so don't waste too much time. You must read carefully and efficiently.

⊘ CONTEXTUAL CLUES

Look for contextual clues. If the question includes a word you are not familiar with, look at the immediate context for some indication of what the word might mean. Contextual clues can often give you all the information you need to decipher the meaning of an unfamiliar word. Even if you can't determine the meaning, you may be able to narrow down the possibilities enough to make a solid guess at the answer to the question.

⊘ PREFIXES

If you're having trouble with a word in the question or answer choices, try dissecting it. Take advantage of every clue that the word might include. Prefixes can be a huge help. Usually, they allow you to determine a basic meaning. *Pre-* means before, *post-* means after, *pro-* is positive, *de-* is negative. From prefixes, you can get an idea of the general meaning of the word and try to put it into context.

⊘ HEDGE WORDS

Watch out for critical hedge words, such as *likely, may, can, sometimes, often, almost, mostly, usually, generally, rarely,* and *sometimes.* Question writers insert these hedge phrases to cover every possibility. Often an answer choice will be wrong simply because it leaves no room for exception. Be on guard for answer choices that have definitive words such as *exactly* and *always.*

⊘ SWITCHBACK WORDS

Stay alert for *switchbacks*. These are the words and phrases frequently used to alert you to shifts in thought. The most common switchback words are *but, although,* and *however.* Others include *nevertheless, on the other hand, even though, while, in spite of, despite,* and *regardless of.* Switchback words are important to catch because they can change the direction of the question or an answer choice.

⊘ FACE VALUE

When in doubt, use common sense. Accept the situation in the problem at face value. Don't read too much into it. These problems will not require you to make wild assumptions. If you have to go beyond creativity and warp time or space in order to have an answer choice fit the question, then you should move on and consider the other answer choices. These are normal problems rooted in reality. The applicable relationship or explanation may not be readily apparent, but it is there for you to figure out. Use your common sense to interpret anything that isn't clear.

Answer Choice Strategies

⊘ ANSWER SELECTION

The most thorough way to pick an answer choice is to identify and eliminate wrong answers until only one is left, then confirm it is the correct answer. Sometimes an answer choice may immediately seem right, but be careful. The test writers will usually put more than one reasonable answer choice on each question, so take a second to read all of them and make sure that the other choices are not equally obvious. As long as you have time left, it is better to read every answer choice than to pick the first one that looks right without checking the others.

⊘ ANSWER CHOICE FAMILIES

An answer choice family consists of two (in rare cases, three) answer choices that are very similar in construction and cannot all be true at the same time. If you see two answer choices that are direct opposites or parallels, one of them is usually the correct answer. For instance, if one answer choice says that quantity x increases and another either says that quantity x decreases (opposite) or says that quantity y increases (parallel), then those answer choices would fall into the same family. An answer choice that doesn't match the construction of the answer choice family is more likely to be incorrect. Most questions will not have answer choice families, but when they do appear, you should be prepared to recognize them.

⊘ ELIMINATE ANSWERS

Eliminate answer choices as soon as you realize they are wrong, but make sure you consider all possibilities. If you are eliminating answer choices and realize that the last one you are left with is also wrong, don't panic. Start over and consider each choice again. There may be something you missed the first time that you will realize on the second pass.

⊘ AVOID FACT TRAPS

Don't be distracted by an answer choice that is factually true but doesn't answer the question. You are looking for the choice that answers the question. Stay focused on what the question is asking for so you don't accidentally pick an answer that is true but incorrect. Always go back to the question and make sure the answer choice you've selected actually answers the question and is not merely a true statement.

⊘ EXTREME STATEMENTS

In general, you should avoid answers that put forth extreme actions as standard practice or proclaim controversial ideas as established fact. An answer choice that states the "process should be used in certain situations, if..." is much more likely to be correct than one that states the "process should be discontinued completely." The first is a calm rational statement and doesn't even make a definitive, uncompromising stance, using a hedge word *if* to provide wiggle room, whereas the second choice is far more extreme.

⊘ Benchmark

As you read through the answer choices and you come across one that seems to answer the question well, mentally select that answer choice. This is not your final answer, but it's the one that will help you evaluate the other answer choices. The one that you selected is your benchmark or standard for judging each of the other answer choices. Every other answer choice must be compared to your benchmark. That choice is correct until proven otherwise by another answer choice beating it. If you find a better answer, then that one becomes your new benchmark. Once you've decided that no other choice answers the question as well as your benchmark, you have your final answer.

⊘ Predict the Answer

Before you even start looking at the answer choices, it is often best to try to predict the answer. When you come up with the answer on your own, it is easier to avoid distractions and traps because you will know exactly what to look for. The right answer choice is unlikely to be word-for-word what you came up with, but it should be a close match. Even if you are confident that you have the right answer, you should still take the time to read each option before moving on.

General Strategies

⊘ Tough Questions

If you are stumped on a problem or it appears too hard or too difficult, don't waste time. Move on! Remember though, if you can quickly check for obviously incorrect answer choices, your chances of guessing correctly are greatly improved. Before you completely give up, at least try to knock out a couple of possible answers. Eliminate what you can and then guess at the remaining answer choices before moving on.

⊘ Check Your Work

Since you will probably not know every term listed and the answer to every question, it is important that you get credit for the ones that you do know. Don't miss any questions through careless mistakes. If at all possible, try to take a second to look back over your answer selection and make sure you've selected the correct answer choice and haven't made a costly careless mistake (such as marking an answer choice that you didn't mean to mark). This quick double check should more than pay for itself in caught mistakes for the time it costs.

⊘ Pace Yourself

It's easy to be overwhelmed when you're looking at a page full of questions; your mind is confused and full of random thoughts, and the clock is ticking down faster than you would like. Calm down and maintain the pace that you have set for yourself. Especially as you get down to the last few minutes of the test, don't let the small numbers on the clock make you panic. As long as you are on track by monitoring your pace, you are guaranteed to have time for each question.

⊘ Don't Rush

It is very easy to make errors when you are in a hurry. Maintaining a fast pace in answering questions is pointless if it makes you miss questions that you would have gotten right otherwise. Test writers like to include distracting information and wrong answers that seem right. Taking a little extra time to avoid careless mistakes can make all the difference in your test score. Find a pace that allows you to be confident in the answers that you select.

⊘ Keep Moving

Panicking will not help you pass the test, so do your best to stay calm and keep moving. Taking deep breaths and going through the answer elimination steps you practiced can help to break through a stress barrier and keep your pace.

Final Notes

The combination of a solid foundation of content knowledge and the confidence that comes from practicing your plan for applying that knowledge is the key to maximizing your performance on test day. As your foundation of content knowledge is built up and strengthened, you'll find that the strategies included in this chapter become more and more effective in helping you quickly sift through the distractions and traps of the test to isolate the correct answer.

Now that you're preparing to move forward into the test content chapters of this book, be sure to keep your goal in mind. As you read, think about how you will be able to apply this information on the test. If you've already seen sample questions for the test and you have an idea of the question format and style, try to come up with questions of your own that you can answer based on what you're reading. This will give you valuable practice applying your knowledge in the same ways you can expect to on test day.

Good luck and good studying!

Mathematical Reasoning

Basic Math

NUMBERS

CLASSIFICATIONS OF NUMBERS

Numbers are the basic building blocks of mathematics. Specific features of numbers are identified by the following terms:

Integer – any positive or negative whole number, including zero. Integers do not include fractions $\left(\frac{1}{3}\right)$, decimals (0.56), or mixed numbers $\left(7\frac{3}{4}\right)$.

Prime number – any whole number greater than 1 that has only two factors, itself and 1; that is, a number that can be divided evenly only by 1 and itself.

Composite number – any whole number greater than 1 that has more than two different factors; in other words, any whole number that is not a prime number. For example: The composite number 8 has the factors of 1, 2, 4, and 8.

Even number – any integer that can be divided by 2 without leaving a remainder. For example: 2, 4, 6, 8, and so on.

Odd number – any integer that cannot be divided evenly by 2. For example: 3, 5, 7, 9, and so on.

Decimal number – any number that uses a decimal point to show the part of the number that is less than one. Example: 1.234.

Decimal point – a symbol used to separate the ones place from the tenths place in decimals or dollars from cents in currency.

Decimal place – the position of a number to the right of the decimal point. In the decimal 0.123, the 1 is in the first place to the right of the decimal point, indicating tenths; the 2 is in the second place, indicating hundredths; and the 3 is in the third place, indicating thousandths.

The **decimal**, or base 10, system is a number system that uses ten different digits (0, 1, 2, 3, 4, 5, 6, 7, 8, 9). An example of a number system that uses something other than ten digits is the **binary**, or base 2, number system, used by computers, which uses only the numbers 0 and 1. It is thought that the decimal system originated because people had only their 10 fingers for counting.

Rational numbers include all integers, decimals, and fractions. Any terminating or repeating decimal number is a rational number.

Irrational numbers cannot be written as fractions or decimals because the number of decimal places is infinite and there is no recurring pattern of digits within the number. For example, pi (π)

begins with 3.141592 and continues without terminating or repeating, so pi is an irrational number.

Real numbers are the set of all rational and irrational numbers.

> **Review Video and Practice: Classification of Numbers**
> Visit mometrix.com/academy and enter code: 461071
>
> **Review Video and Practice: Rational and Irrational Numbers**
> Visit mometrix.com/academy and enter code: 280645
>
> **Review Video and Practice: Prime and Composite Numbers**
> Visit mometrix.com/academy and enter code: 565581

THE NUMBER LINE

A number line is a graph to see the distance between numbers. Basically, this graph shows the relationship between numbers. So a number line may have a point for zero and may show negative numbers on the left side of the line. Any positive numbers are placed on the right side of the line. For example, consider the points labeled on the following number line:

We can use the dashed lines on the number line to identify each point. Each dashed line between two whole numbers is $\frac{1}{4}$. The line halfway between two numbers is $\frac{1}{2}$.

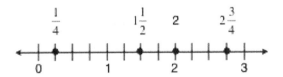

> **Review Video: The Number Line**
> Visit mometrix.com/academy and enter code: 816439

NUMBERS IN WORD FORM AND PLACE VALUE

When writing numbers out in word form or translating word form to numbers, it is essential to understand how a place value system works. In the decimal or base-10 system, each digit of a number represents how many of the corresponding place value – a specific factor of 10 – are contained in the number being represented. To make reading numbers easier, every three digits to the left of the decimal place is preceded by a comma. The following table demonstrates some of the place values:

Power of 10	10^3	10^2	10^1	10^0	10^{-1}	10^{-2}	10^{-3}
Value	1,000	100	10	1	0.1	0.01	0.001
Place	thousands	hundreds	tens	ones	tenths	hundredths	thousandths

For example, consider the number 4,546.09, which can be separated into each place value like this:

4: thousands
5: hundreds
4: tens
6: ones
0: tenths
9: hundredths

This number in word form would be *four thousand five hundred forty-six and nine hundredths*.

> **Review Video: Place Value**
> Visit mometrix.com/academy and enter code: 205433

ABSOLUTE VALUE

A precursor to working with negative numbers is understanding what **absolute values** are. A number's absolute value is simply the distance away from zero a number is on the number line. The absolute value of a number is always positive and is written $|x|$. For example, the absolute value of 3, written as $|3|$, is 3 because the distance between 0 and 3 on a number line is three units. Likewise, the absolute value of –3, written as $|-3|$, is 3 because the distance between 0 and –3 on a number line is three units. So $|3| = |-3|$.

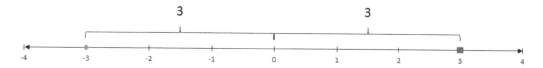

> **Review Video: Absolute Value**
> Visit mometrix.com/academy and enter code: 314669

PRACTICE

P1. Write the place value of each digit in 14,059.826

P2. Write out each of the following in words:

(a) 29
(b) 478
(c) 98,542
(d) 0.06
(e) 13.113

P3. Write each of the following in numbers:

(a) nine thousand four hundred thirty-five
(b) three hundred two thousand eight hundred seventy-six
(c) nine hundred one thousandths
(d) nineteen thousandths
(e) seven thousand one hundred forty-two and eighty-five hundredths

PRACTICE SOLUTIONS

P1. The place value for each digit would be as follows:

Digit	Place Value
1	ten-thousands
4	thousands
0	hundreds
5	tens
9	ones
8	tenths
2	hundredths
6	thousandths

P2. Each written out in words would be:

(a) twenty-nine
(b) four hundred seventy-eight
(c) ninety-eight thousand five hundred forty-two
(d) six hundredths
(e) thirteen and one hundred thirteen thousandths

P3. Each in numeric form would be:

(a) 9,435
(b) 302, 876
(c) 0.901
(d) 0.019
(e) 7,142.85

OPERATIONS

OPERATIONS

An **operation** is simply a mathematical process that takes some value(s) as input(s) and produces an output. Elementary operations are often written in the following form: *value operation value*. For instance, in the expression $1 + 2$ the values are 1 and 2 and the operation is addition. Performing the operation gives the output of 3. In this way we can say that $1 + 2$ and 3 are equal, or $1 + 2 = 3$.

ADDITION

Addition increases the value of one quantity by the value of another quantity (both called **addends**). For example, $2 + 4 = 6$; $8 + 9 = 17$. The result is called the **sum**. With addition, the order does not matter, $4 + 2 = 2 + 4$.

When adding signed numbers, if the signs are the same simply add the absolute values of the addends and apply the original sign to the sum. For example, $(+4) + (+8) = +12$ and $(-4) + (-8) = -12$. When the original signs are different, take the absolute values of the addends and subtract the smaller value from the larger value, then apply the original sign of the larger value to the difference. For instance, $(+4) + (-8) = -4$ and $(-4) + (+8) = +4$.

SUBTRACTION

Subtraction is the opposite operation to addition; it decreases the value of one quantity (the **minuend**) by the value of another quantity (the **subtrahend**). For example, $6 - 4 = 2$; $17 - 8 = 9$. The result is called the **difference**. Note that with subtraction, the order does matter, $6 - 4 \neq 4 - 6$.

For subtracting signed numbers, change the sign of the subtrahend and then follow the same rules used for addition. For example, $(+4) - (+8) = (+4) + (-8) = -4$.

MULTIPLICATION

Multiplication can be thought of as repeated addition. One number (the **multiplier**) indicates how many times to add the other number (the **multiplicand**) to itself. For example, 3×2 (three times two) $= 2 + 2 + 2 = 6$. With multiplication, the order does not matter: $2 \times 3 = 3 \times 2$ or $3 + 3 = 2 + 2 + 2$, either way the result (the **product**) is the same.

If the signs are the same the product is positive when multiplying signed numbers. For example, $(+4) \times (+8) = +32$ and $(-4) \times (-8) = +32$. If the signs are opposite, the product is negative. For example, $(+4) \times (-8) = -32$ and $(-4) \times (+8) = -32$. When more than two factors are multiplied together, the sign of the product is determined by how many negative factors are present. If there are an odd number of negative factors then the product is negative, whereas an even number of negative factors indicates a positive product. For instance, $(+4) \times (-8) \times (-2) = +64$ and $(-4) \times (-8) \times (-2) = -64$.

DIVISION

Division is the opposite operation to multiplication; one number (the **divisor**) tells us how many parts to divide the other number (the **dividend**) into. The result of division is called the **quotient**. For example, $20 \div 4 = 5$; if 20 is split into 4 equal parts, each part is 5. With division, the order of the numbers does matter, $20 \div 4 \neq 4 \div 20$.

The rules for dividing signed numbers are similar to multiplying signed numbers. If the dividend and divisor have the same sign, the quotient is positive. If the dividend and divisor have opposite signs, the quotient is negative. For example, $(-4) \div (+8) = -0.5$.

> **Review Video: Mathematical Operations**
> Visit mometrix.com/academy and enter code: 208095

PARENTHESES

Parentheses are used to designate which operations should be done first when there are multiple operations. Example: $4 - (2 + 1) = 1$; the parentheses tell us that we must add 2 and 1, and then subtract the sum from 4, rather than subtracting 2 from 4 and then adding 1 (this would give us an answer of 3).

> **Review Video: Mathematical Parentheses**
> Visit mometrix.com/academy and enter code: 978600

EXPONENTS

An **exponent** is a superscript number placed next to another number at the top right. It indicates how many times the base number is to be multiplied by itself. Exponents provide a shorthand way to write what would be a longer mathematical expression, for example: $2^4 = 2 \times 2 \times 2 \times 2$. A number with an exponent of 2 is said to be "squared," while a number with an exponent of 3 is said to be "cubed." The value of a number raised to an exponent is called its power. So 8^4 is read as "8 to the 4th power," or "8 raised to the power of 4."

The properties of exponents are as follows:

Property	Description
$a^1 = a$	Any number to the power of 1 is equal to itself
$1^n = 1$	The number 1 raised to any power is equal to 1
$a^0 = 1$	Any number raised to the power of 0 is equal to 1
$a^n \times a^m = a^{n+m}$	Add exponents to multiply powers of the same base number
$a^n \div a^m = a^{n-m}$	Subtract exponents to divide powers of the same base number
$(a^n)^m = a^{n \times m}$	When a power is raised to a power, the exponents are multiplied
$(a \times b)^n = a^n \times b^n$ $(a \div b)^n = a^n \div b^n$	Multiplication and division operations inside parentheses can be raised to a power. This is the same as each term being raised to that power.
$a^{-n} = \dfrac{1}{a^n}$	A negative exponent is the same as the reciprocal of a positive exponent

Note that exponents do not have to be integers. Fractional or decimal exponents follow all the rules above as well. Example: $5^{\frac{1}{4}} \times 5^{\frac{3}{4}} = 5^{\frac{1}{4}+\frac{3}{4}} = 5^1 = 5$.

> **Review Video: What is an Exponent?**
> Visit mometrix.com/academy and enter code: 600998
>
> **Review Video: Properties of Exponents**
> Visit mometrix.com/academy and enter code: 532558

ROOTS

A **root**, such as a square root, is another way of writing a fractional exponent. Instead of using a superscript, roots use the radical symbol ($\sqrt{}$) to indicate the operation. A radical will have a number underneath the bar, and may sometimes have a number in the upper left: $\sqrt[n]{a}$, read as "the nth root of a." The relationship between radical notation and exponent notation can be described by this equation: $\sqrt[n]{a} = a^{\frac{1}{n}}$. The two special cases of $n = 2$ and $n = 3$ are called square roots and cube roots. If there is no number to the upper left, it is understood to be a square root ($n = 2$). Nearly all of the roots you encounter will be square roots. A square root is the same as a number raised to the one-half power. When we say that a is the square root of b ($a = \sqrt{b}$), we mean that a multiplied by itself equals b: ($a \times a = b$).

A **perfect square** is a number that has an integer for its square root. There are 10 perfect squares from 1 to 100: 1, 4, 9, 16, 25, 36, 49, 64, 81, 100 (the squares of integers 1 through 10).

> **Review Video: Roots**
> Visit mometrix.com/academy and enter code: 795655
>
> **Review Video: Square Root and Perfect Squares**
> Visit mometrix.com/academy and enter code: 648063

ORDER OF OPERATIONS

The **order of operations** is a set of rules that dictates the order in which we must perform each operation in an expression so that we will evaluate it accurately. If we have an expression that includes multiple different operations, the order of operations tells us which operations to do first. The most common mnemonic for the order of operations is **PEMDAS**, or "Please Excuse My Dear Aunt Sally." PEMDAS stands for parentheses, exponents, multiplication, division, addition, and subtraction. It is important to understand that multiplication and division have equal precedence, as do addition and subtraction, so those pairs of operations are simply worked from left to right in order.

For example, evaluating the expression $5 + 20 \div 4 \times (2 + 3) - 6$ using the correct order of operations would be done like this:

- **P:** Perform the operations inside the parentheses: $(2 + 3) = 5$
- **E:** Simplify the exponents.
  - The equation now looks like this: $5 + 20 \div 4 \times 5 - 6$
- **MD:** Perform multiplication and division from left to right: $20 \div 4 = 5$; then $5 \times 5 = 25$
  - The equation now looks like this: $5 + 25 - 6$
- **AS:** Perform addition and subtraction from left to right: $5 + 25 = 30$; then $30 - 6 = 24$

> **Review Video: Order of Operations**
> Visit mometrix.com/academy and enter code: 259675

SUBTRACTION WITH REGROUPING

A great way to make use of some of the features built into the decimal system would be regrouping when attempting longform subtraction operations. When subtracting within a place value, sometimes the minuend is smaller than the subtrahend, **regrouping** enables you to 'borrow' a unit from a place value to the left in order to get a positive difference. For example, consider subtracting 189 from 525 with regrouping.

First, set up the subtraction problem in vertical form:

```
    525
-   189
```

Notice that the numbers in the ones and tens columns of 525 are smaller than the numbers in the ones and tens columns of 189. This means you will need to use regrouping to perform subtraction:

```
    5   2   5
-   1   8   9
```

To subtract 9 from 5 in the ones column you will need to borrow from the 2 in the tens columns:

```
    5   1   15
-   1   8    9
                6
```

Next, to subtract 8 from 1 in the tens column you will need to borrow from the 5 in the hundreds column:

```
    4   11   15
-   1    8    9
         3    6
```

Last, subtract the 1 from the 4 in the hundreds column:

$$\begin{array}{r} 4\;\;11\;\;15 \\ -\;\;1\;\;\;\;8\;\;\;\;9 \\ \hline 3\;\;\;\;3\;\;\;\;6 \end{array}$$

PRACTICE

P1. Demonstrate how to subtract 477 from 620 using regrouping.

P2. Simplify the following expressions with exponents:

  (a) 37^0
  (b) 1^{30}
  (c) $2^3 \times 2^4 \times 2^x$
  (d) $(3^x)^3$
  (e) $(12 \div 3)^2$

PRACTICE SOLUTIONS

P1. First, set up the subtraction problem in vertical form:

$$\begin{array}{r} 6\;\;2\;\;0 \\ -\;\;4\;\;7\;\;7 \end{array}$$

To subtract 7 from 0 in the ones column you will need to borrow from the 2 in the tens column:

$$\begin{array}{r} 6\;\;1\;\;10 \\ -\;\;4\;\;7\;\;\;\;7 \\ \hline 3 \end{array}$$

Next, to subtract 7 from the 1 that's still in the tens column you will need to borrow from the 6 in the hundreds column:

$$\begin{array}{r} 5\;\;11\;\;10 \\ -\;\;4\;\;\;\;7\;\;\;\;7 \\ \hline 4\;\;\;\;3 \end{array}$$

Lastly, subtract 4 from the 5 remaining in the hundreds column:

$$\begin{array}{r} 5\;\;11\;\;10 \\ -\;\;4\;\;\;\;7\;\;\;\;7 \\ \hline 1\;\;\;\;4\;\;\;\;3 \end{array}$$

P2. Using the properties of exponents and the proper order of operations:

  (a) Any number raised to the power of 0 is equal to 1: $37^0 = 1$
  (b) The number 1 raised to any power is equal to 1: $1^{30} = 1$
  (c) Add exponents to multiply powers of the same base: $2^3 \times 2^4 \times 2^x = 2^{(3+4+x)} = 2^{(7+x)}$
  (d) When a power is raised to a power, the exponents are multiplied: $(3^x)^3 = 3^{3x}$
  (e) Perform the operation inside the parentheses first: $(12 \div 3)^2 = 4^2 = 16$

FACTORING
FACTORS AND GREATEST COMMON FACTOR

Factors are numbers that are multiplied together to obtain a **product**. For example, in the equation $2 \times 3 = 6$, the numbers 2 and 3 are factors. A **prime number** has only two factors (1 and itself), but other numbers can have many factors.

A **common factor** is a number that divides exactly into two or more other numbers. For example, the factors of 12 are 1, 2, 3, 4, 6, and 12, while the factors of 15 are 1, 3, 5, and 15. The common factors of 12 and 15 are 1 and 3.

A **prime factor** is also a prime number. Therefore, the prime factors of 12 are 2 and 3. For 15, the prime factors are 3 and 5.

The **greatest common factor** (GCF) is the largest number that is a factor of two or more numbers. For example, the factors of 15 are 1, 3, 5, and 15; the factors of 35 are 1, 5, 7, and 35. Therefore, the greatest common factor of 15 and 35 is 5.

> **Review Video: Factors**
> Visit mometrix.com/academy and enter code: 920086
>
> **Review Video: GCF and LCM**
> Visit mometrix.com/academy and enter code: 838699

MULTIPLES AND LEAST COMMON MULTIPLE

Often listed out in multiplication tables, **multiples** are integer increments of a given factor. In other words, dividing a multiple by the factor number will result in an integer. For example, the multiples of 7 include: $1 \times 7 = 7$, $2 \times 7 = 14$, $3 \times 7 = 21$, $4 \times 7 = 28$, $5 \times 7 = 35$. Dividing 7, 14, 21, 28, or 35 by 7 will result in the integers 1, 2, 3, 4, and 5, respectively.

The least common multiple (**LCM**) is the smallest number that is a multiple of two or more numbers. For example, the multiples of 3 include 3, 6, 9, 12, 15, etc.; the multiples of 5 include 5, 10, 15, 20, etc. Therefore, the least common multiple of 3 and 5 is 15.

> **Review Video: Multiples**
> Visit mometrix.com/academy and enter code: 626738

RATIONAL NUMBERS
FRACTIONS

A **fraction** is a number that is expressed as one integer written above another integer, with a dividing line between them $\left(\frac{x}{y}\right)$. It represents the **quotient** of the two numbers "x divided by y." It can also be thought of as x out of y equal parts.

The top number of a fraction is called the **numerator**, and it represents the number of parts under consideration. The 1 in $\frac{1}{4}$ means that 1 part out of the whole is being considered in the calculation. The bottom number of a fraction is called the **denominator**, and it represents the total number of equal parts. The 4 in $\frac{1}{4}$ means that the whole consists of 4 equal parts. A fraction cannot have a denominator of zero; this is referred to as "*undefined.*"

Fractions can be manipulated, without changing the value of the fraction, by multiplying or dividing (but not adding or subtracting) both the numerator and denominator by the same number. If you divide both numbers by a common factor, you are **reducing** or simplifying the fraction. Two fractions that have the same value but are expressed differently are known as **equivalent fractions**. For example, $\frac{2}{10}, \frac{3}{15}, \frac{4}{20}$, and $\frac{5}{25}$ are all equivalent fractions. They can also all be reduced or simplified to $\frac{1}{5}$.

When two fractions are manipulated so that they have the same denominator, this is known as finding a **common denominator**. The number chosen to be that common denominator should be the least common multiple of the two original denominators. Example: $\frac{3}{4}$ and $\frac{5}{6}$; the least common multiple of 4 and 6 is 12. Manipulating to achieve the common denominator: $\frac{3}{4} = \frac{9}{12}; \frac{5}{6} = \frac{10}{12}$.

PROPER FRACTIONS AND MIXED NUMBERS

A fraction whose denominator is greater than its numerator is known as a **proper fraction**, while a fraction whose numerator is greater than its denominator is known as an **improper fraction**. Proper fractions have values *less than one* and improper fractions have values *greater than one*.

A **mixed number** is a number that contains both an integer and a fraction. Any improper fraction can be rewritten as a mixed number. Example: $\frac{8}{3} = \frac{6}{3} + \frac{2}{3} = 2 + \frac{2}{3} = 2\frac{2}{3}$. Similarly, any mixed number can be rewritten as an improper fraction. Example: $1\frac{3}{5} = 1 + \frac{3}{5} = \frac{5}{5} + \frac{3}{5} = \frac{8}{5}$.

> **Review Video: Improper Fractions and Mixed Numbers**
> Visit mometrix.com/academy and enter code: 211077
>
> **Review Video: Overview of Fractions**
> Visit mometrix.com/academy and enter code: 262335

ADDING AND SUBTRACTING FRACTIONS

If two fractions have a common denominator, they can be added or subtracted simply by adding or subtracting the two numerators and retaining the same denominator. If the two fractions do not already have the same denominator, one or both of them must be manipulated to achieve a common denominator before they can be added or subtracted. Example: $\frac{1}{2} + \frac{1}{4} = \frac{2}{4} + \frac{1}{4} = \frac{3}{4}$.

> **Review Video: Adding and Subtracting Fractions**
> Visit mometrix.com/academy and enter code: 378080

MULTIPLYING FRACTIONS

Two fractions can be multiplied by multiplying the two numerators to find the new numerator and the two denominators to find the new denominator. Example: $\frac{1}{3} \times \frac{2}{3} = \frac{1 \times 2}{3 \times 3} = \frac{2}{9}$.

DIVIDING FRACTIONS

Two fractions can be divided by flipping the numerator and denominator of the second fraction and then proceeding as though it were a multiplication. Example: $\frac{2}{3} \div \frac{3}{4} = \frac{2}{3} \times \frac{4}{3} = \frac{8}{9}$.

> **Review Video: Multiplying and Dividing Fractions**
> Visit mometrix.com/academy and enter code: 473632

MULTIPLYING A MIXED NUMBER BY A WHOLE NUMBER OR A DECIMAL

When multiplying a mixed number by something, it is usually best to convert it to an improper fraction first. Additionally, if the multiplicand is a decimal, it is most often simplest to convert it to a fraction. For instance, to multiply $4\frac{3}{8}$ by 3.5, begin by rewriting each quantity as a whole number plus a proper fraction. Remember, a mixed number is a fraction added to a whole number and a decimal is a representation of the sum of fractions, specifically tenths, hundredths, thousandths, and so on:

$$4\frac{3}{8} \times 3.5 = \left(4 + \frac{3}{8}\right) \times \left(3 + \frac{1}{2}\right)$$

Next, the quantities being added need to be expressed with the same denominator. This is achieved by multiplying and dividing the whole number by the denominator of the fraction. Recall that a whole number is equivalent to that number divided by 1:

$$= \left(\frac{4}{1} \times \frac{8}{8} + \frac{3}{8}\right) \times \left(\frac{3}{1} \times \frac{2}{2} + \frac{1}{2}\right)$$

When multiplying fractions, remember to multiply the numerators and denominators separately:

$$= \left(\frac{4 \times 8}{1 \times 8} + \frac{3}{8}\right) \times \left(\frac{3 \times 2}{1 \times 2} + \frac{1}{2}\right)$$
$$= \left(\frac{32}{8} + \frac{3}{8}\right) \times \left(\frac{6}{2} + \frac{1}{2}\right)$$

Now that the fractions have the same denominators, they can be added:

$$= \frac{35}{8} \times \frac{7}{2}$$

Finally, perform the last multiplication and then simplify:

$$= \frac{35 \times 7}{8 \times 2} = \frac{245}{16} = \frac{240}{16} + \frac{5}{16} = 15\frac{5}{16}$$

DECIMALS

Decimals are one way to represent parts of a whole. Using the place value system, each digit to the right of a decimal point denotes the number of units of a corresponding *negative* power of ten. For example, consider the decimal 0.24. We can use a model to represent the decimal. Since a dime is worth one-tenth of a dollar and a penny is worth one-hundredth of a dollar, one possible model to represent this fraction is to have 2 dimes representing the 2 in the tenths place and 4 pennies representing the 4 in the hundredths place:

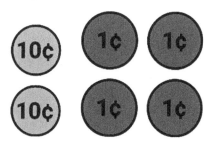

To write the decimal as a fraction, put the decimal in the numerator with 1 in the denominator. Multiply the numerator and denominator by tens until there are no more decimal places. Then simplify the fraction to lowest terms. For example, converting 0.24 to a fraction:

$$0.24 = \frac{0.24}{1} = \frac{0.24 \times 100}{1 \times 100} = \frac{24}{100} = \frac{6}{25}$$

> **Review Video: Decimals**
> Visit mometrix.com/academy and enter code: 837268

Adding and Subtracting Decimals

When adding and subtracting decimals, the decimal points must always be aligned. Adding decimals is just like adding regular whole numbers. Example: $4.5 + 2 = 6.5$.

If the problem-solver does not properly align the decimal points, an incorrect answer of 4.7 may result. An easy way to add decimals is to align all of the decimal points in a vertical column visually. This will allow you to see exactly where the decimal should be placed in the final answer. Begin adding from right to left. Add each column in turn, making sure to carry the number to the left if a column adds up to more than 9. The same rules apply to the subtraction of decimals.

> **Review Video: Adding and Subtracting Decimals**
> Visit mometrix.com/academy and enter code: 381101

Multiplying Decimals

A simple multiplication problem has two components: a **multiplicand** and a **multiplier**. When multiplying decimals, work as though the numbers were whole rather than decimals. Once the final product is calculated, count the number of places to the right of the decimal in both the multiplicand and the multiplier. Then, count that number of places from the right of the product and place the decimal in that position.

For example, 12.3×2.56 has a total of three places to the right of the respective decimals. Multiply 123×256 to get 31488. Now, beginning on the right, count three places to the left and insert the decimal. The final product will be 31.488.

> **Review Video: How to Multiply Decimals**
> Visit mometrix.com/academy and enter code: 731574

Dividing Decimals

Every division problem has a **divisor** and a **dividend**. The dividend is the number that is being divided. In the problem $14 \div 7$, 14 is the dividend and 7 is the divisor. In a division problem with decimals, the divisor must be converted into a whole number. Begin by moving the decimal in the divisor to the right until a whole number is created. Next, move the decimal in the dividend the same number of spaces to the right. For example, 4.9 into 24.5 would become 49 into 245. The decimal was moved one space to the right to create a whole number in the divisor, and then the same was done for the dividend. Once the whole numbers are created, the problem is carried out normally: $245 \div 49 = 5$.

> **Review Video: How to Divide Decimals**
> Visit mometrix.com/academy and enter code: 560690

PERCENTAGES

Percentages can be thought of as fractions that are based on a whole of 100; that is, one whole is equal to 100%. The word **percent** means "per hundred." Percentage problems are often presented in three main ways:

- Find what percentage of some number another number is.
    - Example: What percentage of 40 is 8?
- Find what number is some percentage of a given number.
    - Example: What number is 20% of 40?
- Find what number another number is a given percentage of.
    - Example: What number is 8 20% of?

There are three components in each of these cases: a **whole** (W), a **part** (P), and a **percentage** (%). These are related by the equation: $P = W \times \%$. This can easily be rearranged into other forms that may suit different questions better: $\% = \frac{P}{W}$ and $W = \frac{P}{\%}$. Percentage problems are often also word problems. As such, a large part of solving them is figuring out which quantities are what. For example, consider the following word problem:

In a school cafeteria, 7 students choose pizza, 9 choose hamburgers, and 4 choose tacos. What percentage of student choose tacos?

To find the whole, you must first add all of the parts: $7 + 9 + 4 = 20$. The percentage can then be found by dividing the part by the whole ($\% = \frac{P}{W}$): $\frac{4}{20} = \frac{20}{100} = 20\%$.

CONVERTING BETWEEN PERCENTAGES, FRACTIONS, AND DECIMALS

Converting decimals to percentages and percentages to decimals is as simple as moving the decimal point. To *convert from a decimal to a percentage*, move the decimal point **two places to the right**. To *convert from a percentage to a decimal*, move it **two places to the left**. It may be helpful to remember that the percentage number will always be larger than the equivalent decimal number. For example:

$$0.23 = 23\% \quad 5.34 = 534\% \quad 0.007 = 0.7\%$$
$$700\% = 7.00 \quad 86\% = 0.86 \quad 0.15\% = 0.0015$$

To convert a fraction to a decimal, simply divide the numerator by the denominator in the fraction. To convert a decimal to a fraction, put the decimal in the numerator with 1 in the denominator. Multiply the numerator and denominator by tens until there are no more decimal places. Then simplify the fraction to lowest terms. For example, converting 0.24 to a fraction:

$$0.24 = \frac{0.24}{1} = \frac{0.24 \times 100}{1 \times 100} = \frac{24}{100} = \frac{6}{25}$$

Fractions can be converted to a percentage by finding equivalent fractions with a denominator of 100. Example:

$$\frac{7}{10} = \frac{70}{100} = 70\% \quad \frac{1}{4} = \frac{25}{100} = 25\%$$

To convert a percentage to a fraction, divide the percentage number by 100 and reduce the fraction to its simplest possible terms. Example:

$$60\% = \frac{60}{100} = \frac{3}{5} \quad 96\% = \frac{96}{100} = \frac{24}{25}$$

> **Review Video: Converting Fractions to Percentages and Decimals**
> Visit mometrix.com/academy and enter code: 306233
>
> **Review Video: Converting Percentages to Decimals and Fractions**
> Visit mometrix.com/academy and enter code: 287297
>
> **Review Video: Converting Decimals to Fractions and Percentages**
> Visit mometrix.com/academy and enter code: 986765
>
> **Review Video: Converting Decimals, Improper Fractions, and Mixed Numbers**
> Visit mometrix.com/academy and enter code: 696924

RATIONAL NUMBERS

The term **rational** means that the number can be expressed as a ratio or fraction. That is, a number, r, is rational if and only if it can be represented by a fraction $\frac{a}{b}$ where a and b are integers and b does not equal 0. The set of rational numbers includes integers and decimals. If there is no finite way to represent a value with a fraction of integers, then the number is **irrational**. Common examples of irrational numbers include: $\sqrt{5}, (1 + \sqrt{2})$, and π.

> **Review Video: Rational and Irrational Numbers**
> Visit mometrix.com/academy and enter code: 280645

PRACTICE

P1. What is 30% of 120?

P2. What is 150% of 20?

P3. What is 14.5% of 96?

P4. Simplify the following expressions:

(a) $\left(\frac{2}{5}\right)/\left(\frac{4}{7}\right)$
(b) $\frac{7}{8} - \frac{8}{16}$
(c) $\frac{1}{2} + \left(3\left(\frac{3}{4}\right) - 2\right) + 4$
(d) $0.22 + 0.5 - (5.5 + 3.3 \div 3)$
(e) $\frac{3}{2} + (4(0.5) - 0.75) + 2$

P5. Convert the following to a fraction and to a decimal: **(a)** 15%; **(b)** 24.36%

P6. Convert the following to a decimal and to a percentage. **(a)** 4/5; **(b)** $3\frac{2}{5}$

P7. A woman's age is thirteen more than half of 60. How old is the woman?

P8. A patient was given pain medicine at a dosage of 0.22 grams. The patient's dosage was then increased to 0.80 grams. By how much was the patient's dosage increased?

P9. At a hotel, $\frac{3}{4}$ of the 100 rooms are occupied today. Yesterday, $\frac{4}{5}$ of the 100 rooms were occupied. On which day were more of the rooms occupied and by how much more?

P10. At a school, 40% of the teachers teach English. If 20 teachers teach English, how many teachers work at the school?

P11. A patient was given blood pressure medicine at a dosage of 2 grams. The patient's dosage was then decreased to 0.45 grams. By how much was the patient's dosage decreased?

P12. Two weeks ago, $\frac{2}{3}$ of the 60 customers at a skate shop were male. Last week, $\frac{3}{6}$ of the 80 customers were male. During which week were there more male customers?

P13. Jane ate lunch at a local restaurant. She ordered a $4.99 appetizer, a $12.50 entrée, and a $1.25 soda. If she wants to tip her server 20%, how much money will she spend in all?

P14. According to a survey, about 82% of engineers were highly satisfied with their job. If 145 engineers were surveyed, how many reported that they were highly satisfied?

P15. A patient was given 40 mg of a certain medicine. Later, the patient's dosage was increased to 45 mg. What was the percent increase in his medication?

P16. Order the following rational numbers from least to greatest: 0.55, 17%, $\sqrt{25}$, $\frac{64}{4}$, $\frac{25}{50}$, 3.

P17. Order the following rational numbers from greatest to least: 0.3, 27%, $\sqrt{100}$, $\frac{72}{9}$, $\frac{1}{9}$, 4.5.

P18. Perform the following multiplication. Write each answer as a mixed number.

(a) $\left(1\frac{11}{16}\right) \times 4$

(b) $\left(12\frac{1}{3}\right) \times 1.1$

(c) $3.71 \times \left(6\frac{1}{5}\right)$

P19. Suppose you are making doughnuts and you want to triple the recipe you have. If the following list is the original amounts for the ingredients, what would be the amounts for the tripled recipe?

$1\frac{3}{4}$	cup	Flour
$1\frac{1}{4}$	tsp	Baking powder
$\frac{3}{4}$	tsp	Salt
$\frac{3}{8}$	cup	Sugar
$1\frac{1}{2}$	Tbsp	Butter
2	large	Eggs
$\frac{3}{4}$	tsp	Vanilla extract
$\frac{3}{8}$	cup	Sour cream

PRACTICE SOLUTIONS

P1. The word *of* indicates multiplication, so 30% of 120 is found by multiplying 120 by 30%. Change 30% to a decimal, then multiply: $120 \times 0.3 = 36$

P2. The word *of* indicates multiplication, so 150% of 20 is found by multiplying 20 by 150%. Change 150% to a decimal, then multiply: $20 \times 1.5 = 30$

P3. Change 14.5% to a decimal before multiplying. $0.145 \times 96 = 13.92$.

P4. Follow the order of operations and utilize properties of fractions to solve each:

(a) Rewrite the problem as a multiplication problem: $\frac{2}{5} \times \frac{7}{4} = \frac{2 \times 7}{5 \times 4} = \frac{14}{20}$. Make sure the fraction is reduced to lowest terms. Both 14 and 20 can be divided by 2.

$$\frac{14}{20} = \frac{14 \div 2}{20 \div 2} = \frac{7}{10}$$

(b) The denominators of $\frac{7}{8}$ and $\frac{8}{16}$ are 8 and 16, respectively. The lowest common denominator of 8 and 16 is 16 because 16 is the least common multiple of 8 and 16. Convert the first fraction to its equivalent with the newly found common denominator of 16: $\frac{7 \times 2}{8 \times 2} = \frac{14}{16}$. Now that the fractions have the same denominator, you can subtract them.

$$\frac{14}{16} - \frac{8}{16} = \frac{6}{16} = \frac{3}{8}$$

(c) When simplifying expressions, first perform operations within groups. Within the set of parentheses are multiplication and subtraction operations. Perform the multiplication first to get $\frac{1}{2} + \left(\frac{9}{4} - 2\right) + 4$. Then, subtract two to obtain $\frac{1}{2} + \frac{1}{4} + 4$. Finally, perform addition from left to right:

$$\frac{1}{2} + \frac{1}{4} + 4 = \frac{2}{4} + \frac{1}{4} + \frac{16}{4} = \frac{19}{4} = 4\frac{3}{4}$$

(d) First, evaluate the terms in the parentheses $(5.5 + 3.3 \div 3)$ using order of operations. $3.3 \div 3 = 1.1$, and $5.5 + 1.1 = 6.6$. Next, rewrite the problem: $0.22 + 0.5 - 6.6$. Finally, add and subtract from left to right: $0.22 + 0.5 = 0.72$; $0.72 - 6.6 = -5.88$. The answer is -5.88.

(e) First, simplify within the parentheses, then change the fraction to a decimal and perform addition from left to right:

$$\frac{3}{2} + (2 - 0.75) + 2 =$$
$$\frac{3}{2} + 1.25 + 2 =$$
$$1.5 + 1.25 + 2 = 4.75$$

P5. (a) 15% can be written as $\frac{15}{100}$. Both 15 and 100 can be divided by 5: $\frac{15 \div 5}{100 \div 5} = \frac{3}{20}$

When converting from a percentage to a decimal, drop the percent sign and move the decimal point two places to the left: $15\% = 0.15$

(b) 24.36% written as a fraction is $\frac{24.36}{100}$, or $\frac{2436}{10,000}$, which reduces to $\frac{609}{2500}$. 24.36% written as a decimal is 0.2436. Recall that dividing by 100 moves the decimal two places to the left.

P6. (a) Recall that in the decimal system the first decimal place is one tenth: $\frac{4 \times 2}{5 \times 2} = \frac{8}{10} = 0.8$

Percent means "per hundred." $\frac{4 \times 20}{5 \times 20} = \frac{80}{100} = 80\%$

(b) The mixed number $3\frac{2}{5}$ has a whole number and a fractional part. The fractional part $\frac{2}{5}$ can be written as a decimal by dividing 5 into 2, which gives 0.4. Adding the whole to the part gives 3.4.

To find the equivalent percentage, multiply the decimal by 100. $3.4(100) = 340\%$. Notice that this percentage is greater than 100%. This makes sense because the original mixed number $3\frac{2}{5}$ is greater than 1.

P7. "More than" indicates addition, and "of" indicates multiplication. The expression can be written as $\frac{1}{2}(60) + 13$. So the woman's age is equal to $\frac{1}{2}(60) + 13 = 30 + 13 = 43$. The woman is 43 years old.

P8. The first step is to determine what operation (addition, subtraction, multiplication, or division) the problem requires. Notice the keywords and phrases "by how much" and "increased." "Increased" means that you go from a smaller amount to a larger amount. This change can be found by subtracting the smaller amount from the larger amount: 0.80 grams$- 0.22$ grams $= 0.58$ grams.

Remember to line up the decimal when subtracting:

$$\begin{array}{r} 0.80 \\ -\ 0.22 \\ \hline 0.58 \end{array}$$

P9. First, find the number of rooms occupied each day. To do so, multiply the fraction of rooms occupied by the number of rooms available:

$$\text{Number occupied} = \text{Fraction occupied} \times \text{Total number}$$
$$\text{Number of rooms occupied today} = \frac{3}{4} \times 100 = 75$$
$$\text{Number of rooms occupied} = \frac{4}{5} \times 100 = 80$$

The difference in the number of rooms occupied is: $80 - 75 = 5$ rooms

P10. To answer this problem, first think about the number of teachers that work at the school. Will it be more or less than the number of teachers who work in a specific department such as English? More teachers work at the school, so the number you find to answer this question will be greater than 20.

40% of the teachers are English teachers. "Of" indicates multiplication, and words like "is" and "are" indicate equivalence. Translating the problem into a mathematical sentence gives $40\% \times t = 20$, where t represents the total number of teachers. Solving for t gives $t = \frac{20}{40\%} = \frac{20}{0.40} = 50$. Fifty teachers work at the school.

P11. The decrease is represented by the difference between the two amounts:

$$2 \text{ grams} - 0.45 \text{ grams} = 1.55 \text{ grams}.$$

Remember to line up the decimal point before subtracting.

$$\begin{array}{r} 2.00 \\ -\ 0.45 \\ \hline 1.55 \end{array}$$

P12. First, you need to find the number of male customers that were in the skate shop each week. You are given this amount in terms of fractions. To find the actual number of male customers, multiply the fraction of male customers by the number of customers in the store.

$$\text{Actual number of male customers} = \text{fraction of male customers} \times \text{total customers}$$
$$\text{Number of male customers two weeks ago} = \frac{2}{3} \times 60 = \frac{120}{3} = 40$$
$$\text{Number of male customers last week} = \frac{3}{6} \times 80 = \frac{1}{2} \times 80 = \frac{80}{2} = 40$$

The number of male customers was the same both weeks.

P13. To find total amount, first find the sum of the items she ordered from the menu and then add 20% of this sum to the total.

$$\$4.99 + \$12.50 + \$1.25 = \$18.74$$

$$\$18.74 \times 20\% = (0.20)(\$18.74) = \$3.748 \approx \$3.75$$

$$\text{Total} = \$18.74 + \$3.75 = \$22.49$$

P14. 82% of 145 is $0.82 \times 145 = 118.9$. Because you can't have 0.9 of a person, we must round up to say that 119 engineers reported that they were highly satisfied with their jobs.

P15. To find the percent increase, first compare the original and increased amounts. The original amount was 40 mg, and the increased amount is 45 mg, so the dosage of medication was increased by 5 mg ($45 - 40 = 5$). Note, however, that the question asks not by how much the dosage increased but by what percentage it increased.

$$\text{Percent increase} = \frac{\text{new amount} - \text{original amount}}{\text{original amount}} \times 100\%$$
$$= \frac{45 \text{ mg} - 40 \text{ mg}}{40 \text{ mg}} \times 100\% = \frac{5}{40} \times 100\% = 0.125 \times 100\% = 12.5\%$$

P16. Recall that the term rational simply means that the number can be expressed as a ratio or fraction. Notice that each of the numbers in the problem can be written as a decimal or integer:

$$17\% = 0.1717$$
$$\sqrt{25} = 5$$
$$\frac{64}{4} = 16$$
$$\frac{25}{50} = \frac{1}{2} = 0.5$$

So, the answer is $17\%, \frac{25}{50}, 0.55, 3, \sqrt{25}, \frac{64}{4}$.

P17. Converting all the numbers to integers and decimals makes it easier to compare the values:

$$27\% = 0.27$$
$$\sqrt{100} = 10$$
$$\frac{72}{9} = 8$$
$$\frac{1}{9} \approx 0.11$$

So, the answer is $\sqrt{100}, \frac{72}{9}, 4.5, 0.3, 27\%, \frac{1}{9}$.

> **Review Video: Ordering Rational Numbers**
> Visit mometrix.com/academy and enter code: 419578

P18. For each, convert improper fractions, adjust to a common denominator, perform the operations, and then simplify:

(a) Sometimes, you can skip converting the denominator and just distribute the multiplication.

$$\left(1\frac{11}{16}\right) \times 4 = \left(1 + \frac{11}{16}\right) \times 4$$
$$= 1 \times 4 + \frac{11}{16} \times 4$$
$$= 4 + \frac{11}{16} \times \frac{4}{1}$$
$$= 4 + \frac{44}{16} = 4 + \frac{11}{4} = 4 + 2\frac{3}{4} = 6\frac{3}{4}$$

(b)

$$\left(12\frac{1}{3}\right) \times 1.1 = \left(12 + \frac{1}{3}\right) \times \left(1 + \frac{1}{10}\right)$$
$$= \left(\frac{12}{1} \times \frac{3}{3} + \frac{1}{3}\right) \times \left(\frac{10}{10} + \frac{1}{10}\right)$$
$$= \left(\frac{36}{3} + \frac{1}{3}\right) \times \frac{11}{10}$$
$$= \frac{37}{3} \times \frac{11}{10}$$
$$= \frac{407}{30} = \frac{390}{30} + \frac{17}{30} = 13\frac{17}{30}$$

(c)

$$3.71 \times \left(6\frac{1}{5}\right) = \left(3 + \frac{71}{100}\right) \times \left(6 + \frac{1}{5}\right)$$
$$= \left(\frac{300}{100} + \frac{71}{100}\right) \times \left(\frac{6}{1} \times \frac{5}{5} + \frac{1}{5}\right)$$
$$= \frac{371}{100} \times \left(\frac{30}{5} + \frac{1}{5}\right)$$
$$= \frac{371}{100} \times \frac{31}{5}$$
$$= \frac{11501}{500} = \frac{11500}{500} + \frac{1}{500} = 23\frac{1}{500}$$

P19. Fortunately, some of the amounts are duplicated, so we do not need to figure out every amount.

$$1\frac{3}{4} \times 3 = (1 \times 3) + \left(\frac{3}{4} \times 3\right)$$
$$= 3 + \frac{9}{4}$$
$$= 3 + 2\frac{1}{4}$$
$$= 5\frac{1}{4}$$

$$1\frac{1}{4} \times 3 = (1 \times 3) + \left(\frac{1}{4} \times 3\right)$$
$$= 3 + \frac{3}{4}$$
$$= 3\frac{3}{4}$$

$$\frac{3}{4} \times 3 = \frac{3}{4} \times 3$$
$$= \frac{9}{4}$$
$$= 2\frac{1}{4}$$

$$\frac{3}{8} \times 3 = \frac{3}{8} \times 3$$
$$= \frac{9}{8}$$
$$= 1\frac{1}{8}$$

$$1\frac{1}{2} \times 3 = 1 \times 3 + \frac{1}{2} \times 3$$
$$= 3 + \frac{3}{2}$$
$$= 3 + 1\frac{1}{2}$$
$$= 4\frac{1}{2}$$

$$2 \times 3 = 6$$

So, the result for the triple recipe is:

$5\frac{1}{4}$	cup	Flour
$3\frac{3}{4}$	tsp	Baking powder
$2\frac{1}{4}$	tsp	Salt
$1\frac{1}{8}$	cup	Sugar
$4\frac{1}{2}$	Tbsp	Butter
6	large	Eggs
$2\frac{1}{4}$	tsp	Vanilla extract
$1\frac{1}{8}$	cup	Sour cream

PROPORTIONS AND RATIOS
PROPORTIONS

A proportion is a relationship between two quantities that dictates how one changes when the other changes. A **direct proportion** describes a relationship in which a quantity increases by a set amount for every increase in the other quantity, or decreases by that same amount for every decrease in the other quantity. Example: Assuming a constant driving speed, the time required for a car trip increases as the distance of the trip increases. The distance to be traveled and the time required to travel are directly proportional.

An **inverse proportion** is a relationship in which an increase in one quantity is accompanied by a decrease in the other, or vice versa. Example: the time required for a car trip decreases as the speed increases, and increases as the speed decreases, so the time required is inversely proportional to the speed of the car.

> **Review Video: Proportions**
> Visit mometrix.com/academy and enter code: 505355

RATIOS

A **ratio** is a comparison of two quantities in a particular order. Example: If there are 14 computers in a lab, and the class has 20 students, there is a student to computer ratio of 20 to 14, commonly written as 20:14. Ratios are normally reduced to their smallest whole number representation, so 20:14 would be reduced to 10:7 by dividing both sides by 2.

> **Review Video: Ratios**
> Visit mometrix.com/academy and enter code: 996914

CONSTANT OF PROPORTIONALITY

When two quantities have a proportional relationship, there exists a **constant of proportionality** between the quantities. The product of this constant and one of the quantities is equal to the other quantity. For example, if one lemon costs $0.25, two lemons cost $0.50, and three lemons cost $0.75, there is a proportional relationship between the total cost of lemons and the number of lemons purchased. The constant of proportionality is the **unit price**, namely $0.25/lemon. Notice that the total price of lemons, t, can be found by multiplying the unit price of lemons, p, and the number of lemons, n: $t = pn$.

WORK/UNIT RATE

Unit rate expresses a quantity of one thing in terms of one unit of another. For example, if you travel 30 miles every two hours, a unit rate expresses this comparison in terms of one hour: in one hour you travel 15 miles, so your unit rate is 15 miles per hour. Other examples are how much one ounce of food costs (price per ounce) or figuring out how much one egg costs out of the dozen (price per 1 egg, instead of price per 12 eggs). The denominator of a unit rate is always 1. Unit rates are used to compare different situations to solve problems. For example, to make sure you get the best deal when deciding which kind of soda to buy, you can find the unit rate of each. If soda #1 costs $1.50 for a 1-liter bottle, and soda #2 costs $2.75 for a 2-liter bottle, it would be a better deal to buy soda #2, because its unit rate is only $1.375 per 1-liter, which is cheaper than soda #1. Unit rates can also help determine the length of time a given event will take. For example, if you can paint 2 rooms in 4.5 hours, you can determine how long it will take you to paint 5 rooms by solving for the unit rate per room and then multiplying that by 5.

> **Review Video: Rates and Unit Rates**
> Visit mometrix.com/academy and enter code: 185363

SLOPE

On a graph with two points, (x_1, y_1) and (x_2, y_2), the **slope** is found with the formula $m = \frac{y_2 - y_1}{x_2 - x_1}$; where $x_1 \neq x_2$ and m stands for slope. If the value of the slope is **positive**, the line has an *upward direction* from left to right. If the value of the slope is **negative**, the line has a *downward direction* from left to right. Consider the following example:

A new book goes on sale in bookstores and online stores. In the first month, 5,000 copies of the book are sold. Over time, the book continues to grow in popularity. The data for the number of copies sold is in the table below.

# of Months on Sale	1	2	3	4	5
# of Copies Sold (In Thousands)	5	10	15	20	25

So, the number of copies that are sold and the time that the book is on sale is a proportional relationship. In this example, an equation can be used to show the data: $y = 5x$, where x is the number of months that the book is on sale, and y is the number of copies sold. So the slope of the corresponding line is $\frac{\text{rise}}{\text{run}} = \frac{5}{1} = 5$.

> **Review Video: Finding the Slope of a Line**
> Visit mometrix.com/academy and enter code: 766664

FINDING AN UNKNOWN IN EQUIVALENT EXPRESSIONS

It is often necessary to apply information given about a rate or proportion to a new scenario. For example, if you know that Jedha can run a marathon (26 miles) in 3 hours, how long would it take her to run 10 miles at the same pace? Start by setting up equivalent expressions:

$$\frac{26 \text{ mi}}{3 \text{ hr}} = \frac{10 \text{ mi}}{x \text{ hr}}$$

Now, cross multiply and, solve for x:

$$26x = 30$$
$$x = \frac{30}{26} = \frac{15}{13}$$
$$x \cong 1.15 \text{ hrs } or \text{ 1 hr 9 min}$$

So, at this pace, Jedha could run 10 miles in about 1.15 hours or about 1 hour and 9 minutes.

PRACTICE

P1. Solve the following for x.

(a) $\frac{45}{12} = \frac{15}{x}$

(b) $\frac{0.50}{2} = \frac{1.50}{x}$

(c) $\frac{40}{8} = \frac{x}{24}$

P2. At a school, for every 20 female students there are 15 male students. This same student ratio happens to exist at another school. If there are 100 female students at the second school, how many male students are there?

P3. In a hospital emergency room, there are 4 nurses for every 12 patients. What is the ratio of nurses to patients? If the nurse-to-patient ratio remains constant, how many nurses must be present to care for 24 patients?

P4. In a bank, the banker-to-customer ratio is 1:2. If seven bankers are on duty, how many customers are currently in the bank?

P5. Janice made $40 during the first 5 hours she spent babysitting. She will continue to earn money at this rate until she finishes babysitting in 3 more hours. Find how much money Janice earns per hour and the total she earned babysitting.

P6. The McDonalds are taking a family road trip, driving 300 miles to their cabin. It took them 2 hours to drive the first 120 miles. They will drive at the same speed all the way to their cabin. Find the speed at which the McDonalds are driving and how much longer it will take them to get to their cabin.

P7. It takes Andy 10 minutes to read 6 pages of his book. He has already read 150 pages in his book that is 210 pages long. Find how long it takes Andy to read 1 page and also find how long it will take him to finish his book if he continues to read at the same speed.

PRACTICE SOLUTIONS

P1. First, cross multiply; then, solve for x:

(a) $45x = 12 \times 15$
$45x = 180$
$x = \frac{180}{45} = 4$

(b) $0.5x = 1.5 \times 2$
$0.5x = 3$
$x = \frac{3}{0.5} = 6$

(c) $8x = 40 \times 24$
$8x = 960$
$x = \frac{960}{8} = 120$

P2. One way to find the number of male students is to set up and solve a proportion.

$$\frac{\text{number of female students}}{\text{number of male students}} = \frac{20}{15} = \frac{100}{\text{number of male students}}$$

Represent the unknown number of male students as the variable x: $\frac{20}{15} = \frac{100}{x}$.

Cross multiply and then solve for x:

$$20x = 15 \times 100$$
$$x = \frac{1500}{20}$$
$$x = 75$$

P3. The ratio of nurses to patients can be written as 4 to 12, 4:12, or $\frac{4}{12}$. Because four and twelve have a common factor of four, the ratio should be reduced to 1:3, which means that there is one nurse present for every three patients. If this ratio remains constant, there must be eight nurses present to care for 24 patients.

P4. Use proportional reasoning or set up a proportion to solve. Because there are twice as many customers as bankers, there must be fourteen customers when seven bankers are on duty. Setting up and solving a proportion gives the same result:

$$\frac{\text{number of bankers}}{\text{number of customers}} = \frac{1}{2} = \frac{7}{\text{number of customers}}$$

Represent the unknown number of customers as the variable x: $\frac{1}{2} = \frac{7}{x}$.

To solve for x, cross multiply: $1 \times x = 7 \times 2$, so $x = 14$.

P5. Janice earns $8 per hour. This can be found by taking her initial amount earned, $40, and dividing it by the number of hours worked, 5. Since $\frac{40}{5} = 8$, Janice makes $8 in one hour. This can also be found by finding the unit rate, money earned per hour: $\frac{40}{5} = \frac{x}{1}$. Since cross multiplying yields $5x = 40$, and division by 5 shows that $x = 8$, Janice earns $8 per hour.

Janice will earn $64 babysitting in her 8 total hours (adding the first 5 hours to the remaining 3 gives the 8-hour total). Since Janice earns $8 per hour and she worked 8 hours, $\frac{\$8}{\text{hr}} \times 8 \text{ hrs} = \$64$. This can also be found by setting up a proportion comparing money earned to babysitting hours. Since she earns $40 for 5 hours and since the rate is constant, she will earn a proportional amount in 8 hours: $\frac{40}{5} = \frac{x}{8}$. Cross multiplying will yield $5x = 320$, and division by 5 shows that $x = 64$.

P6. The McDonalds are driving 60 miles per hour. This can be found by setting up a proportion to find the unit rate, the number of miles they drive per one hour: $\frac{120}{2} = \frac{x}{1}$. Cross multiplying yields $2x = 120$ and division by 2 shows that $x = 60$.

Since the McDonalds will drive this same speed for the remaining miles, it will take them another 3 hours to get to their cabin. This can be found by first finding how many miles the McDonalds have left to drive, which is $300 - 120 = 180$. The McDonalds are driving at 60 miles per hour, so a proportion can be set up to determine how many hours it will take them to drive 180 miles: $\frac{180}{x} = \frac{60}{1}$. Cross multiplying yields $60x = 180$, and division by 60 shows that $x = 3$. This can also be found by using the formula $D = r \times t$ (or distance = rate × time), where $180 = 60 \times t$, and division by 60 shows that $t = 3$.

P7. It takes Andy 10 minutes to read 6 pages, $\frac{10}{6} = 1\frac{2}{3}$ minutes, which is 1 minute and 40 seconds.

Next, determine how many pages Andy has left to read, $210 - 150 = 60$. Since it is now known that it takes him $1\frac{2}{3}$ minutes to read each page, then that rate must be multiplied by however many pages he has left to read (60) to find the time he'll need: $60 \times 1\frac{2}{3} = 100$, so it will take him 100 minutes, or 1 hour and 40 minutes, to read the rest of his book.

Geometry

LINES AND PLANES

A **point** is a fixed location in space, has no size or dimensions, and is commonly represented by a dot. A **line** is a set of points that extends infinitely in two opposite directions. It has length, but no width or depth. A line can be defined by any two distinct points that it contains. A **line segment** is a portion of a line that has definite endpoints. A **ray** is a portion of a line that extends from a single point on that line in one direction along the line. It has a definite beginning, but no ending.

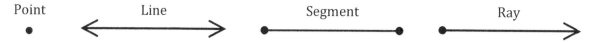

Intersecting lines are lines that have exactly one point in common. **Concurrent lines** are multiple lines that intersect at a single point. **Perpendicular lines** are lines that intersect at right angles. They are represented by the symbol ⊥. The shortest distance from a line to a point not on the line is a perpendicular segment from the point to the line. **Parallel lines** are lines in the same plane that have no points in common and never meet. It is possible for lines to be in different planes, have no points in common, and never meet, but they are not parallel because they are in different planes.

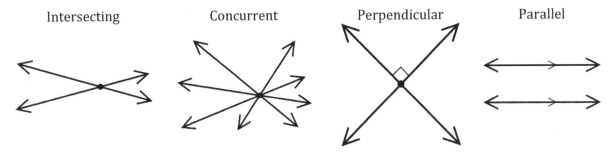

A **transversal** is a line that intersects at least two other lines, which may or may not be parallel to one another. A transversal that intersects parallel lines is a common occurrence in geometry. A **bisector** is a line or line segment that divides another line segment into two equal lengths. A **perpendicular bisector** of a line segment is composed of points that are equidistant from the endpoints of the segment it is dividing.

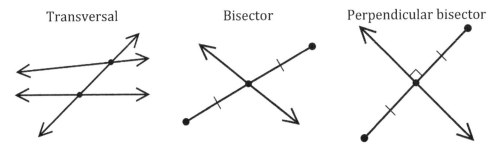

The **projection of a point on a line** is the point at which a perpendicular line drawn from the given point to the given line intersects the line. This is also the shortest distance from the given point to the line. The **projection of a segment on a line** is a segment whose endpoints are the points formed when perpendicular lines are drawn from the endpoints of the given segment to the given line. This is similar to the length a diagonal line appears to be when viewed from above.

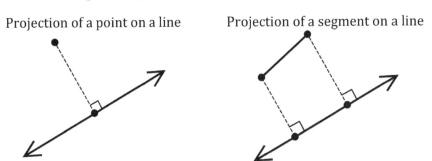

A **plane** is a two-dimensional flat surface defined by three non-collinear points. A plane extends an infinite distance in all directions in those two dimensions. It contains an infinite number of points, parallel lines and segments, intersecting lines and segments, as well as parallel or intersecting rays. A plane will never contain a three-dimensional figure or skew lines, which are lines that don't intersect and are not parallel. Two given planes are either parallel or they intersect at a line. A plane may intersect a circular conic surface to form **conic sections**, such as a parabola, hyperbola, circle or ellipse.

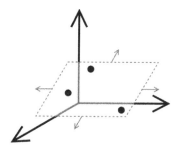

Review Video: Lines and Planes
Visit mometrix.com/academy and enter code: 554267

ANGLES

An **angle** is formed when two lines or line segments meet at a common point. It may be a common starting point for a pair of segments or rays, or it may be the intersection of lines. Angles are represented by the symbol ∠.

The **vertex** is the point at which two segments or rays meet to form an angle. If the angle is formed by intersecting rays, lines, and/or line segments, the vertex is the point at which four angles are formed. The pairs of angles opposite one another are called vertical angles, and their measures are equal.

- An **acute** angle is an angle with a degree measure less than 90°.
- A **right** angle is an angle with a degree measure of exactly 90°.
- An **obtuse** angle is an angle with a degree measure greater than 90° but less than 180°.
- A **straight angle** is an angle with a degree measure of exactly 180°. This is also a semicircle.
- A **reflex angle** is an angle with a degree measure greater than 180° but less than 360°.

A **full angle** is an angle with a degree measure of exactly 360°. This is also a circle.

Review Video: Angles
Visit mometrix.com/academy and enter code: 264624

Two angles whose sum is exactly 90° are said to be **complementary**. The two angles may or may not be adjacent. In a right triangle, the two acute angles are complementary.

Two angles whose sum is exactly 180° are said to be **supplementary**. The two angles may or may not be adjacent. Two intersecting lines always form two pairs of supplementary angles. Adjacent supplementary angles will always form a straight line.

Two angles that have the same vertex and share a side are said to be **adjacent**. Vertical angles are not adjacent because they share a vertex but no common side.

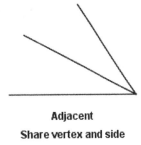
Adjacent
Share vertex and side

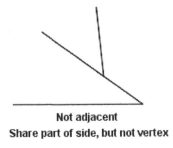
Not adjacent
Share part of side, but not vertex

When two parallel lines are cut by a transversal, the angles that are between the two parallel lines are **interior angles**. In the diagram below, angles 3, 4, 5, and 6 are interior angles.

When two parallel lines are cut by a transversal, the angles that are outside the parallel lines are **exterior angles**. In the diagram below, angles 1, 2, 7, and 8 are exterior angles.

When two parallel lines are cut by a transversal, the angles that are in the same position relative to the transversal and a parallel line are **corresponding angles**. The diagram below has four pairs of corresponding angles: angles 1 and 5; angles 2 and 6; angles 3 and 7; and angles 4 and 8. Corresponding angles formed by parallel lines are congruent.

When two parallel lines are cut by a transversal, the two interior angles that are on opposite sides of the transversal are called **alternate interior angles**. In the diagram below, there are two pairs of alternate interior angles: angles 3 and 6, and angles 4 and 5. Alternate interior angles formed by parallel lines are congruent.

When two parallel lines are cut by a transversal, the two exterior angles that are on opposite sides of the transversal are called **alternate exterior angles**.

In the diagram below, there are two pairs of alternate exterior angles: angles 1 and 8, and angles 2 and 7. Alternate exterior angles formed by parallel lines are congruent.

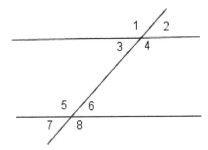

When two lines intersect, four angles are formed. The non-adjacent angles at this vertex are called vertical angles. Vertical angles are congruent. In the diagram, $\angle ABD \cong \angle CBE$ and $\angle ABC \cong \angle DBE$.

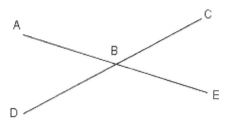

PRACTICE

P1. Find the measure of angles **(a)**, **(b)**, and **(c)** based on the figure with two parallel lines, two perpendicular lines and one transversal:

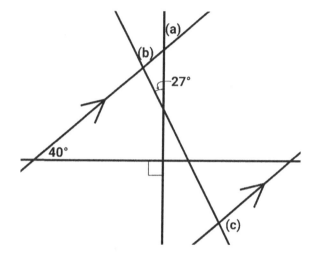

PRACTICE SOLUTIONS

P1. (a) The vertical angle paired with (a) is part of a right triangle with the 40° angle. Thus the measure can be found:

$$90° = 40° + a$$
$$a = 50°$$

(b) The triangle formed by the supplementary angle to (b) is part of a triangle with the vertical angle paired with (a) and the given angle of 27°. Since $a = 50°$:

$$180° = (180° - b) + 50° + 27°$$
$$103° = 180° - b$$
$$-77° = -b$$
$$77° = b$$

(c) As they are part of a transversal crossing parallel lines, angles (b) and (c) are supplementary. Thus $c = 103°$

$$V = \frac{1}{3}\pi r^2 h = \frac{1}{3}\pi (5 \text{ yd})^2 (7 \text{ yd}) = \frac{35\pi}{3} \text{ yd}^3 \cong 36.65 \text{ yd}^3$$

Two-Dimensional Shapes
Polygons

A **polygon** is a closed, two-dimensional figure with three or more straight line segments called **sides**. The point at which two sides of a polygon intersect is called the **vertex**. In a polygon, the number of sides is always equal to the number of vertices. A polygon with all sides congruent and all angles equal is called a **regular polygon**. Common polygons are:

$$\text{Triangle} = 3 \text{ sides}$$
$$\text{Quadrilateral} = 4 \text{ sides}$$
$$\text{Pentagon} = 5 \text{ sides}$$
$$\text{Hexagon} = 6 \text{ sides}$$
$$\text{Heptagon} = 7 \text{ sides}$$
$$\text{Octagon} = 8 \text{ sides}$$
$$\text{Nonagon} = 9 \text{ sides}$$
$$\text{Decagon} = 10 \text{ sides}$$
$$\text{Dodecagon} = 12 \text{ sides}$$

More generally, an n-gon is a polygon that has n angles and n sides.

The sum of the interior angles of an n-sided polygon is $(n - 2) \times 180°$. For example, in a triangle $n = 3$. So the sum of the interior angles is $(3 - 2) \times 180° = 180°$. In a quadrilateral, $n = 4$, and the sum of the angles is $(4 - 2) \times 180° = 360°$.

A line segment from the center of a polygon that is perpendicular to a side of the polygon is called the **apothem**. A line segment from the center of a polygon to a vertex of the polygon is called a **radius**. In a regular polygon, the apothem can be used to find the area of the polygon using the formula $A = \frac{1}{2}ap$, where a is the apothem, and p is the perimeter.

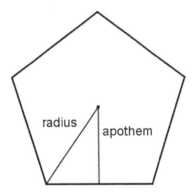

A **diagonal** is a line segment that joins two non-adjacent vertices of a polygon. The number of diagonals a polygon has can be found by using the formula:

$$\text{number of diagonals} = \frac{n(n - 3)}{2}$$

Note that n is the number of sides in the polygon. This formula works for all polygons, not just regular polygons.

A **convex polygon** is a polygon whose diagonals all lie within the interior of the polygon. A **concave polygon** is a polygon with a least one diagonal that is outside the polygon. In the diagram below, quadrilateral *ABCD* is concave because diagonal $\overline{AC}$ lies outside the polygon and quadrilateral *EFGH* is convex because both diagonals lie inside the polygon

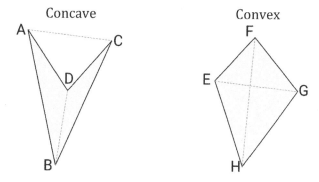

Congruent figures are geometric figures that have the same size and shape. All corresponding angles are equal, and all corresponding sides are equal. Congruence is indicated by the symbol ≅.

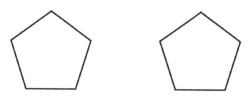

Congruent polygons

Similar figures are geometric figures that have the same shape, but do not necessarily have the same size. All corresponding angles are equal, and all corresponding sides are proportional, but they do not have to be equal. It is indicated by the symbol ~.

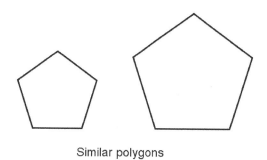

Similar polygons

Note that all congruent figures are also similar, but not all similar figures are congruent.

Review Video: Intro to Polygons
Visit mometrix.com/academy and enter code: 271869

LINE OF SYMMETRY

A line that divides a figure or object into congruent parts is called a **line of symmetry**. An object may have no lines of symmetry, one line of symmetry, or multiple (i.e., more than one) lines of symmetry.

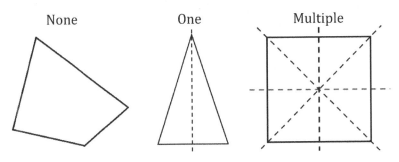

Review Video: Symmetry
Visit mometrix.com/academy and enter code: 528106

TRIANGLES

A triangle is a three-sided figure with the sum of its interior angles being 180° The **perimeter of any triangle** is found by summing the three side lengths; $P = a + b + c$. For an equilateral triangle, this is the same as $P = 3a$, where a is any side length, since all three sides are the same length.

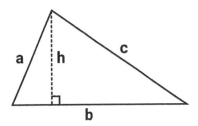

The **area of any triangle** can be found by taking half the product of one side length, referred to as the base and often given the variable b, and the perpendicular distance from that side to the opposite vertex, called the altitude or height and given the variable h. In equation form that is $A = \frac{1}{2}bh$. Another formula that works for any triangle is $A = \sqrt{s(s-a)(s-b)(s-c)}$, where s is the semiperimeter: $\frac{a+b+c}{2}$, and a, b, and c are the lengths of the three sides. Special cases include isosceles triangles: $A = \frac{1}{2}b\sqrt{a^2 - \frac{b^2}{4}}$, where b is the unique side and a is the length of one of the two congruent sides, and equilateral triangles: $A = \frac{\sqrt{3}}{4}a^2$, where a is the length of a side.

Review Video: Area and Perimeter of a Triangle
Visit mometrix.com/academy and enter code: 853779

PARTS OF A TRIANGLE

An **altitude** of a triangle is a line segment drawn from one vertex perpendicular to the opposite side. In the diagram below, $\overline{BE}$, $\overline{AD}$, and $\overline{CF}$ are altitudes. The length of an altitude is also called the height of the triangle. The three altitudes in a triangle are always concurrent. The point of concurrency of the altitudes of a triangle, O, is called the **orthocenter**. Note that in an obtuse triangle, the orthocenter will be outside the triangle, and in a right triangle, the orthocenter is the vertex of the right angle.

A **median** of a triangle is a line segment drawn from one vertex to the midpoint of the opposite side. In the diagram below, $\overline{BH}$, $\overline{AG}$, and $\overline{CI}$ are medians. This is not the same as the altitude, except the altitude to the base of an isosceles triangle and all three altitudes of an equilateral triangle. The point of concurrency of the medians of a triangle, T, is called the **centroid**. This is the same point as the orthocenter only in an equilateral triangle. Unlike the orthocenter, the centroid is always inside the triangle. The centroid can also be considered the exact center of the triangle. Any shape triangle can be perfectly balanced on a tip placed at the centroid. The centroid is also the point that is two-thirds the distance from the vertex to the opposite side.

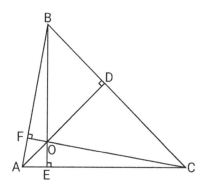
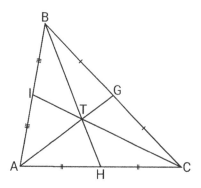

Review Video: Incenter, Circumcenter, Orthocenter, and Centroid
Visit mometrix.com/academy and enter code: 598260

QUADRILATERALS

A **quadrilateral** is a closed two-dimensional geometric figure that has four straight sides. The sum of the interior angles of any quadrilateral is 360°.

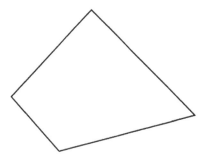

A **kite** is a quadrilateral with two pairs of adjacent sides that are congruent. A result of this is perpendicular diagonals. A kite can be concave or convex and has one line of symmetry.

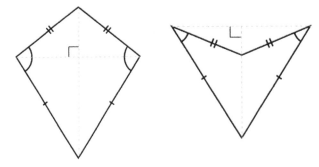

Trapezoid: A trapezoid is defined as a quadrilateral that has at least one pair of parallel sides. There are no rules for the second pair of sides. So there are no rules for the diagonals and no lines of symmetry for a trapezoid.

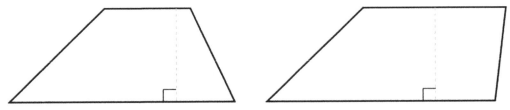

The **area of a trapezoid** is found by the formula $A = \frac{1}{2}h(b_1 + b_2)$, where h is the height (segment joining and perpendicular to the parallel bases), and b_1 and b_2 are the two parallel sides (bases). Do not use one of the other two sides as the height unless that side is also perpendicular to the parallel bases.

The **perimeter of a trapezoid** is found by the formula $P = a + b_1 + c + b_2$, where a, b_1, c, and b_2 are the four sides of the trapezoid.

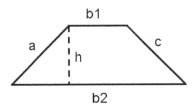

> **Review Video: Area and Perimeter of a Trapezoid**
> Visit mometrix.com/academy and enter code: 587523

Parallelogram: A quadrilateral that has two pairs of opposite parallel sides. As such it is a special type of trapezoid. The sides that are parallel are also congruent. The opposite interior angles are always congruent, and the consecutive interior angles are supplementary. The diagonals of a parallelogram divide each other. Each diagonal divides the parallelogram into two congruent triangles. A parallelogram has no line of symmetry, but does have 180-degree rotational symmetry about the midpoint.

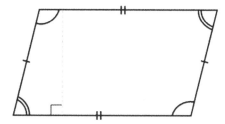

The **area of a parallelogram** is found by the formula $A = bh$, where b is the length of the base, and h is the height. Note that the base and height correspond to the length and width in a rectangle, so this formula would apply to rectangles as well. Do not confuse the height of a parallelogram with the length of the second side. The two are only the same measure in the case of a rectangle.

The **perimeter of a parallelogram** is found by the formula $P = 2a + 2b$ or $P = 2(a + b)$, where a and b are the lengths of the two sides.

> **Review Video: How to Find the Area and Perimeter of a Parallelogram**
> Visit mometrix.com/academy and enter code: 718313

Isosceles trapezoid: A trapezoid with equal base angles. This gives rise to other properties including: the two nonparallel sides have the same length, the two non-base angles are also equal, and there is one line of symmetry through the midpoints of the parallel sides.

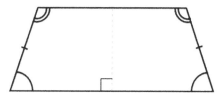

Rectangle: A quadrilateral with four right angles. All rectangles are parallelograms and trapezoids, but not all parallelograms or trapezoids are rectangles. The diagonals of a rectangle are congruent. Rectangles have 2 lines of symmetry (through each pair of opposing midpoints) and 180-degree rotational symmetry about the midpoint.

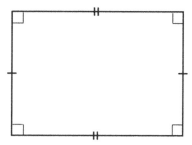

The **area of a rectangle** is found by the formula $A = lw$, where A is the area of the rectangle, l is the length (usually considered to be the longer side) and w is the width (usually considered to be the shorter side). The numbers for l and w are interchangeable.

The **perimeter of a rectangle** is found by the formula $P = 2l + 2w$ or $P = 2(l + w)$, where l is the length, and w is the width. It may be easier to add the length and width first and then double the result, as in the second formula.

Rhombus: A quadrilateral with four congruent sides. All rhombuses are parallelograms and kites; thus, they inherit all the properties of both types of quadrilaterals. The diagonals of a rhombus are perpendicular to each other. Rhombi have 2 lines of symmetry (along each of the diagonals) and 180-degree rotational symmetry. The **area of a rhombus** is half the product of the diagonals: $A = \frac{d_1 d_2}{2}$ and the perimeter of a rhombus is: $P = 2\sqrt{(d_1)^2 + (d_2)^2}$

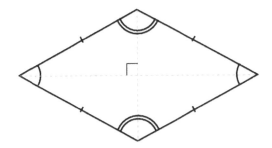

Review Video: Diagonals of Parallelograms, Rectangles, and Rhombi
Visit mometrix.com/academy and enter code: 320040

Square: A quadrilateral with four right angles and four congruent sides. Squares satisfy the criteria of all other types of quadrilaterals. The diagonals of a square are congruent and perpendicular to each other. Squares have 4 lines of symmetry (through each pair of opposing midpoints and along each of the diagonals) as well as 90-degree rotational symmetry about the midpoint.

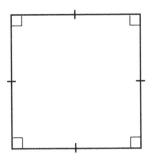

The **area of a square** is found by using the formula $A = s^2$, where s is the length of one side. The **perimeter of a square** is found by using the formula $P = 4s$, where s is the length of one side. Because all four sides are equal in a square, it is faster to multiply the length of one side by 4 than to add the same number four times. You could use the formulas for rectangles and get the same answer.

The hierarchy of quadrilaterals can be shown as follows:

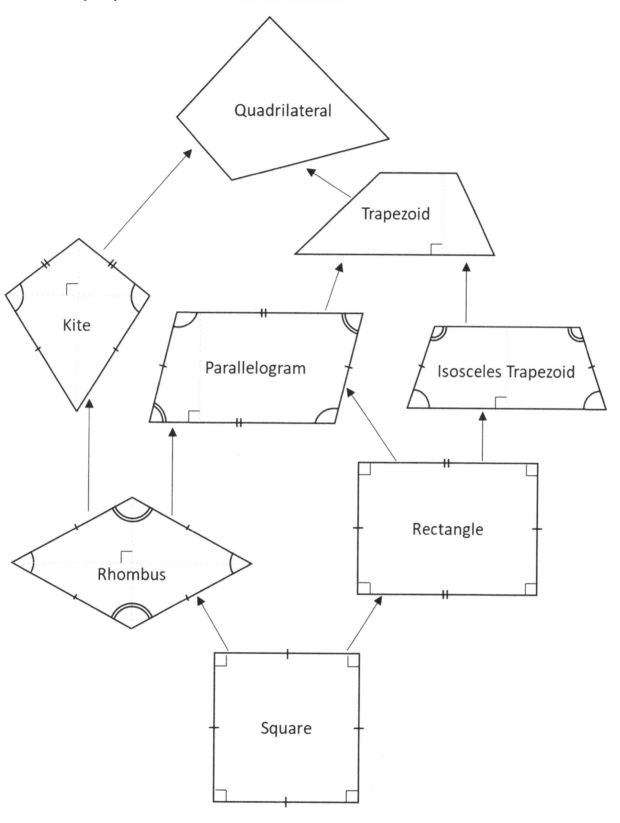

CIRCLES

The **center** of a circle is the single point from which every point on the circle is **equidistant**. The **radius** is a line segment that joins the center of the circle and any one point on the circle. All radii of a circle are equal. Circles that have the same center, but not the same length of radii are **concentric**. The **diameter** is a line segment that passes through the center of the circle and has both endpoints on the circle. The length of the diameter is exactly twice the length of the radius. Point O in the diagram below is the center of the circle, segments $\overline{OX}$, $\overline{OY}$, and $\overline{OZ}$ are radii, and segment $\overline{XZ}$ is a diameter.

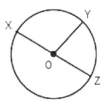

> **Review Video: Points of a Circle**
> Visit mometrix.com/academy and enter code: 420746
>
> **Review Video: The Diameter, Radius, and Circumference of Circles**
> Visit mometrix.com/academy and enter code: 448988

The **area of a circle** is found by the formula $A = \pi r^2$, where r is the length of the radius. If the diameter of the circle is given, remember to divide it in half to get the length of the radius before proceeding.

The **circumference** of a circle is found by the formula $C = 2\pi r$, where r is the radius. Again, remember to convert the diameter if you are given that measure rather than the radius.

> **Review Video: Area and Circumference of a Circle**
> Visit mometrix.com/academy and enter code: 243015

INSCRIBED AND CIRCUMSCRIBED FIGURES

These terms can both be used to describe a given arrangement of figures, depending on perspective. If each of the vertices of figure A lie on figure B, then it can be said that figure A is **inscribed** in figure B, but it can also be said that figure B is **circumscribed** about figure A. The following table and examples help to illustrate the concept. Note that the figures cannot both be circles, as they would be completely overlapping and neither would be inscribed or circumscribed.

Given	Description	Equivalent Description	Figures
Each of the sides of a pentagon is tangent to a circle	The circle is inscribed in the pentagon	The pentagon is circumscribed about the circle	
Each of the vertices of a pentagon lie on a circle	The pentagon is inscribed in the circle	The circle is circumscribed about the pentagon	

PRACTICE

P1. Find the area and perimeter of the following quadrilaterals:

(a) A square with side length 2.5 cm.

(b) A parallelogram with height 3 m, base 4 m, and other side 6 m.

(c) A rhombus with diagonals 15 in and 20 in.

P2. Calculate the area of a triangle with side lengths of 7 ft, 8 ft, and 9 ft.

P3. Square ABCD is inscribed in a circle with radius 20 m. What is the area of the part of the circle outside of the square?

PRACTICE SOLUTIONS

P1. (a) $A = s^2 = (2.5 \text{ cm})^2 = 6.25 \text{ cm}^2$; $P = 4s = 4 \times 2.5 \text{ cm} = 10 \text{ cm}$

(b) $A = bh = (3 \text{ m})(4 \text{ m}) = 12 \text{ m}^2$; $P = 2a + 2b = 2 \times 6 \text{ m} + 2 \times 4 \text{ m} = 20 \text{ m}$

(c) $A = \frac{d_1 d_2}{2} = \frac{(15 \text{ in})(20 \text{ in})}{2} = 150 \text{ in}^2$;
$P = 2\sqrt{(d_1)^2 + (d_2)^2} = 2\sqrt{(15 \text{ in})^2 + (20 \text{ in})^2} = 2\sqrt{625 \text{ in}^2} = 50 \text{ in}$

P2. Given only side lengths, we can use the semi perimeter to the find the area based on the formula, $A = \sqrt{s(s-a)(s-b)(s-c)}$, where s is the semiperimeter, $\frac{a+b+c}{2} = \frac{7+8+9}{2} = 12$ ft:

$$A = \sqrt{12(12-7)(12-8)(12-9)}$$
$$= \sqrt{(12)(5)(4)(3)}$$
$$= 12\sqrt{5} \text{ ft}^2$$

P3. Begin by drawing a diagram of the situation, where we want to find the shaded area:

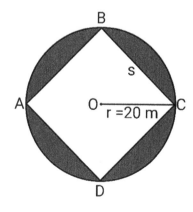
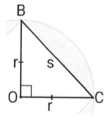

The area of the square is s^2, so the area we want to find is: $\pi r^2 - s^2$. Since the inscribed figure is a square, the triangle BCO is a 45-45-90 right triangle. Now we can find $s^2 = r^2 + r^2 = 2r^2$. So the shaded area is:

$$A = \pi r^2 - s^2$$
$$= \pi r^2 - 2r^2$$
$$= (\pi - 2)r^2$$
$$= (\pi - 2) \times 400$$
$$\cong 456.6 \text{ m}^2$$

THREE-DIMENSIONAL SHAPES
SOLIDS

The **surface area of a solid object** is the area of all sides or exterior surfaces. For objects such as prisms and pyramids, a further distinction is made between base surface area (B) and lateral surface area (LA). For a prism, the total surface area (SA) is $SA = LA + 2B$. For a pyramid or cone, the total surface area is $SA = LA + B$.

> **Review Video: How to Calculate the Volume of 3D Objects**
> Visit mometrix.com/academy and enter code: 163343

The **surface area of a sphere** can be found by the formula $A = 4\pi r^2$, where r is the radius. The volume is given by the formula $V = \frac{4}{3}\pi r^3$, where r is the radius. Both quantities are generally given in terms of π.

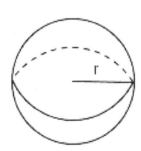

The **volume of any prism** is found by the formula $V = Bh$, where B is the area of the base, and h is the height (perpendicular distance between the bases). The surface area of any prism is the sum of the areas of both bases and all sides. It can be calculated as $SA = 2B + Ph$, where P is the perimeter of the base.

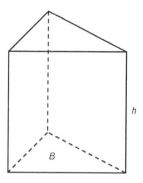

Review Video: Volume and Surface Area of a Prism
Visit mometrix.com/academy and enter code: 420158

For a **rectangular prism**, the volume can be found by the formula $V = lwh$, where V is the volume, l is the length, w is the width, and h is the height. The surface area can be calculated as $SA = 2lw + 2hl + 2wh$ or $SA = 2(lw + hl + wh)$.

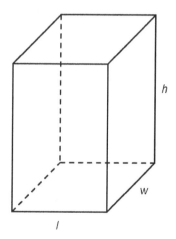

Review Video: Volume and Surface Area of a Rectangular Prism
Visit mometrix.com/academy and enter code: 282814

The **volume of a cube** can be found by the formula $V = s^3$, where s is the length of a side. The surface area of a cube is calculated as $SA = 6s^2$, where SA is the total surface area and s is the length of a side. These formulas are the same as the ones used for the volume and surface area of a rectangular prism, but simplified since all three quantities (length, width, and height) are the same.

Review Video: Volume and Surface Area of a Cube
Visit mometrix.com/academy and enter code: 664455

The **volume of a cylinder** can be calculated by the formula $V = \pi r^2 h$, where r is the radius, and h is the height. The surface area of a cylinder can be found by the formula $SA = 2\pi r^2 + 2\pi rh$. The first term is the base area multiplied by two, and the second term is the perimeter of the base multiplied by the height.

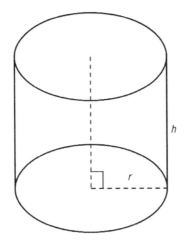

Review Video: Finding the Volume and Surface Area of a Right Circular Cylinder
Visit mometrix.com/academy and enter code: 226463

The **volume of a pyramid** is found by the formula $V = \frac{1}{3}Bh$, where B is the area of the base, and h is the height (perpendicular distance from the vertex to the base). Notice this formula is the same as $\frac{1}{3}$ times the volume of a prism. Like a prism, the base of a pyramid can be any shape.

Finding the **surface area of a pyramid** is not as simple as the other shapes we've looked at thus far. If the pyramid is a right pyramid, meaning the base is a regular polygon and the vertex is directly over the center of that polygon, the surface area can be calculated as $SA = B + \frac{1}{2}Ph_s$, where P is the perimeter of the base, and h_s is the slant height (distance from the vertex to the midpoint of one side of the base). If the pyramid is irregular, the area of each triangle side must be calculated individually and then summed, along with the base.

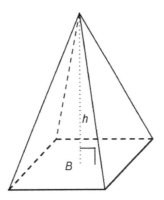

Review Video: Finding the Volume and Surface Area of a Pyramid
Visit mometrix.com/academy and enter code: 621932

The **volume of a cone** is found by the formula $V = \frac{1}{3}\pi r^2 h$, where r is the radius, and h is the height. Notice this is the same as $\frac{1}{3}$ times the volume of a cylinder. The surface area can be calculated as $SA = \pi r^2 + \pi r s$, where s is the slant height. The slant height can be calculated using the Pythagorean theorem to be $\sqrt{r^2 + h^2}$, so the surface area formula can also be written as $SA = \pi r^2 + \pi r\sqrt{r^2 + h^2}$.

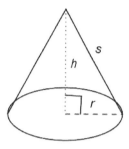

Review Video: Volume and Surface Area of a Right Circular Cone
Visit mometrix.com/academy and enter code: 573574

PRACTICE

P1. Find the surface area and volume of the following solids:

(a) A cylinder with radius 5 m and height 0.5 m.

(b) A trapezoidal prism with base area of 254 mm², base perimeter 74 mm, and height 10 mm.

(c) A half sphere (radius 5 yds) on the base of an inverted cone with the same radius and a height of 7 yds.

PRACTICE SOLUTIONS

P1. (a) $SA = 2\pi r^2 + 2\pi r h = 2\pi(5 \text{ m})^2 + 2\pi(5 \text{ m})(0.5 \text{ m}) = 55\pi \text{ m}^2 \cong 172.79 \text{ m}^2$;
$V = \pi r^2 h = \pi(5 \text{ m})^2(0.5 \text{ m}) = 12.5\pi \text{ m}^3 \cong 39.27 \text{ m}^3$

(b) $SA = 2B + Ph = 2(254 \text{ mm}^2) + (74 \text{ mm})(10 \text{ mm}) = 1248 \text{ mm}^2$;
$V = Bh = (254 \text{ mm}^2)(10 \text{ mm}) = 2540 \text{ mm}^3$

(c) We can find s, the slant height using the Pythagorean theorem, and since this solid is made of parts of simple solids, we can combine the formulas to find surface area and volume:

$$s = \sqrt{r^2 + h^2} = \sqrt{(5 \text{ yd})^2 + (7 \text{ yd})^2} = \sqrt{74} \text{ yd}$$

$$\begin{aligned}SA_{Total} &= (SA_{sphere})/2 + SA_{cone} - SA_{base} \\ &= \frac{4\pi r^2}{2} + (\pi r s + \pi r^2) - \pi r^2 \\ &= 2\pi(5 \text{ yd})^2 + \pi(5 \text{ yd})(\sqrt{74} \text{ yd}) \\ &= 5\pi(10 + \sqrt{74}) \text{ yd}^2 \\ &\cong 292.20 \text{ yd}^2\end{aligned}$$

$$\begin{aligned}V_{Total} &= (V_{sphere})/2 + V_{cone} \\ &= \frac{\frac{4}{3}\pi r^3}{2} + \frac{1}{3}\pi r^2 h \\ &= \frac{2}{3}\pi(5 \text{ yd})^3 + \frac{1}{3}\pi(5 \text{ yd})^2(7 \text{ yd}) \\ &= \frac{5^2 \times \pi}{3}(10 + 7) \text{ yd}^3 \\ &\cong 445.06 \text{ yd}^3\end{aligned}$$

TRIANGLE CLASSIFICATION AND PROPERTIES

A **scalene triangle** is a triangle with no congruent sides. A scalene triangle will also have three angles of different measures. The angle with the largest measure is opposite the longest side, and the angle with the smallest measure is opposite the shortest side. An **acute triangle** is a triangle whose three angles are all less than 90°. If two of the angles are equal, the acute triangle is also an **isosceles triangle**. An isosceles triangle will also have two congruent angles opposite the two congruent sides. If the three angles are all equal, the acute triangle is also an **equilateral triangle**. An equilateral triangle will also have three congruent angles, each 60°. All equilateral triangles are also acute triangles. An **obtuse triangle** is a triangle with exactly one angle greater than 90°. The other two angles may or may not be equal. If the two remaining angles are equal, the obtuse triangle is also an isosceles triangle. A **right triangle** is a triangle with exactly one angle equal to 90°. All right triangles follow the Pythagorean theorem. A right triangle can never be acute or obtuse.

The table below illustrates how each descriptor places a different restriction on the triangle:

Sides \ Angles	Acute: All angles < 90°	Obtuse: One angle > 90°	Right: One angle = 90°
Scalene: No equal side lengths	$90° > \angle a > \angle b > \angle c$ $x > y > z$	$\angle a > 90° > \angle b > \angle c$ $x > y > z$	$90° = \angle a > \angle b > \angle c$ $x > y > z$
Isosceles: Two equal side lengths	$90° > \angle a, \angle b, \text{or } \angle c$ $\angle b = \angle c, \quad y = z$	$\angle a > 90° > \angle b = \angle c$ $x > y = z$	$\angle a = 90°, \angle b = \angle c$ $= 45°$ $x > y = z$
Equilateral: Three equal side lengths	$60° = \angle a = \angle b = \angle c$ $x = y = z$		

Review Video: Introduction to Types of Triangles
Visit mometrix.com/academy and enter code: 511711

SIMILARITY AND CONGRUENCE RULES

Similar triangles are triangles whose corresponding angles are equal and whose corresponding sides are proportional. Represented by AAA. Similar triangles whose corresponding sides are congruent are also congruent triangles.

Triangles can be shown to be **congruent** in 5 ways:

- **SSS**: Three sides of one triangle are congruent to the three corresponding sides of the second triangle.
- **SAS**: Two sides and the included angle (the angle formed by those two sides) of one triangle are congruent to the corresponding two sides and included angle of the second triangle.
- **ASA**: Two angles and the included side (the side that joins the two angles) of one triangle are congruent to the corresponding two angles and included side of the second triangle.
- **AAS**: Two angles and a non-included side of one triangle are congruent to the corresponding two angles and non-included side of the second triangle.
- **HL**: The hypotenuse and leg of one right triangle are congruent to the corresponding hypotenuse and leg of the second right triangle.

> **Review Video: Similar Triangles**
> Visit mometrix.com/academy and enter code: 398538

GENERAL RULES FOR TRIANGLES

The **triangle inequality theorem** states that the sum of the measures of any two sides of a triangle is always greater than the measure of the third side. If the sum of the measures of two sides were equal to the third side, a triangle would be impossible because the two sides would lie flat across the third side and there would be no vertex. If the sum of the measures of two of the sides was less than the third side, a closed figure would be impossible because the two shortest sides would never meet. In other words, for a triangle with sides lengths A, B, and C: $A + B > C$, $B + C > A$, and $A + C > B$

The sum of the measures of the interior angles of a triangle is always 180°. Therefore, a triangle can never have more than one angle greater than or equal to 90°.

In any triangle, the angles opposite congruent sides are congruent, and the sides opposite congruent angles are congruent. The largest angle is always opposite the longest side, and the smallest angle is always opposite the shortest side.

The line segment that joins the midpoints of any two sides of a triangle is always parallel to the third side and exactly half the length of the third side.

PYTHAGOREAN THEOREM

The side of a triangle opposite the right angle is called the **hypotenuse**. The other two sides are called the legs. The Pythagorean theorem states a relationship among the legs and hypotenuse of a right triangle: $a^2 + b^2 = c^2$, where a and b are the lengths of the legs of a right triangle, and c is the length of the hypotenuse. Note that this formula will only work with right triangles.

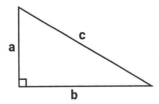

Review Video: Pythagorean Theorem
Visit mometrix.com/academy and enter code: 906576

PRACTICE

P1. Given the following pairs of triangles, determine whether they are similar, congruent, or neither (note that the figures are not drawn to scale):

(a).

(b).

(c).

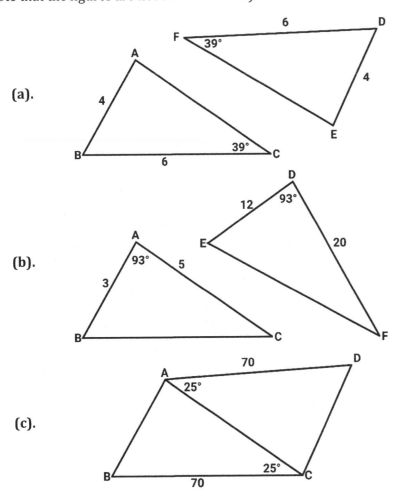

P2. Calculate the following values based on triangle MNO:

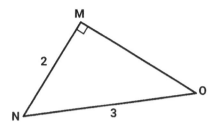

(a) length of $\overline{MO}$

(b) $\sin(\angle NOM)$

(c) area of the triangle, if the units of the measurements are in miles

Practice Solutions

P1. (a). Neither: We are given that two sides lengths and an angle are equal, however, the angle given is not between the given side lengths. That means there are two possible triangles that could satisfy the given measurements. Thus, we cannot be certain of congruence:

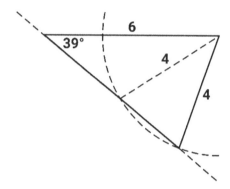

(b) Similar: Since we are given a side-angle-side of each triangle and the side lengths given are scaled evenly $\left(\frac{3}{5} \times \frac{4}{4} = \frac{12}{20}\right)$ and the angles are equal. Thus, $\triangle ABC \sim \triangle DEF$. If the side lengths were equal, then they would be congruent.

(c) Congruent: Even though we aren't given a measurement for the shared side of the figure, since it is shared it is equal. So, this is a case of SAS. Thus, $\triangle ABC \cong \triangle CDA$

P2. (a) Since triangle MNO is a right triangle, we can use the simple form of Pythagoras theorem to find the missing side length:

$$\left(\overline{MO}\right)^2 + 2^2 = 3^2$$
$$\left(\overline{MO}\right)^2 = 9 - 4$$
$$\overline{MO} = \sqrt{5}$$

(b) Recall that sine of an angle in a right triangle is the ratio of the opposite side to the hypotenuse. So, $\sin(\angle NOM) = 2/3$

(c) Since triangle MNO is a right triangle, we can use either of the legs as the height and the other as the base in the simple formula for the area of a triangle:

$$A = \frac{bh}{2}$$
$$= \frac{(2 \text{ mi})(\sqrt{5} \text{ mi})}{2}$$
$$= \sqrt{5} \text{ mi}^2$$

Statistics and Probability

DISPLAYING INFORMATION
FREQUENCY TABLES

Frequency tables show how frequently each unique value appears in a set. A **relative frequency table** is one that shows the proportions of each unique value compared to the entire set. Relative frequencies are given as percentages; however, the total percent for a relative frequency table will not necessarily equal 100 percent due to rounding. An example of a frequency table with relative frequencies is below.

Favorite Color	Frequency	Relative Frequency
Blue	4	13%
Red	7	22%
Green	3	9%
Purple	6	19%
Cyan	12	38%

> **Review Video: Data Interpretation of Graphs**
> Visit mometrix.com/academy and enter code: 200439

CIRCLE GRAPHS

Circle graphs, also known as *pie charts*, provide a visual depiction of the relationship of each type of data compared to the whole set of data. The circle graph is divided into sections by drawing radii to create central angles whose percentage of the circle is equal to the individual data's percentage of the whole set. Each 1% of data is equal to 3.6° in the circle graph. Therefore, data represented by a 90° section of the circle graph makes up 25% of the whole. When complete, a circle graph often looks like a pie cut into uneven wedges. The pie chart below shows the data from the frequency table referenced earlier where people were asked their favorite color.

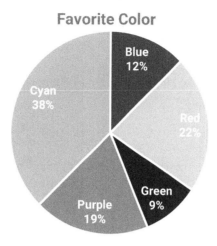

Pictographs

A **pictograph** is a graph, generally in the horizontal orientation, that uses pictures or symbols to represent the data. Each pictograph must have a key that defines the picture or symbol and gives the quantity each picture or symbol represents. Pictures or symbols on a pictograph are not always shown as whole elements. In this case, the fraction of the picture or symbol shown represents the same fraction of the quantity a whole picture or symbol stands for. For example, a row with $3\frac{1}{2}$ ears of corn, where each ear of corn represents 100 stalks of corn in a field, would equal $3\frac{1}{2} \times 100 = 350$ stalks of corn in the field.

Line Graphs

Line graphs have one or more lines of varying styles (solid or broken) to show the different values for a set of data. The individual data are represented as ordered pairs, much like on a Cartesian plane. In this case, the x- and y-axes are defined in terms of their units, such as dollars or time. The individual plotted points are joined by line segments to show whether the value of the data is increasing (line sloping upward), decreasing (line sloping downward) or staying the same (horizontal line). Multiple sets of data can be graphed on the same line graph to give an easy visual comparison. An example of this would be graphing achievement test scores for different groups of students over the same time period to see which group had the greatest increase or decrease in performance from year-to-year (as shown below).

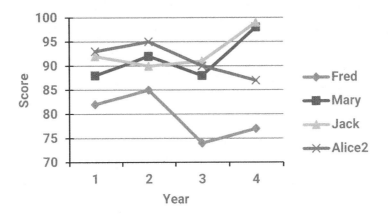

Review Video: **How to Create a Line Graph**
Visit mometrix.com/academy and enter code: 480147

LINE PLOTS

A **line plot**, also known as a *dot plot*, has plotted points that are not connected by line segments. In this graph, the horizontal axis lists the different possible values for the data, and the vertical axis lists the number of times the individual value occurs. A single dot is graphed for each value to show the number of times it occurs. This graph is more closely related to a bar graph than a line graph. Do not connect the dots in a line plot or it will misrepresent the data.

Review Video: **Line Plot**
Visit mometrix.com/academy and enter code: 754610

STEM AND LEAF PLOTS

A **stem and leaf plot** is useful for depicting groups of data that fall into a range of values. Each piece of data is separated into two parts: the first, or left, part is called the stem; the second, or right, part is called the leaf. Each stem is listed in a column from smallest to largest. Each leaf that has the common stem is listed in that stem's row from smallest to largest. For example, in a set of two-digit numbers, the digit in the tens place is the stem, and the digit in the ones place is the leaf. With a stem and leaf plot, you can easily see which subset of numbers (10s, 20s, 30s, etc.) is the largest. This information is also readily available by looking at a histogram, but a stem and leaf plot also allows you to look closer and see exactly which values fall in that range. Using all of the test scores from above, we can assemble a stem and leaf plot like the one below.

Test Scores

7	4	8						
8	2	5	7	8	8			
9	0	0	1	2	2	3	5	8	9

Review Video: **Stem-and-Leaf Plots**
Visit mometrix.com/academy and enter code: 302339

BAR GRAPHS

A **bar graph** is one of the few graphs that can be drawn correctly in two different configurations – both horizontally and vertically. A bar graph is similar to a line plot in the way the data is organized on the graph. Both axes must have their categories defined for the graph to be useful. Rather than placing a single dot to mark the point of the data's value, a bar, or thick line, is drawn from zero to the exact value of the data, whether it is a number, percentage, or other numerical value. Longer bar lengths correspond to greater data values. To read a bar graph, read the labels for the axes to find the units being reported. Then look where the bars end in relation to the scale given on the corresponding axis and determine the associated value.

The bar chart below represents the responses from our favorite color survey.

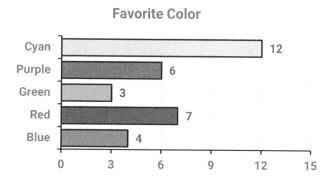

HISTOGRAMS

At first glance, a **histogram** looks like a vertical bar graph. The difference is that a bar graph has a separate bar for each piece of data and a histogram has one continuous bar for each *range* of data. For example, a histogram may have one bar for the range 0–9, one bar for 10–19, etc. While a bar graph has numerical values on one axis, a histogram has numerical values on both axes. Each range is of equal size, and they are ordered left to right from lowest to highest. The height of each column on a histogram represents the number of data values within that range. Like a stem and leaf plot, a histogram makes it easy to glance at the graph and quickly determine which range has the greatest quantity of values. A simple example of a histogram is below.

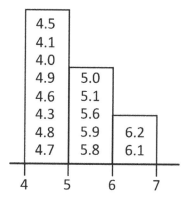

BIVARIATE DATA

Bivariate data is simply data from two different variables. (The prefix *bi-* means *two*.) In a *scatter plot*, each value in the set of data is plotted on a grid similar to a Cartesian plane, where each axis represents one of the two variables. By looking at the pattern formed by the points on the grid, you can often determine whether or not there is a relationship between the two variables, and what that relationship is, if it exists. The variables may be directly proportionate, inversely proportionate, or show no proportion at all. It may also be possible to determine if the data is linear, and if so, to find an equation to relate the two variables. The following scatter plot shows the relationship between preference for brand "A" and the age of the consumers surveyed.

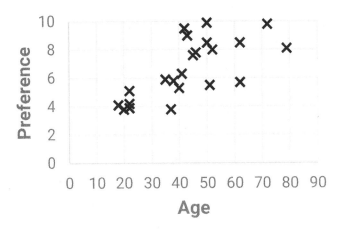

Scatter Plots

Scatter plots are also useful in determining the type of function represented by the data and finding the simple regression. Linear scatter plots may be positive or negative. Nonlinear scatter plots are generally exponential or quadratic. Below are some common types of scatter plots:

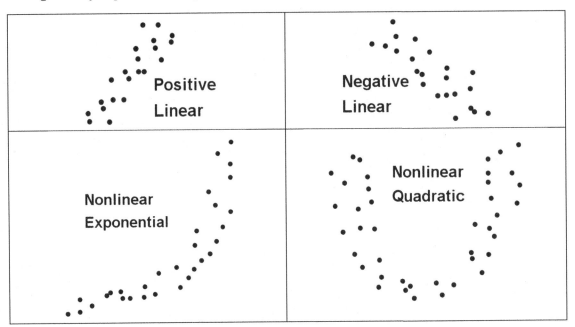

Review Video: **What is a Scatter Plot?**
Visit mometrix.com/academy and enter code: 596526

5-NUMBER SUMMARY

The **5-number summary** of a set of data gives a very informative picture of the set. The five numbers in the summary include the minimum value, maximum value, and the three quartiles. This information gives the reader the range and median of the set, as well as an indication of how the data is spread about the median.

BOX AND WHISKER PLOTS

A **box-and-whisker plot** is a graphical representation of the 5-number summary. To draw a box-and-whiskers plot, plot the points of the 5-number summary on a number line. Draw a box whose ends are through the points for the first and third quartiles. Draw a vertical line in the box through the median to divide the box in half. Draw a line segment from the first quartile point to the minimum value, and from the third quartile point to the maximum value.

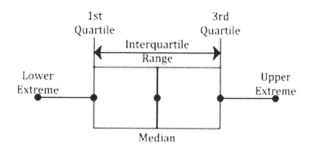

> **Review Video: Box and Whisker Plots**
> Visit mometrix.com/academy and enter code: 810817

68-95-99.7 RULE

The **68–95–99.7 rule** describes how a normal distribution of data should appear when compared to the mean. This is also a description of a normal bell curve. According to this rule, 68 percent of the data values in a normally distributed set should fall within one standard deviation of the mean (34 percent above and 34 percent below the mean), 95 percent of the data values should fall within two standard deviations of the mean (47.5 percent above and 47.5 percent below the mean), and 99.7 percent of the data values should fall within three standard deviations of the mean, again, equally distributed on either side of the mean. This means that only 0.3 percent of all data values should fall more than three standard deviations from the mean. On the graph below, the normal curve is centered on the y-axis. The x-axis labels are how many standard deviations away from the center you are. Therefore, it is easy to see how the 68-95-99.7 rule can apply.

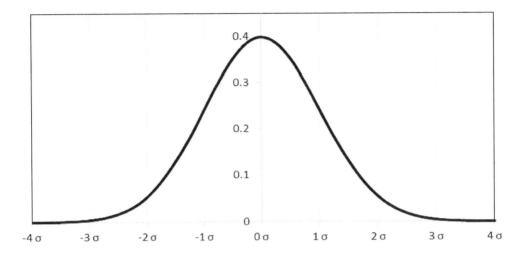

STATISTICAL ANALYSIS
MEASURES OF CENTRAL TENDENCY

A **measure of central tendency** is a statistical value that gives a reasonable estimate for the center of a group of data. There are several different ways of describing the measure of central tendency. Each one has a unique way it is calculated, and each one gives a slightly different perspective on the data set. Whenever you give a measure of central tendency, always make sure the units are the same. If the data has different units, such as hours, minutes, and seconds, convert all the data to the same unit, and use the same unit in the measure of central tendency. If no units are given in the data, do not give units for the measure of central tendency.

MEAN

The **statistical mean** of a group of data is the same as the arithmetic average of that group. To find the mean of a set of data, first convert each value to the same units, if necessary. Then find the sum of all the values, and count the total number of data values, making sure you take into consideration each individual value. If a value appears more than once, count it more than once. Divide the sum of the values by the total number of values and apply the units, if any. Note that the mean does not have to be one of the data values in the set, and may not divide evenly.

$$\text{mean} = \frac{\text{sum of the data values}}{\text{quantity of data values}}$$

For instance, the mean of the data set {88, 72, 61, 90, 97, 68, 88, 79, 86, 93, 97, 71, 80, 84, 89} would be the sum of the fifteen numbers divided by 15:

$$\frac{88 + 72 + 61 + 90 + 97 + 68 + 88 + 79 + 86 + 93 + 97 + 71 + 80 + 84 + 88}{15} = \frac{1242}{15} = 82.8$$

While the mean is relatively easy to calculate and averages are understood by most people, the mean can be very misleading if it is used as the sole measure of central tendency. If the data set has outliers (data values that are unusually high or unusually low compared to the rest of the data values), the mean can be very distorted, especially if the data set has a small number of values. If unusually high values are countered with unusually low values, the mean is not affected as much. For example, if five of twenty students in a class get a 100 on a test, but the other 15 students have an average of 60 on the same test, the class average would appear as 70. Whenever the mean is skewed by outliers, it is always a good idea to include the median as an alternate measure of central tendency.

A **weighted mean**, or weighted average, is a mean that uses "weighted" values. The formula is weighted mean $= \frac{w_1 x_1 + w_2 x_2 + w_3 x_3 \ldots + w_n x_n}{w_1 + w_2 + w_3 + \cdots + w_n}$. Weighted values, such as $w_1, w_2, w_3, \ldots w_n$ are assigned to each member of the set $x_1, x_2, x_3, \ldots x_n$. When calculating the weighted mean, make sure a weight value for each member of the set is used.

MEDIAN

The **statistical median** is the value in the middle of the set of data. To find the median, list all data values in order from smallest to largest or from largest to smallest. Any value that is repeated in the set must be listed the number of times it appears. If there are an odd number of data values, the median is the value in the middle of the list. If there is an even number of data values, the median is the arithmetic mean of the two middle values.

For example, the median of the data set {88, 72, 61, 90, 97, 68, 88, 79, 86, 93, 97, 71, 80, 84, 88} is 86 since the ordered set is {61, 68, 71, 72, 79, 80, 84, **86**, 88, 88, 88, 90, 93, 97, 97}.

The big disadvantage of using the median as a measure of central tendency is that is relies solely on a value's relative size as compared to the other values in the set. When the individual values in a set of data are evenly dispersed, the median can be an accurate tool. However, if there is a group of rather large values or a group of rather small values that are not offset by a different group of values, the information that can be inferred from the median may not be accurate because the distribution of values is skewed.

MODE

The **statistical mode** is the data value that occurs the greatest number of times in the data set. It is possible to have exactly one mode, more than one mode, or no mode. To find the mode of a set of data, arrange the data like you do to find the median (all values in order, listing all multiples of data values). Count the number of times each value appears in the data set. If all values appear an equal number of times, there is no mode. If one value appears more than any other value, that value is the mode. If two or more values appear the same number of times, but there are other values that appear fewer times and no values that appear more times, all of those values are the modes.

For example, the mode of the data set {**88**, 72, 61, 90, 97, 68, **88**, 79, 86, 93, 97, 71, 80, 84, **88**} is 88.

The main disadvantage of the mode is that the values of the other data in the set have no bearing on the mode. The mode may be the largest value, the smallest value, or a value anywhere in between in the set. The mode only tells which value or values, if any, occurred the greatest number of times. It does not give any suggestions about the remaining values in the set.

> **Review Video: Mean, Median, and Mode**
> Visit mometrix.com/academy and enter code: 286207

DISPERSION

The **measure of dispersion** is a single value that helps to "interpret" the measure of central tendency by providing more information about how the data values in the set are distributed about the measure of central tendency. The measure of dispersion helps to eliminate or reduce the disadvantages of using the mean, median, or mode as a single measure of central tendency, and give a more accurate picture of the dataset as a whole. To have a measure of dispersion, you must know or calculate the range, standard deviation, or variance of the data set.

RANGE

The **range** of a set of data is the difference between the greatest and lowest values of the data in the set. To calculate the range, you must first make sure the units for all data values are the same, and then identify the greatest and lowest values. If there are multiple data values that are equal for the highest or lowest, just use one of the values in the formula. Write the answer with the same units as the data values you used to do the calculations.

> **Review Video: Statistical Range**
> Visit mometrix.com/academy and enter code: 778541

PERCENTILE

Percentiles and quartiles are other methods of describing data within a set. **Percentiles** tell what percentage of the data in the set fall below a specific point. For example, achievement test scores are often given in percentiles. A score at the 80th percentile is one which is equal to or higher than 80 percent of the scores in the set. In other words, 80 percent of the scores were lower than that score.

Quartiles are percentile groups that make up quarter sections of the data set. The first quartile is the 25th percentile. The second quartile is the 50th percentile; this is also the median of the dataset. The third quartile is the 75th percentile.

OUTLIER

An outlier is an extremely high or extremely low value in the data set. It may be the result of measurement error, in which case, the outlier is not a valid member of the data set. However, it may also be a valid member of the distribution. Unless a measurement error is identified, the experimenter cannot know for certain if an outlier is or is not a member of the distribution. There are arbitrary methods that can be employed to designate an extreme value as an outlier. One method designates an outlier (or possible outlier) to be any value less than $Q_1 - 1.5(IQR)$ or any value greater than $Q_3 + 1.5(IQR)$.

PRACTICE

P1. Given the following graph, determine the range of patient ages:

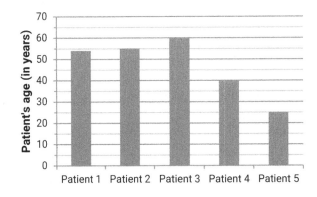

PRACTICE SOLUTIONS

P1. Patient 1 is 54 years old; Patient 2 is 55 years old; Patient 3 is 60 years old; Patient 4 is 40 years old; and Patient 5 is 25 years old. The range of patient ages is the age of the oldest patient minus the age of the youngest patient. In other words, $60 - 25 = 35$. The range of ages is 35 years.

PROBABILITY

Probability is the likelihood of a certain outcome occurring for a given event. An **event** is a situation that produces a result; that could be something as simple as flipping a coin or as complex as launching a rocket. Determining the probability of an outcome for an event can be equally simple or complex. As such there are specific terms used in the study of probability that need to be understood:

- **Compound event**—an event that involves two or more independent events (rolling a pair of dice and taking the sum)
- **Desired outcome** (or success)—an outcome that meets a particular set of criteria (a roll of 1 or 2 if we are looking for numbers less than 3)
- **Independent events**—two or more events whose outcomes do not affect one another (two coins tossed at the same time)
- **Dependent events**—two or more events whose outcomes affect one another (two cards drawn consecutively from the same deck)
- **Certain outcome**—probability of outcome is 100% or 1
- **Impossible outcome**—probability of outcome is 0% or 0
- **Mutually exclusive outcomes**—two or more outcomes whose criteria cannot all be satisfied in a single event (a coin coming up heads and tails on the same toss)
- **Random variable**—refers to all possible outcomes of a single event which may be discrete or continuous.

> **Review Video: Intro to Probability**
> Visit mometrix.com/academy and enter code: 212374

THEORETICAL AND EXPERIMENTAL PROBABILITY

Theoretical probability can usually be determined without actually performing the event. The likelihood of an outcome occurring, or the probability of an outcome occurring, is given by the formula:

$$P(A) = \frac{\text{Number of acceptable outcomes}}{\text{Number of possible outcomes}}$$

Note that $P(A)$ is the probability of an outcome A occurring, and each outcome is just as likely to occur as any other outcome. If each outcome has the same probability of occurring as every other possible outcome, the outcomes are said to be equally likely to occur. The total number of acceptable outcomes must be less than or equal to the total number of possible outcomes. If the two are equal, then the outcome is certain to occur and the probability is 1. If the number of acceptable outcomes is zero, then the outcome is impossible and the probability is 0. For example, if there are 20 marbles in a bag and 5 are red, then the theoretical probability of randomly selecting a red marble is 5 out of 20, ($\frac{5}{20} = \frac{1}{4}$, 0.25, or 25%).

If the theoretical probability is unknown or too complicated to calculate, it can be estimated by an experimental probability. **Experimental probability**, also called empirical probability, is an estimate of the likelihood of a certain outcome based on repeated experiments or collected data. In other words, while theoretical probability is based on what *should* happen, experimental probability is based on what *has* happened. Experimental probability is calculated in the same way as theoretical probability, except that actual outcomes are used instead of possible outcomes. The more experiments performed or datapoints gathered, the better the estimate should be.

Theoretical and experimental probability do not always line up with one another. Theoretical probability says that out of 20 coin-tosses, 10 should be heads. However, if we were actually to toss 20 coins, we might record just 5 heads. This doesn't mean that our theoretical probability is incorrect; it just means that this particular experiment had results that were different from what was predicted. A practical application of empirical probability is the insurance industry. There are no set functions that define lifespan, health, or safety. Insurance companies look at factors from hundreds of thousands of individuals to find patterns that they then use to set the formulas for insurance premiums.

> **Review Video: Empirical Probability**
> Visit mometrix.com/academy and enter code: 513468

PERMUTATIONS AND COMBINATIONS

When trying to calculate the probability of an event using the $\frac{\text{desired outcomes}}{\text{total outcomes}}$ formula, you may frequently find that there are too many outcomes to individually count them. **Permutation** and **combination formulas** offer a shortcut to counting outcomes. A permutation is an arrangement of a specific number of a set of objects in a specific order. The number of **permutations** of r items given a set of n items can be calculated as $_nP_r = \frac{n!}{(n-r)!}$. Combinations are similar to permutations, except there are no restrictions regarding the order of the elements. While ABC is considered a different permutation than BCA, ABC and BCA are considered the same combination. The number of **combinations** of r items given a set of n items can be calculated as $_nC_r = \frac{n!}{r!(n-r)!}$ or $_nC_r = \frac{nP_r}{r!}$.

Suppose you want to calculate how many different 5-card hands can be drawn from a deck of 52 cards. This is a combination since the order of the cards in a hand does not matter. There are 52 cards available, and 5 to be selected. Thus, the number of different hands is $_{52}C_5 = \frac{52!}{5! \times 47!} = 2{,}598{,}960$.

> **Review Video: Probability - Permutation and Combination**
> Visit mometrix.com/academy and enter code: 907664

COMPLEMENT OF AN EVENT

Sometimes it may be easier to calculate the possibility of something not happening, or the **complement of an event**. Represented by the symbol $\bar{A}$, the complement of A is the probability that event A does not happen. When you know the probability of event A occurring, you can use the formula $P(\bar{A}) = 1 - P(A)$, where $P(\bar{A})$ is the probability of event A not occurring, and $P(A)$ is the probability of event A occurring.

ADDITION RULE

The **addition rule** for probability is used for finding the probability of a compound event. Use the formula $P(A \text{ or } B) = P(A) + P(B) - P(A \text{ and } B)$, where $P(A \text{ and } B)$ is the probability of both events occurring to find the probability of a compound event. The probability of both events occurring at the same time must be subtracted to eliminate any overlap in the first two probabilities.

CONDITIONAL PROBABILITY

Given two events A and B, the **conditional probability** $P(A|B)$ is the probability that event A will occur, given that event B has occurred. The conditional probability cannot be calculated simply from $P(A)$ and $P(B)$; these probabilities alone do not give sufficient information to determine the conditional probability. It can, however, be determined if you are also given the probability of the intersection of events A and B, $P(A \cap B)$, the probability that events A and B both occur. Specifically, $P(A|B) = \frac{P(A \cap B)}{P(B)}$. For instance, suppose you have a jar containing two red marbles and two blue marbles, and you draw two marbles at random. Consider event A being the event that the first marble drawn is red, and event B being the event that the second marble drawn is blue. $P(A)$ is $\frac{1}{2}$, and $P(A \cap B)$ is $\frac{1}{3}$. (The latter may not be obvious, but may be determined by finding the product of $\frac{1}{2}$ and $\frac{2}{3}$). Therefore $P(A|B) = \frac{1/3}{1/2} = \frac{2}{3}$.

CONDITIONAL PROBABILITY IN EVERYDAY SITUATIONS

Conditional probability often arises in everyday situations in, for example, estimating the risk or benefit of certain activities. The conditional probability of having a heart attack given that you exercise daily may be smaller than the overall probability of having a heart attack. The conditional probability of having lung cancer given that you are a smoker is larger than the overall probability of having lung cancer. Note that changing the order of the conditional probability changes the meaning: the conditional probability of having lung cancer given that you are a smoker is a very different thing from the probability of being a smoker given that you have lung cancer. In an extreme case, suppose that a certain rare disease is caused only by eating a certain food, but even then, it is unlikely. Then the conditional probability of having that disease given that you eat the dangerous food is nonzero but low, but the conditional probability of having eaten that food given that you have the disease is 100%!

> **Review Video: Conditional Probability**
> Visit mometrix.com/academy and enter code: 397924

MULTIPLICATION RULE

The **multiplication rule** can be used to find the probability of two independent events occurring using the formula $P(A \text{ and } B) = P(A) \times P(B)$, where $P(A \text{ and } B)$ is the probability of two independent events occurring, $P(A)$ is the probability of the first event occurring, and $P(B)$ is the probability of the second event occurring.

The multiplication rule can also be used to find the probability of two dependent events occurring using the formula $P(A \text{ and } B) = P(A) \times P(B|A)$, where $P(A \text{ and } B)$ is the probability of two dependent events occurring and $P(B|A)$ is the probability of the second event occurring after the first event has already occurred. Before using the multiplication rule, you MUST first determine whether the two events are *dependent* or *independent*.

Use a **combination of the multiplication** rule and the rule of complements to find the probability that at least one outcome of the element will occur. This is given by the general formula $P(\text{at least one event occurring}) = 1 - P(\text{no outcomes occurring})$. For example, to find the probability that at least one even number will show when a pair of dice is rolled, find the probability that two odd numbers will be rolled (no even numbers) and subtract from one. You can always use a tree diagram or make a chart to list the possible outcomes when the sample space is small, such as in the dice-rolling example, but in most cases it will be much faster to use the multiplication and complement formulas.

> **Review Video: Multiplication Rule**
> Visit mometrix.com/academy and enter code: 782598

EXPECTED VALUE

Expected value is a method of determining the expected outcome in a random situation. It is a sum of the weighted probabilities of the possible outcomes. Multiply the probability of an event occurring by the weight assigned to that probability (such as the amount of money won or lost). A practical application of the expected value is to determine whether a game of chance is really fair. If the sum of the weighted probabilities is equal to zero, the game is generally considered fair because the player has a fair chance to at least break even. If the expected value is less than zero, then players lose more than they win. For example, a lottery drawing might allow the player to choose any three-digit number, 000–999. The probability of choosing the winning number is 1:1000. If it costs $1 to play, and a winning number receives $500, the expected value is $\left(-\$1 \times \frac{999}{1,000}\right) + \left(\$499 \times \frac{1}{1,000}\right) = -\$0.50$. You can expect to lose on average 50 cents for every dollar you spend.

> **Review Video: Expected Value**
> Visit mometrix.com/academy and enter code: 643554

PRACTICE

P1. Determine the theoretical probability of the following events:

(a) Rolling an even number on a regular 6-sided die.

(b) Not getting a red ball when selecting one from a bag of 3 red balls, 4 black balls, and 2 green balls.

(c) Rolling a standard die and then selecting a card from a standard deck that is less than the value rolled.

P2. There is a game of chance involving a standard deck of cards that has been shuffled and then laid on a table. The player wins $10 if they can turn over 2 cards of matching color (black or red), $50 for 2 cards with matching value (A-K), and $100 for 2 cards with both matching color and value. What is the expected value of playing this game?

P3. Today, there were two food options for lunch at a local college cafeteria. Given the following survey data, what is the probability that a junior selected at random from the sample had a sandwich?

	Freshman	Sophomore	Junior	Senior
Salad	15	12	27	36
Sandwich	24	40	43	35
Nothing	42	23	23	30

PRACTICE SOLUTIONS

P1. (a). The values on the faces of a regular die are 1, 2, 3, 4, 5, and 6. Since three of these are even numbers (2, 4, 6), The probability of rolling an even number is $\frac{3}{6} = \frac{1}{2} = 0.5 = 50\%$.

(b) The bag contains a total of 9 balls, 6 of which are not red, so the probability of selecting one non-red ball would be $\frac{6}{9} = \frac{2}{3} \cong 0.667 \cong 66.7\%$.

(c) In this scenario, we need to determine how many cards could satisfy the condition for each possible value of the die roll. If a one is rolled, there is no way to achieve the desired outcome, since no cards in a standard deck are less than 1. If a two is rolled, then any of the four aces would achieve the desired result. If a three is rolled, then either an ace or a two would satisfy the condition, and so on. Note that any value on the die is equally likely to occur, meaning that the probability of each roll is $\frac{1}{6}$. Putting all this in a table can help:

Roll	Cards < Roll	Probability of Card	Probability of Event
1	-	$\frac{0}{52} = 0$	$\frac{1}{6} \times 0 = 0$
2	1	$\frac{4}{52} = \frac{1}{13}$	$\frac{1}{6} \times \frac{1}{13} = \frac{1}{78}$
3	1,2	$\frac{8}{52} = \frac{2}{13}$	$\frac{1}{6} \times \frac{2}{13} = \frac{2}{78}$
4	1,2,3	$\frac{12}{52} = \frac{3}{13}$	$\frac{1}{6} \times \frac{3}{13} = \frac{3}{78}$
5	1,2,3,4	$\frac{16}{52} = \frac{4}{13}$	$\frac{1}{6} \times \frac{4}{13} = \frac{4}{78}$
6	1,2,3,4,5	$\frac{20}{52} = \frac{5}{13}$	$\frac{1}{6} \times \frac{5}{13} = \frac{5}{78}$

Assuming that each value of the die is equally likely, then the probability of selecting a card less than the value of the die is the sum of the probabilities of each way to achieve the desired outcome: $\frac{0+1+2+3+4+5}{78} = \frac{15}{78} = \frac{5}{26} \cong 0.192 \cong 19.2\%$.

P2. First, determine the probability of each way of winning. In each case, the first card simply determines which of the remaining 51 cards in the deck correspond to a win. For the color of the cards to match, there are 25 cards remaining in the deck that match the color of the first, but one of the 25 also matches the value, so only 24 are left in this category. For the value of the cards to match, there are 3 cards remaining in the deck that match the value of the first, but one of the three also matches the color, so only 2 are left in this category. There is only one card in the deck that will match both the color and value. Finally, there are 24 cards left that don't match at all.

Now we can find the expected value of playing the game, where we multiply the value of each event by the probability it will occur and sum over all of them:

$$\$10 \times \frac{24}{51} = \$4.71$$
$$\$50 \times \frac{2}{51} = \$1.96$$
$$\$100 \times \frac{1}{51} = \$1.96$$
$$\$0 \times \frac{24}{51} = \$0$$

$$\$4.71 + \$1.96 + \$1.96 = \$8.63$$

This game therefore has an expected value of $8.63 each time you play, which means if the cost to play is less than $8.63 then you would, on average, *gain* money. However, if the cost to play is more than $8.63, then you would, on average, *lose* money.

P3. With two-way tables it is often most helpful to start by totaling the rows and columns:

	Freshman	Sophomore	Junior	Senior	Total
Salad	15	12	27	36	90
Sandwich	24	40	43	35	142
Nothing	42	23	23	30	118
Total	81	75	93	101	350

Since the question is focused on juniors, we can focus on that column. There was a total of 93 juniors surveyed and 43 of them had a sandwich for lunch. Thus, the probability that a junior selected at random had a sandwich would be $\frac{43}{93} \cong 0.462 \cong 46.2\%$.

Algebra

UNITS OF MEASUREMENT
METRIC MEASUREMENT PREFIXES

Giga-: one billion (1 *giga*watt is one billion watts)
Mega-: one million (1 *mega*hertz is one million hertz)
Kilo-: one thousand (1 *kilo*gram is one thousand grams)
Deci-: one tenth (1 *deci*meter is one tenth of a meter)
Centi-: one hundredth (1 *centi*meter is one hundredth of a meter)
Milli-: one thousandth (1 *milli*liter is one thousandth of a liter)
Micro-: one millionth (1 *micro*gram is one millionth of a gram)

MEASUREMENT CONVERSION

When converting between units, the goal is to maintain the same meaning but change the way it is displayed. In order to go from a larger unit to a smaller unit, multiply the number of the known amount by the equivalent amount. When going from a smaller unit to a larger unit, divide the number of the known amount by the equivalent amount.

> **Review Video: Metric System Conversions**
> Visit mometrix.com/academy and enter code: 163709

For complicated conversions, it may be helpful to set up conversion fractions. In these fractions, one fraction is the **conversion factor**. The other fraction has the unknown amount in the numerator. So, the known value is placed in the denominator. Sometimes the second fraction has the known value from the problem in the numerator, and the unknown in the denominator. Multiply the two fractions to get the converted measurement. Note that since the numerator and the denominator of the factor are equivalent, the value of the fraction is 1. That is why we can say that the result in the new units is equal to the result in the old units even though they have different numbers.

It can often be necessary to chain known conversion factors together. As an example, consider converting 512 square inches to square meters. We know that there are 2.54 centimeters in an inch and 100 centimeters in a meter, and that we will need to square each of these factors to achieve the conversion we are looking for.

$$\frac{512 \text{ in}^2}{1} \times \left(\frac{2.54 \text{ cm}}{1 \text{ in}}\right)^2 \times \left(\frac{1 \text{ m}}{100 \text{ cm}}\right)^2 = \frac{512 \text{ in}^2}{1} \times \left(\frac{6.4516 \text{ cm}^2}{1 \text{ in}^2}\right) \times \left(\frac{1 \text{ m}^2}{10000 \text{ cm}^2}\right) = 0.330 \text{ m}^2$$

> **Review Video: Measurement Conversions**
> Visit mometrix.com/academy and enter code: 316703

COMMON UNITS AND EQUIVALENTS
METRIC EQUIVALENTS

1000 µg (microgram)	1 mg
1000 mg (milligram)	1 g
1000 g (gram)	1 kg
1000 kg (kilogram)	1 metric ton
1000 mL (milliliter)	1 L
1000 µm (micrometer)	1 mm
1000 mm (millimeter)	1 m
100 cm (centimeter)	1 m
1000 m (meter)	1 km

DISTANCE AND AREA MEASUREMENT

Unit	Abbreviation	U.S. equivalent	Metric equivalent
Inch	in	1 inch	2.54 centimeters
Foot	ft	12 inches	0.305 meters
Yard	yd	3 feet	0.914 meters
Mile	mi	5280 feet	1.609 kilometers
Acre	ac	4840 square yards	0.405 hectares
Square Mile	mi^2	640 acres	2.590 square kilometers

CAPACITY MEASUREMENTS

Unit	Abbreviation	U.S. equivalent	Metric equivalent
Fluid Ounce	fl oz	8 fluid drams	29.573 milliliters
Cup	cp	8 fluid ounces	0.237 liter
Pint	pt	16 fluid ounces	0.473 liter
Quart	qt	2 pints	0.946 liter
Gallon	gal	4 quarts	3.785 liters
Teaspoon	t or tsp	1 fluid dram	5 milliliters
Tablespoon	T or tbsp	4 fluid drams	15 or 16 milliliters
Cubic Centimeter	cc or cm^3	0.271 drams	1 milliliter

WEIGHT MEASUREMENTS

Unit	Abbreviation	U.S. equivalent	Metric equivalent
Ounce	oz	16 drams	28.35 grams
Pound	lb	16 ounces	453.6 grams
Ton	t	2,000 pounds	907.2 kilograms

VOLUME AND WEIGHT MEASUREMENT CLARIFICATIONS

Always be careful when using ounces and fluid ounces. They are not equivalent.

$$1 \text{ pint} = 16 \text{ fluid ounces} \quad 1 \text{ fluid ounce} \neq 1 \text{ ounce}$$
$$1 \text{ pound} = 16 \text{ ounces} \quad 1 \text{ pint} \neq 1 \text{ pound}$$

Having one pint of something does not mean you have one pound of it. In the same way, just because something weighs one pound does not mean that its volume is one pint.

In the United States, the word "ton" by itself refers to a short ton or a net ton. Do not confuse this with a long ton (also called a gross ton) or a metric ton (also spelled *tonne*), which have different measurement equivalents.

$$1 \text{ U.S. ton} = 2000 \text{ pounds} \quad \neq \quad 1 \text{ metric ton} = 1000 \text{ kilograms}$$

SCIENTIFIC NOTATION

Scientific notation is a way of writing large numbers in a shorter form. The form $a \times 10^n$ is used in scientific notation, where a is greater than or equal to 1 but less than 10, and n is the number of places the decimal must move to get from the original number to a. Example: The number 230,400,000 is cumbersome to write. To write the value in scientific notation, place a decimal point between the first and second numbers, and include all digits through the last non-zero digit ($a = 2.304$). To find the appropriate power of 10, count the number of places the decimal point had to move ($n = 8$). The number is positive if the decimal moved to the left, and negative if it moved to the right. We can then write 230,400,000 as 2.304×10^8. If we look instead at the number 0.00002304, we have the same value for a, but this time the decimal moved 5 places to the right ($n = -5$). Thus, 0.00002304 can be written as 2.304×10^{-5}. Using this notation makes it simple to compare very large or very small numbers. By comparing exponents, it is easy to see that 3.28×10^4 is smaller than 1.51×10^5, because 4 is less than 5.

> **Review Video: Scientific Notation**
> Visit mometrix.com/academy and enter code: 976454

SIMPLE INTEREST

Simple Interest: Interest that is paid once per year for the principal amount. The principal amount is the original amount that someone borrows from another person or a bank. The formula is $I = Prt$, where I is the amount of interest, P is the principal, r is the annual interest rate, and t is the amount of time in years.

ACTUAL DRAWINGS AND SCALE DRAWINGS

A map has a key for measurements to compare real distances with a scale distance.

Example: The key on one map says that 2 inches on the map is 12 real miles. Find the distance of a route that is 5 inches long on the map.

A proportion is needed to show the map measurements and real distances. First, write a ratio that has the information in the key. The map measurement can be in the numerator, and the real distance can be in the denominator.

$$\frac{2 \text{ inches}}{12 \text{ miles}}$$

Next, write a ratio with the known map distance and the unknown real distance. The unknown number for miles can be represented with the letter m.

$$\frac{5 \text{ inches}}{m \text{ miles}}$$

Then, write out the ratios in a proportion and solve it for m.

$$\frac{2 \text{ inches}}{12 \text{ miles}} = \frac{5 \text{ inches}}{m \text{ miles}}$$

Now, you have $2m = 60$. So you are left with $m = 30$. Thus, the route is 30 miles long.

PRACTICE

P1. Perform the following conversions:

(a) 1.4 meters to centimeters

(b) 218 centimeters to meters

(c) 42 inches to feet

(d) 15 kilograms to pounds

(e) 80 ounces to pounds

(f) 2 miles to kilometers

(g) 5 feet to centimeters

(h) 15.14 liters to gallons

(i) 8 quarts to liters

(j) 13.2 pounds to grams

PRACTICE SOLUTIONS

P1. (a) $\frac{100 \text{ cm}}{1 \text{ m}} = \frac{x \text{ cm}}{1.4 \text{ m}}$ Cross multiply to get $x = 140$

(b) $\frac{100 \text{ cm}}{1 \text{ m}} = \frac{218 \text{ cm}}{x \text{ m}}$ Cross multiply to get $100x = 218$, or $x = 2.18$

(c) $\frac{12 \text{ in}}{1 \text{ ft}} = \frac{42 \text{ in}}{x \text{ ft}}$ Cross multiply to get $12x = 42$, or $x = 3.5$

(d) $15 \text{ kilograms} \times \frac{2.2 \text{ pounds}}{1 \text{ kilogram}} = 33 \text{ pounds}$

(e) $80 \text{ ounces} \times \frac{1 \text{ pound}}{16 \text{ ounces}} = 5 \text{ pounds}$

(f) $2 \text{ miles} \times \frac{1.609 \text{ kilometers}}{1 \text{ mile}} = 3.218 \text{ kilometers}$

(g) $5 \text{ feet} \times \frac{12 \text{ inches}}{1 \text{ foot}} \times \frac{2.54 \text{ centimeters}}{1 \text{ inch}} = 152.4 \text{ centimeters}$

(h) $15.14 \text{ liters} \times \frac{1 \text{ gallon}}{3.785 \text{ liters}} = 4 \text{ gallons}$

(i) $8 \text{ quarts} \times \frac{1 \text{ gallon}}{4 \text{ quarts}} \times \frac{3.785 \text{ liters}}{1 \text{ gallon}} = 7.57 \text{ liters}$

(j) $13.2 \text{ pounds} \times \frac{1 \text{ kilogram}}{2.2 \text{ pounds}} \times \frac{1000 \text{ grams}}{1 \text{ kilogram}} = 6000 \text{ grams}$

EXPRESSIONS

TERMS AND COEFFICIENTS

Mathematical expressions consist of a combination of one or more values arranged in terms that are added together. As such, an expression could be just a single number, including zero. A **variable term** is the product of a real number, also called a **coefficient**, and one or more variables, each of which may be raised to an exponent. Expressions may also include numbers without a variable, called **constants** or **constant terms**. The expression $6s^2$, for example, is a single term where the coefficient is the real number 6 and the variable term is s^2. Note that if a term is written as simply a variable to some exponent, like t^2, then the coefficient is 1, because $t^2 = 1t^2$.

LINEAR EXPRESSIONS

A **single variable linear expression** is the sum of a single variable term, where the variable has no exponent, and a constant, which may be zero. For instance, the expression $2w + 7$ has $2w$ as the variable term and 7 as the constant term. It is important to realize that terms are separated by addition or subtraction. Since an expression is a sum of terms, expressions such as $5x - 3$ can be written as $5x + (-3)$ to emphasize that the constant term is negative. A real-world example of a single variable linear expression is the perimeter of a square, four times the side length, often expressed: $4s$.

In general, a **linear expression** is the sum of any number of variable terms so long as none of the variables have an exponent. For example, $3m + 8n - \frac{1}{4}p + 5.5q - 1$ is a linear expression, but $3y^3$ is not. In the same way, the expression for the perimeter of a general triangle, the sum of the side lengths $(a + b + c)$ is considered to be linear, but the expression for the area of a square, the side length squared (s^2) is not.

WRITING AN EXPRESSION FROM WORD-TO-SYMBOL

To write an expression, you must first put variables with the unknown values in the problem. Then, translate the words and phrases into expressions that have numbers and symbols.

INEQUALITIES

To write out an inequality, you may need to translate a sentence into an inequality. This translation is putting the words into symbols. When translating, choose a variable to stand for the unknown value. Then, change the words or phrases into symbols. For example, the sum of 2 and a number is at most 12. So, you would write: $2 + b \leq 12$.

Example: A farm sells vegetables and dairy products. One third of the sales from dairy products plus half of the sales from vegetables should be greater than the monthly payment (P) for the farm.

Let d stand for the sales from dairy products. Let v stand for the sales from vegetables. One third of the sales from dairy products is the expression $\frac{d}{3}$. One half of the sales from vegetables is the expression $\frac{v}{2}$. The sum of these expressions should be greater than the monthly payment for the farm. An inequality for this is $\frac{d}{3} + \frac{v}{2} > P$.

RATIONAL EXPRESSIONS

John and Luke play basketball every week. John can make 5 free throws per minute faster than Luke can make three-point shots. On one day, John made 30 free throws in the same time that it took Luke to make 20 three-point shots. So, how fast are Luke and John scoring points?

First, set up what you know. You know that John made 30 free throws, and he had a rate of 5 free throws per minute faster than Luke's three-point shots: $\frac{30}{x+5}$. The x is for Luke's speed. Also, you know that Luke made 20 three-point shots in the same amount of time that John scored his free throws: $\frac{20}{x}$. So, we can set up proportions because their times are equal.

$$\frac{30}{x+5} = \frac{20}{x}$$

Cross factor the proportion: $30x = 20(x + 5)$

Then distribute the 20 across the values in the parentheses: $30x = 20x + 100$

Now you can subtract 20x from both sides of the equation, and you are left with: $10x = 100$

Divide both sides by 10: $\frac{10x}{10} = \frac{100}{10}$

Now you are left with: $x = 10$. So Luke's speed was 10 three-point shots per minute and John's speed was 15 free throws per minute.

POLYNOMIAL EXPRESSIONS

Fred buys some CDs for $12 each. He also buys two DVDs. The total that Fred spent is $60. Write an equation that shows the connection between the number of CDs and the average cost of a DVD.

Let c stand for the number of CDs that Fred buys. Also, let d stand for the average cost of one of the DVDs that Fred buys. The expression $12c$ gives the cost of the CDs and the expression $2d$ gives the cost of the DVDs. So the equation $12c + 2d = 60$ states the number of CDs and the average cost of a DVD.

EQUATIONS

LINEAR EQUATIONS

Equations that can be written as $ax + b = 0$, where $a \neq 0$, are referred to as **one variable linear equations**. A solution to such an equation is called a **root**. In the case where we have the equation $5x + 10 = 0$, if we solve for x we get a solution of $x = -2$. In other words, the root of the equation is -2. This is found by first subtracting 10 from both sides, which gives $5x = -10$. Next, simply divide both sides by the coefficient of the variable, in this case 5, to get $x = -2$. This can be checked by plugging -2 back into the original equation $(5)(-2) + 10 = -10 + 10 = 0$.

The **solution set** is the set of all solutions of an equation. In our example, the solution set would simply be -2. If there were more solutions (there usually are in multivariable equations) then they would also be included in the solution set. When an equation has no true solutions, it is referred to as an **empty set**. Equations with identical solution sets are **equivalent equations**. An **identity** is a term whose value or determinant is equal to 1.

> **Review Video: Linear Equations Basics**
> Visit mometrix.com/academy and enter code: 793005

Linear equations can be written many ways. Below is a list of some forms linear equations can take:

- **Standard Form**: $Ax + By = C$; the slope is $\frac{-A}{B}$ and the y-intercept is $\frac{C}{B}$
- **Slope Intercept Form**: $y = mx + b$, where m is the slope and b is the y-intercept
- **Point-Slope Form**: $y - y_1 = m(x - x_1)$, where m is the slope and (x_1, y_1) is a point on the line
- **Two-Point Form**: $\frac{y - y_1}{x - x_1} = \frac{y_2 - y_1}{x_2 - x_1}$, where (x_1, y_1) and (x_2, y_2) are two points on the given line
- **Intercept Form**: $\frac{x}{x_1} + \frac{y}{y_1} = 1$, where $(x_1, 0)$ is the point at which a line intersects the x-axis, and $(0, y_1)$ is the point at which the same line intersects the y-axis

> **Review Video: Slope-Intercept and Point-Slope Forms**
> Visit mometrix.com/academy and enter code: 113216

SOLVING ONE-VARIABLE LINEAR EQUATIONS

Multiply all terms by the lowest common denominator to eliminate any fractions. Look for addition or subtraction to undo so you can isolate the variable on one side of the equal sign. Divide both sides by the coefficient of the variable. When you have a value for the variable, substitute this value into the original equation to make sure you have a true equation. Consider the following example:

Kim's savings are represented by the table below. Represent her savings using an equation.

X (Months)	Y (Total Savings)
2	$1300
5	$2050
9	$3050
11	$3550
16	$4800

The table shows a function with a constant rate of change, or slope, of 250. Given the points on the table, the slopes can be calculated as $(2050 - 1300)/(5 - 2)$, $(3050 - 2050)/(9 - 5)$, $(3550 - 3050)/(11 - 9)$, and $(4800 - 3550)/(16 - 11)$, each of which equals 250. Thus, the table shows a constant rate of change, indicating a linear function. The slope-intercept form of a linear equation is written as $y = mx + b$, where m represents the slope and b represents the y-intercept. Substituting the slope into this form gives $y = 250x + b$. Substituting corresponding x- and y-values from any point into this equation will give the y-intercept, or b. Using the point, (2, 1300), gives $1300 = 250(2) + b$, which simplifies as b = 800. Thus, her savings may be represented by the equation $y = 250x + 800$.

RULES FOR MANIPULATING EQUATIONS

LIKE TERMS

Like terms are terms in an equation that have the same variable, regardless of whether or not they also have the same coefficient. This includes terms that *lack* a variable; all constants (i.e. numbers without variables) are considered like terms. If the equation involves terms with a variable raised to different powers, the like terms are those that have the variable raised to the same power.

For example, consider the equation $x^2 + 3x + 2 = 2x^2 + x - 7 + 2x$. In this equation, 2 and −7 are like terms; they are both constants. $3x$, x, and $2x$ are like terms; they all include the variable x raised to the first power. x^2 and $2x^2$ are like terms; they both include the variable x, raised to the second power. $2x$ and $2x^2$ are not like terms; although they both involve the variable x, the variable is not raised to the same power in both terms. The fact that they have the same coefficient, 2, is not relevant.

> **Review Video: Rules for Manipulating Equations**
> Visit mometrix.com/academy and enter code: 838871

CARRYING OUT THE SAME OPERATION ON BOTH SIDES OF AN EQUATION

When solving an equation, the general procedure is to carry out a series of operations on both sides of an equation, choosing operations that will tend to simplify the equation when doing so. The reason why the same operation must be carried out on both sides of the equation is because that leaves the meaning of the equation unchanged, and yields a result that is equivalent to the original equation. This would not be the case if we carried out an operation on one side of an equation and not the other. Consider what an equation means: it is a statement that two values or expressions are equal. If we carry out the same operation on both sides of the equation—add 3 to both sides, for example—then the two sides of the equation are changed in the same way, and so remain equal. If we do that to only one side of the equation—add 3 to one side but not the other—then that wouldn't be true; if we change one side of the equation but not the other then the two sides are no longer equal.

ADVANTAGE OF COMBINING LIKE TERMS

Combining like terms refers to adding or subtracting like terms—terms with the same variable—and therefore reducing sets of like terms to a single term. The main advantage of doing this is that it simplifies the equation. Often combining like terms can be done as the first step in solving an equation, though it can also be done later, such as after distributing terms in a product.

For example, consider the equation $2(x + 3) + 3(2 + x + 3) = -4$. The 2 and the 3 in the second set of parentheses are like terms, and we can combine them, yielding $2(x + 3) + 3(x + 5) = -4$. Now we can carry out the multiplications implied by the parentheses, distributing outer 2 and 3 accordingly: $2x + 6 + 3x + 15 = -4$. The $2x$ and the $3x$ are like terms, and we can add them together: $5x + 6 + 15 = -4$. Now, the constants 6, 15, and −4 are also like terms, and we can combine them as well: subtracting 6 and 15 from both sides of the equation, we get $5x = -4 - 6 - 15$, or $5x = -25$, which simplifies further to $x = -5$.

> **Review Video: Simplifying Equations by Combining Like Terms**
> Visit mometrix.com/academy and enter code: 668506

CANCELING TERMS ON OPPOSITE SIDES OF AN EQUATION

Two terms on opposite sides of an equation can be canceled if and only if they *exactly* match each other. They must have the same variable raised to the same power and the same coefficient. For example, in the equation $3x + 2x^2 + 6 = 2x^2 - 6$, $2x^2$ appears on both sides of the equation, and can be canceled, leaving $3x + 6 = -6$. The 6 on each side of the equation can*not* be canceled, because it is added on one side of the equation and subtracted on the other. While they cannot be canceled, however, the 6 and –6 are like terms and can be combined, yielding $3x = -12$, which simplifies further to $x = -4$.

It's also important to note that the terms to be canceled must be independent terms and cannot be part of a larger term. For example, consider the equation $2(x + 6) = 3(x + 4) + 1$. We cannot cancel the xs, because even though they match each other they are part of the larger terms $2(x + 6)$ and $3(x + 4)$. We must first distribute the 2 and 3, yielding $2x + 12 = 3x + 12 + 1$. Now we see that the terms with the x's do not match, but the 12s do, and can be canceled, leaving $2x = 3x + 1$, which simplifies to $x = -1$.

PROCESS FOR MANIPULATING EQUATIONS
ISOLATING VARIABLES

To **isolate a variable** means to manipulate the equation so that the variable appears by itself on one side of the equation, and does not appear at all on the other side. Generally, an equation or inequality is considered to be solved once the variable is isolated and the other side of the equation or inequality is simplified as much as possible. In the case of a two-variable equation or inequality, only one variable needs to be isolated; it will not usually be possible to simultaneously isolate both variables.

For a linear equation—an equation in which the variable only appears raised to the first power—isolating a variable can be done by first moving all the terms with the variable to one side of the equation and all other terms to the other side. (*Moving* a term really means adding the inverse of the term to both sides; when a term is *moved* to the other side of the equation its sign is flipped.) Then combine like terms on each side. Finally, divide both sides by the coefficient of the variable, if applicable. The steps need not necessarily be done in this order, but this order will always work.

> **Review Video: Solving Equations with Variables on Both Sides**
> Visit mometrix.com/academy and enter code: 402497

EQUATIONS WITH MORE THAN ONE SOLUTION

Some types of non-linear equations, such as equations involving squares of variables, may have more than one solution. For example, the equation $x^2 = 4$ has two solutions: 2 and –2. Equations with absolute values can also have multiple solutions: $|x| = 1$ has the solutions $x = 1$ and $x = -1$.

It is also possible for a linear equation to have more than one solution, but only if the equation is true regardless of the value of the variable. In this case, the equation is considered to have infinitely many solutions, because any possible value of the variable is a solution. We know a linear equation has infinitely many solutions if when we combine like terms the variables cancel, leaving a true statement. For example, consider the equation $2(3x + 5) = x + 5(x + 2)$. Distributing, we get $6x + 10 = x + 5x + 10$; combining like terms gives $6x + 10 = 6x + 10$, and the $6x$ terms cancel to leave $10 = 10$. This is clearly true, so the original equation is true for any value of x. We could also have canceled the 10s leaving $0 = 0$, but again this is clearly true—in general if both sides of the equation match exactly, it has infinitely many solutions.

EQUATIONS WITH NO SOLUTION

Some types of non-linear equations, such as equations involving squares of variables, may have no solution. For example, the equation $x^2 = -2$ has no solutions in the real numbers, because the square of any real number must be positive. Similarly, $|x| = -1$ has no solution, because the absolute value of a number is always positive.

It is also possible for an equation to have no solution even if does not involve any powers greater than one or absolute values or other special functions. For example, the equation $2(x + 3) + x = 3x$ has no solution. We can see that if we try to solve it. First, we distribute, leaving $2x + 6 + x = 3x$. But now if we try to combine all the terms with the variable, we find that they cancel: we have $3x$ on the left and $3x$ on the right, canceling to leave us with $6 = 0$. This is clearly false. In general, whenever the variable terms in an equation cancel, leaving different constants on both sides, it means that the equation has no solution. (If we are left with the *same* constant on both sides, the equation has infinitely many solutions instead.)

FEATURES OF EQUATIONS THAT REQUIRE SPECIAL TREATMENT
LINEAR EQUATIONS

A linear equation is an equation in which variables only appear by themselves; they are not multiplied together, not with exponents other than one, and not inside absolute value signs or any other functions. For example, the equation $x + 1 - 3x = 5 - x$ is a linear equation; while x appears multiple times, it never appears with an exponent other than one, or inside any function. The two-variable equation $2x - 3y = 5 + 2x$ is also a linear equation. In contrast, the equation $x^2 - 5 = 3x$ is *not* a linear equation, because it involves the term x^2. $\sqrt{x} = 5$ is not a linear equation, because it involves a square root. $(x - 1)^2 = 4$ is not a linear equation because even though there's no exponent on the x directly, it appears as part of an expression that is squared. The two-variable equation $x + xy - y = 5$ is not a linear equation because it includes the term xy, where two variables are multiplied together.

Linear equations can always be solved (or shown to have no solution) by combining like terms and performing simple operations on both sides of the equation. Some non-linear equations can be solved by similar methods, but others may require more advanced methods of solution, if they can be solved analytically at all.

SOLVING EQUATIONS INVOLVING ROOTS

In an equation involving roots, the first step is to isolate the term with the root, if possible, and then raise both sides of the equation to the appropriate power to eliminate it. Consider an example equation, $2\sqrt{x + 1} - 1 = 3$. In this case, begin by adding 1 to both sides, yielding $2\sqrt{x + 1} = 4$, and then dividing both sides by 2, yielding $\sqrt{x + 1} = 2$. Now square both sides, yielding $x + 1 = 4$. Finally, subtracting 1 from both sides yields $x = 3$.

Squaring both sides of an equation may, however, yield a spurious solution—a solution to the squared equation that is *not* a solution of the original equation. It's therefore necessary to plug the solution back into the original equation to make sure it works. In this case, it does: $2\sqrt{3 + 1} - 1 = 2\sqrt{4} - 1 = 2(2) - 1 = 4 - 1 = 3$.

The same procedure applies for other roots as well. For example, given the equation $3 + \sqrt[3]{2x} = 5$, we can first subtract 3 from both sides, yielding $\sqrt[3]{2x} = 2$ and isolating the root. Raising both sides to the third power yields $2x = 2^3$, i.e. $2x = 8$. We can now divide both sides by 2 to get $x = 4$.

> **Review Video: Solving Equations Involving Roots**
> Visit mometrix.com/academy and enter code: 297670

Solving Equations with Exponents

To solve an equation involving an exponent, the first step is to isolate the variable with the exponent. We can then take the appropriate root of both sides to eliminate the exponent. For instance, for the equation $2x^3 + 17 = 5x^3 - 7$, we can subtract $5x^3$ from both sides to get $-3x^3 + 17 = -7$, and then subtract 17 from both sides to get $-3x^3 = -24$. Finally, we can divide both sides by –3 to get $x^3 = 8$. Finally, we can take the cube root of both sides to get $x = \sqrt[3]{8} = 2$.

One important but often overlooked point is that equations with an exponent greater than 1 may have more than one answer. The solution to $x^2 = 9$ isn't simply $x = 3$; it's $x = \pm 3$: that is, $x = 3$ or $x = -3$. For a slightly more complicated example, consider the equation $(x - 1)^2 - 1 = 3$. Adding one to both sides yields $(x - 1)^2 = 4$; taking the square root of both sides yields $x - 1 = 2$. We can then add 1 to both sides to get $x = 3$. However, there's a second solution: we also have the possibility that $x - 1 = -2$, in which case $x = -1$. Both $x = 3$ and $x = -1$ are valid solutions, as can be verified by substituting them both into the original equation.

> **Review Video: Solving Equations with Exponents**
> Visit mometrix.com/academy and enter code: 514557

Solving Equations with Absolute Values

When solving an equation with an absolute value, the first step is to isolate the absolute value term. We then consider two possibilities: when the expression inside the absolute value is positive or when it is negative. In the former case, the expression in the absolute value equals the expression on the other side of the equation; in the latter, it equals the additive inverse of that expression—the expression times negative one. We consider each case separately and finally check for spurious solutions.

For instance, consider solving $|2x - 1| + x = 5$ for x. We can first isolate the absolute value by moving the x to the other side: $|2x - 1| = -x + 5$. Now, we have two possibilities. First, that $2x - 1$ is positive, and hence $2x - 1 = -x + 5$. Rearranging and combining like terms yields $3x = 6$, and hence $x = 2$. The other possibility is that $2x - 1$ is negative, and hence $2x - 1 = -(-x + 5) = x - 5$. In this case, rearranging and combining like terms yields $x = -4$. Substituting $x = 2$ and $x = -4$ back into the original equation, we see that they are both valid solutions.

Note that the absolute value of a sum or difference applies to the sum or difference as a whole, not to the individual terms; in general, $|2x - 1|$ is not equal to $|2x + 1|$ or to $|2x| - 1$.

Spurious Solutions

A **spurious solution** may arise when we square both sides of an equation as a step in solving it, or under certain other operations on the equation. It is a solution to the squared or otherwise modified equation that is *not* a solution of the original equation. To identify a spurious solution, it's useful when you solve an equation involving roots or absolute values to plug the solution back into the original equation to make sure it's valid.

Choosing Which Variable to Isolate in Two-Variable Equations

Similar to methods for a one-variable equation, solving a two-variable equation involves isolating a variable: manipulating the equation so that a variable appears by itself on one side of the equation, and not at all on the other side. However, in a two-variable equation, you will usually only be able to isolate one of the variables; the other variable may appear on the other side along with constant terms, or with exponents or other functions.

Often one variable will be much more easily isolated than the other, and therefore that's the variable you should choose. If one variable appears with various exponents, and the other only raised it to the first power, the latter variable is the one to isolate. Given the equation $a^2 + 2b = a^3 + b + 3$, the b only appears to the first power, whereas a appears squared and cubed, so b is the variable that can be solved for: combining like terms and isolating the b on the left side of the equation, we get $b = a^3 - a^2 + 3$. If both variables are equally easy to isolate, then it's best to isolate the independent variable, if one is defined. If the two variables are x and y, the convention is that y is the independent variable.

PRACTICE

P1. Seeing the equation $2x + 4 = 4x + 7$, a student divides the first terms on each side by 2, yielding $x + 4 = 2x + 7$, and then combines like terms to get $x = -3$. However, this is incorrect, as can be seen by substituting –3 into the original equation. Explain what is wrong with the student's reasoning.

P2. Describe the steps necessary to solve the equation $2x + 1 - x = 4 + 3x + 7$.

P3. Describe the steps necessary to solve the equation $2(x + 5) = 7(4 - x)$.

P4. Find all real solutions to the equation $1 - \sqrt{x} = 2$.

P5. Find all real solutions to the equation $|x + 1| = 2x + 5$.

P6. Solve for x: $-x + 2\sqrt{x + 5} + 1 = 3$.

P7. Ray earns $10 an hour at his job. Write an equation for his earnings as a function of time spent working. Determine how long Ray has to work in order to earn $360.

P8. Simplify the following: $3x + 2 + 2y = 5y - 7 + |2x - 1|$

PRACTICE SOLUTIONS

P1. As stated, it's easy to verify that the student's solution is incorrect: $2(-3) + 4 = -2$ and $4(-3) + 7 = -5$; clearly $-2 \neq -5$. The mistake was in the first step, which illustrates a common type of error in solving equations. The student tried to simplify the two variable terms by dividing them by 2. However, it's not valid to multiply or divide only one term on each side of an equation by a number; when multiplying or dividing, the operation must be applied to *every* term in the equation. So, dividing by 2 would yield not $x + 4 = 2x + 7$, but $x + 2 = 2x + \frac{7}{2}$. While this is now valid, that fraction is inconvenient to work with, so this may not be the best first step in solving the equation. Rather, it may have been better to first combine like terms: subtracting $4x$ from both sides yields $-2x + 4 = 7$; subtracting 4 from both sides yields $-2x = 3$; and *now* we can divide both sides by –2 to get $x = -\frac{3}{2}$.

P2. Our ultimate goal is to isolate the variable, x. To that end we first move all the terms containing x to the left side of the equation, and all the constant terms to the right side. Note that when we move a term to the other side of the equation its sign changes. We are therefore now left with $2x - x - 3x = 4 + 7 - 1$.

Next, we combine the like terms on each side of the equation, adding and subtracting the terms as appropriate. This leaves us with $-2x = 10$.

At this point, we're almost done; all that remains is to divide both sides by -2 to leave the x by itself. We now have our solution, $x = -5$. We can verify that this is a correct solution by substituting it back into the original equation.

P3. Generally, in equations that have a sum or difference of terms multiplied by another value or expression, the first step is to multiply those terms, distributing as necessary: $2(x + 5) = 2(x) + 2(5) = 2x + 10$, and $7(4 - x) = 7(4) - 7(x) = 28 - 7x$. So, the equation becomes $2x + 10 = 28 - 7x$. We can now add $7x$ to both sides to eliminate the variable from the right-hand side: $9x + 10 = 28$. Similarly, we can subtract 10 from both sides to move all the constants to the right: $9x = 18$. Finally, we can divide both sides by 9, yielding the final answer, $x = 2$.

P4. It's not hard to isolate the root: subtract one from both sides, yielding $-\sqrt{x} = 1$. Finally, multiply both sides by -1, yielding $\sqrt{x} = -1$. Squaring both sides of the equation yields $x = 1$. However, if we plug this back into the original equation, we get $1 - \sqrt{1} = 2$, which is false. Therefore $x = 1$ is a spurious solution, and the equation has no real solutions.

P5. This equation has two possibilities: $x + 1 = 2x + 5$, which simplifies to $x = -4$; or $x + 1 = -(2x + 5) = -2x - 5$, which simplifies to $x = -2$. However, if we try substituting both values back into the original equation, we see that only $x = -2$ yields a true statement. $x = -4$ is a spurious solution; $x = -2$ is the only valid solution to the equation.

P6. Start by isolating the term with the root. We can do that by moving the $-x$ and the 1 to the other side, yielding $2\sqrt{x + 5} = 3 + x - 1$, or $2\sqrt{x + 5} = x + 2$. Dividing both sides of the equation by 2 would give us a fractional term that could be messy to deal with, so we won't do that for now. Instead, we square both sides of the equation; note that on the left-hand side the 2 is outside the square root sign, so we have to square it. As a result, we get $4(x + 5) = (x + 2)^2$. Expanding both sides gives us $4x + 20 = x^2 + 4x + 4$. In this case, we see that we have $4x$ on both sides, so we can cancel the $4x$ (which is what allows us to solve this equation despite the different powers of x). We now have $20 = x^2 + 4$, or $x^2 = 16$. Since the variable is raised to an even power, we need to take the positive and negative roots, so $x = \pm 4$: that is, $x = 4$ or $x = -4$. Substituting both values into the original equation, we see that $x = 4$ satisfies the equation but $x = -4$ does not; hence $x = -4$ is a spurious solution, and the only solution to the equation is $x = 4$.

P7. The number of dollars that Ray earns is dependent on the number of hours he works, so earnings will be represented by the dependent variable y and hours worked will be represented by the independent variable x. He earns 10 dollars per hour worked, so his earnings can be calculated as $y = 10x$. To calculate the number of hours Ray must work in order to earn \$360, plug in 360 for y and solve for x:

$$360 = 10x$$
$$x = \frac{360}{10} = 36$$

P8. To simplify this equation, we must isolate one of its variables on one side of the equation. In this case, the x appears under an absolute value sign, which makes it difficult to isolate. The y, on the other hand, only appears without an exponent—the equation is linear in y. We will therefore choose to isolate the y. The first step, then, is to move all the terms with y to the left side of the equation, which we can do by subtracting $5y$ from both sides:

$$3x + 2 - 3y = -7 + |2x - 1|$$

We can then move all the terms that do *not* include y to the right side of the equation, by subtracting $3x$ and 2 from both sides of the equation:

$$-3y = -3x - 9 + |2x - 1|$$

Finally, we can isolate the y by dividing both sides by –3.

$$y = x + 3 - \frac{1}{3}|2x - 1|$$

This is as far as we can simplify the equation; we cannot combine the terms inside and outside the absolute value sign. We can therefore consider the equation to be solved.

INEQUALITIES
WORKING WITH INEQUALITIES

Commonly in algebra and other upper-level fields of math you find yourself working with mathematical expressions that do not equal each other. The statement comparing such expressions with symbols such as < (less than) or > (greater than) is called an *inequality*. An example of an inequality is $7x > 5$. To solve for x, simply divide both sides by 7 and the solution is shown to be $x > \frac{5}{7}$. Graphs of the solution set of inequalities are represented on a number line. Open circles are used to show that an expression approaches a number but is never quite equal to that number.

> **Review Video: Solving Multi-Step Inequalities**
> Visit mometrix.com/academy and enter code: 347842

Conditional inequalities are those with certain values for the variable that will make the condition true and other values for the variable where the condition will be false. **Absolute inequalities** can have any real number as the value for the variable to make the condition true, while there is no real number value for the variable that will make the condition false. Solving inequalities is done by following the same rules as for solving equations with the exception that when multiplying or dividing by a negative number the direction of the inequality sign must be flipped or reversed. **Double inequalities** are situations where two inequality statements apply to the same variable expression. An example of this is $-c < ax + b < c$.

> **Review Video: Conditional and Absolute Inequalities**
> Visit mometrix.com/academy and enter code: 980164

DETERMINING SOLUTIONS TO INEQUALITIES

To determine whether a coordinate is a solution of an inequality, you can substitute the values of the coordinate into the inequality, simplify, and check whether the resulting statement holds true. For instance, to determine whether $(-2, 4)$ is a solution of the inequality $y \geq -2x + 3$, substitute the values into the inequality, $4 \geq -2(-2) + 3$. Simplify the right side of the inequality and the result is $4 \geq 7$, which is a false statement. Therefore, the coordinate is not a solution of the inequality. You can also use this method to determine which part of the graph of an inequality is shaded. The graph of $y \geq -2x + 3$ includes the solid line $y = -2x + 3$ and, since it excludes the point $(-2, 4)$ to the left of the line, it is shaded to the right of the line.

FLIPPING INEQUALITY SIGNS

When given an inequality, we can always turn the entire inequality around, swapping the two sides of the inequality and changing the inequality sign. For instance, $x + 2 > 2x - 3$ is equivalent to

$2x - 3 < x + 2$. Aside from that, normally the inequality does not change if we carry out the same operation on both sides of the inequality. There is, however, one principal exception: if we *multiply* or *divide* both sides of the inequality by a *negative number*, the inequality is flipped. For example, if we take the inequality $-2x < 6$ and divide both sides by -2, the inequality flips and we are left with $x > -3$. This *only* applies to multiplication and division, and only with negative numbers. Multiplying or dividing both sides by a positive number, or adding or subtracting any number regardless of sign, does not flip the inequality.

COMPOUND INEQUALITIES

A **compound inequality** is an equality that consists of two inequalities combined with *and* or *or*. The two components of a proper compound inequality must be of opposite type: that is, one must be greater than (or greater than or equal to), the other less than (or less than or equal to). For instance, "$x + 1 < 2$ or $x + 1 > 3$" is a compound inequality, as is "$2x \geq 4$ and $2x \leq 6$." An *and* inequality can be written more compactly by having one inequality on each side of the common part: "$2x \geq 1$ and $2x \leq 6$," can also be written as $1 \leq 2x \leq 6$.

In order for the compound inequality to be meaningful, the two parts of an *and* inequality must overlap; otherwise no numbers satisfy the inequality. On the other hand, if the two parts of an *or* inequality overlap, then *all* numbers satisfy the inequality and as such the inequality is usually not meaningful.

Solving a compound inequality requires solving each part separately. For example, given the compound inequality "$x + 1 < 2$ or $x + 1 > 3$," the first inequality, $x + 1 < 2$, reduces to $x < 1$, and the second part, $x + 1 > 3$, reduces to $x > 2$, so the whole compound inequality can be written as "$x < 1$ or $x > 2$." Similarly, $1 \leq 2x \leq 6$ can be solved by dividing each term by 2, yielding $\frac{1}{2} \leq x \leq 3$.

> **Review Video: Compound Inequalities**
> Visit mometrix.com/academy and enter code: 786318

SOLVING INEQUALITIES INVOLVING ABSOLUTE VALUES

To solve an inequality involving an absolute value, first isolate the term with the absolute value. Then proceed to treat the two cases separately as with an absolute value equation, but flipping the inequality in the case where the expression in the absolute value is negative (since that essentially involves multiplying both sides by -1.) The two cases are then combined into a compound inequality; if the absolute value is on the greater side of the inequality, then it is an *or* compound inequality, if on the lesser side, then it's an *and*.

Consider the inequality $2 + |x - 1| \geq 3$. We can isolate the absolute value term by subtracting 2 from both sides: $|x - 1| \geq 1$. Now, we're left with the two cases $x - 1 \geq 1$ or $x - 1 \leq -1$: note that in the latter, negative case, the inequality is flipped. $x - 1 \geq 1$ reduces to $x \geq 2$, and $x - 1 \leq -1$ reduces to $x \leq 0$. Since in the inequality $|x - 1| \geq 1$ the absolute value is on the greater side, the two cases combine into an *or* compound inequality, so the final, solved inequality is "$x \leq 0$ or $x \geq 2$."

SOLVING INEQUALITIES INVOLVING SQUARE ROOTS

Solving an inequality with a square root involves two parts. First, we solve the inequality as if it were an equation, isolating the square root and then squaring both sides of the equation. Second, we restrict the solution to the set of values of x for which the value inside the square root sign is non-negative.

For example, in the inequality, $\sqrt{x-2} + 1 < 5$, we can isolate the square root by subtracting 1 from both sides, yielding $\sqrt{x-2} < 4$. Squaring both sides of the inequality yields $x - 2 < 16$, so $x < 18$. Since we can't take the square root of a negative number, we also require the part inside the square root to be non-negative. In this case, that means $x - 2 \geq 0$. Adding 2 to both sides of the inequality yields $x \geq 2$. Our final answer is a compound inequality combining the two simple inequalities: $x \geq 2$ and $x < 18$, or $2 \leq x < 18$.

Note that we only get a compound inequality if the two simple inequalities are in opposite directions; otherwise we take the one that is more restrictive.

The same technique can be used for other even roots, such as fourth roots. It is *not*, however, used for cube roots or other odd roots—negative numbers *do* have cube roots, so the condition that the quantity inside the root sign cannot be negative does not apply.

> **Review Video: Solving Inequalities Involving Square Roots**
> Visit mometrix.com/academy and enter code: 800288

SPECIAL CIRCUMSTANCES

Sometimes an inequality involving an absolute value or an even exponent is true for all values of x, and we don't need to do any further work to solve it. This is true if the inequality, once the absolute value or exponent term is isolated, says that term is greater than a negative number (or greater than or equal to zero). Since an absolute value or a number raised to an even exponent is *always* non-negative, this inequality is always true.

GRAPHICAL SOLUTIONS TO EQUATIONS AND INEQUALITIES

When equations are shown graphically, they are usually shown on a **Cartesian coordinate plane**. The Cartesian coordinate plane consists of two number lines placed perpendicular to each other, and intersecting at the zero point, also known as the origin. The horizontal number line is known as the x-axis, with positive values to the right of the origin, and negative values to the left of the origin. The vertical number line is known as the y-axis, with positive values above the origin, and negative values below the origin. Any point on the plane can be identified by an ordered pair in the form (x, y), called coordinates. The x-value of the coordinate is called the abscissa, and the y-value of the coordinate is called the ordinate. The two number lines divide the plane into **four quadrants**: I, II, III, and IV.

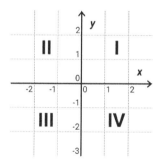

Note that in quadrant I $x > 0$ and $y > 0$, in quadrant II $x < 0$ and $y > 0$, in quadrant III $x < 0$ and $y < 0$, and in quadrant IV $x > 0$ and $y < 0$.

Recall that if the value of the slope of a line is positive, the line slopes upward from left to right. If the value of the slope is negative, the line slopes downward from left to right. If the y-coordinates are the same for two points on a line, the slope is 0 and the line is a **horizontal line**. If the x-

coordinates are the same for two points on a line, there is no slope and the line is a **vertical line**. Two or more lines that have equivalent slopes are **parallel lines**. **Perpendicular lines** have slopes that are negative reciprocals of each other, such as $\frac{a}{b}$ and $\frac{-b}{a}$.

GRAPHING SIMPLE INEQUALITIES

To graph a simple inequality, we first mark on the number line the value that signifies the end point of the inequality. If the inequality is strict (involves a less than or greater than), we use a hollow circle; if it is not strict (less than or equal to or greater than or equal to), we use a solid circle. We then fill in the part of the number line that satisfies the inequality: to the left of the marked point for less than (or less than or equal to), to the right for greater than (or greater than or equal to).

For example, we would graph the inequality $x < 5$ by putting a hollow circle at 5 and filling in the part of the line to the left:

GRAPHING COMPOUND INEQUALITIES

To graph a compound inequality, we fill in both parts of the inequality for an *or* inequality, or the overlap between them for an *and* inequality. More specifically, we start by plotting the endpoints of each inequality on the number line. For an *or* inequality, we then fill in the appropriate side of the line for each inequality. Typically, the two component inequalities do not overlap, that means the shaded part is *outside* the two points. For an *and* inequality, we instead fill in the part of the line that meets both inequalities.

For the inequality "$x \leq -3$ or $x > 4$," we first put a solid circle at –3 and a hollow circle at 4. We then fill the parts of the line *outside* these circles:

GRAPHING INEQUALITIES INCLUDING ABSOLUTE VALUES

An inequality with an absolute value can be converted to a compound inequality. To graph the inequality, first convert it to a compound inequality, and then graph that normally. If the absolute value is on the greater side of the inequality, we end up with an *or* inequality; we plot the endpoints of the inequality on the number line and fill in the part of the line *outside* those points. If the absolute value is on the smaller side of the inequality, we end up with an *and* inequality; we plot the endpoints of the inequality on the number line and fill in the part of the line *between* those points.

For example, the inequality $|x + 1| \geq 4$ can be rewritten as $x \geq 3$ or $x \leq -5$. We place solid circles at the points 3 and -5 and fill in the part of the line *outside* them:

GRAPHING EQUATIONS IN TWO VARIABLES

One way of graphing an equation in two variables is to plot enough points to get an idea for its shape, and then draw the appropriate curve through those points. A point can be plotted by substituting in a value for one variable and solving for the other. If the equation is linear, we only need two points, and can then draw a straight line between them.

> **Review Video: Linear Function**
> Visit mometrix.com/academy and enter code: 699478

For example, consider the equation $y = 2x - 1$. This is a linear equation—both variables only appear raised to the first power—so we only need two points. When $x = 0$, $y = 2(0) - 1 = -1$. When $x = 2$, $y = 2(2) - 1 = 3$. We can therefore choose the points $(0, -1)$ and $(2, 3)$, and draw a line between them:

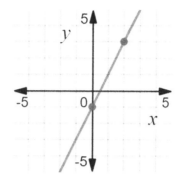

GRAPHING INEQUALITIES IN TWO VARIABLES

To graph an inequality in two variables, we first graph the border of the inequality. This means graphing the equation that we get if we replace the inequality sign with an equals sign. If the inequality is strict (> or <), we graph the border with a dashed or dotted line; if it is not strict (≥ or ≤), we use a solid line. We can then test any point not on the border to see if it satisfies the inequality. If it does, we shade in that side of the border; if not, we shade in the other side. As an example, consider $y > 2x + 2$. To graph this inequality, we first graph the border, $y = 2x + 2$. Since it is a strict inequality, we use a dashed line. Then, we choose a test point. This can be any point not on the border; in this case, we will choose the origin, $(0, 0)$. (This makes the calculation easy and is generally a good choice unless the border passes through the origin.) Putting this into the original inequality, we get $0 > 2(0) + 2$, i.e. $0 > 2$. This is *not* true, so we shade in the side of the border that does *not* include the point $(0, 0)$:

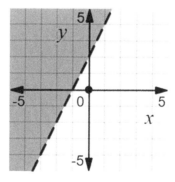

GRAPHING COMPOUND INEQUALITIES IN TWO VARIABLES

One way to graph a compound inequality in two variables is to first graph each of the component inequalities. For an *and* inequality, we then shade in only the parts where the two graphs overlap; for an *or* inequality, we shade in any region that pertains to either of the individual inequalities.

Consider the graph of "$y \geq x - 1$ and $y \leq -x$":

We first shade in the individual inequalities:

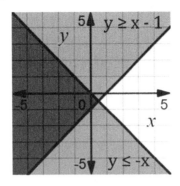

Now, since the compound inequality has an *and*, we only leave shaded the overlap—the part that pertains to *both* inequalities:

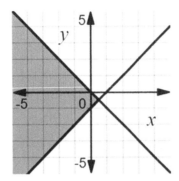

If instead the inequality had been "$y \geq x - 1$ or $y \leq -x$," our final graph would involve the *total* shaded area:

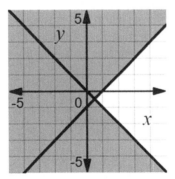

> **Review Video: Graphing Solutions to Inequalities**
> Visit mometrix.com/academy and enter code: 391281

PRACTICE

P1. Analyze the following inequalities:

(a) $2 - |x + 1| < 3$
(b) $2(x - 1)^2 + 7 \leq 1$

P2. Graph the following on a number line:

(a) $x \geq 3$
(b) $-2 \leq x \leq 6$
(c) $|x| < 2$

PRACTICE SOLUTIONS

P1. (a) Subtracting 2 from both sides yields $-|x+1| < 1$; multiplying by -1 and flipping the inequality, since we're multiplying by a negative number, yields $|x+1| > -1$. But since the absolute value cannot be negative, it's *always* greater than -1, so this inequality is true for all values of x.

(b) Subtracting 7 from both sides yields $2(x-1)^2 \leq -6$; dividing by 2 yields $(x-1)^2 \leq -3$. But $(x-1)^2$ must be nonnegative, and hence cannot be less than or equal to -3; this inequality has no solution.

P2. (a) We would graph the inequality $x \geq 3$ by putting a solid circle at 3 and filling in the part of the line to the right:

(b) The inequality $-2 \leq x \leq 6$ is equivalent to "$x \geq -2$ and $x \leq 6$." To plot this compound inequality, we first put solid circles at -2 and 6, and then fill in the part of the line *between* these circles:

(c) The inequality $|x| < 2$ can be rewritten as "$x > -2$ and $x < 2$." We place hollow circles at the points -2 and 2 and fill in the part of the line between them:

SYSTEMS OF EQUATIONS
SOLVING SYSTEMS OF EQUATIONS

Systems of equations are sets of simultaneous equations that all use the same variables. A solution to a system of equations must be true for each equation in the system. **Consistent systems** are those with at least one solution. **Inconsistent systems** are systems of equations that have no solution.

> **Review Video: Solving Linear Equations**
> Visit mometrix.com/academy and enter code: 746745

SUBSTITUTION

To solve a system of linear equations by **substitution**, start with the easier equation and solve for one of the variables. Express this variable in terms of the other variable. Substitute this expression in the other equation, and solve for the other variable. The solution should be expressed in the form

(x, y). Substitute the values into both of the original equations to check your answer. Consider the following system of equations:

$$x + 6y = 15$$
$$3x - 12y = 18$$

Solving the first equation for x: $x = 15 - 6y$

Substitute this value in place of x in the second equation, and solve for y:

$$3(15 - 6y) - 12y = 18$$
$$45 - 18y - 12y = 18$$
$$30y = 27$$
$$y = \frac{27}{30} = \frac{9}{10} = 0.9$$

Plug this value for y back into the first equation to solve for x:

$$x = 15 - 6(0.9) = 15 - 5.4 = 9.6$$

Check both equations if you have time:

$$9.6 + 6(0.9) = 15 \qquad 3(9.6) - 12(0.9) = 18$$
$$9.6 + 5.4 = 15 \qquad 28.8 - 10.8 = 18$$
$$15 = 15 \qquad 18 = 18$$

Therefore, the solution is (9.6, 0.9).

> **Review Video: What is the Substitution Method?**
> Visit mometrix.com/academy and enter code: 565151

ELIMINATION

To solve a system of equations using **elimination**, begin by rewriting both equations in standard form $Ax + By = C$. Check to see if the coefficients of one pair of like variables add to zero. If not, multiply one or both of the equations by a non-zero number to make one set of like variables add to zero. Add the two equations to solve for one of the variables. Substitute this value into one of the original equations to solve for the other variable. Check your work by substituting into the other equation. Now, let's look at solving the following system using the elimination method:

$$5x + 6y = 4$$
$$x + 2y = 4$$

If we multiply the second equation by -3, we can eliminate the y terms:

$$5x + 6y = 4$$
$$-3x - 6y = -12$$

Add the equations together and solve for x:

$$2x = -8$$
$$x = \frac{-8}{2} = -4$$

Plug the value for x back in to either of the original equations and solve for y:

$$-4 + 2y = 4$$
$$y = \frac{4+4}{2} = 4$$

Check both equations if you have time:

$$5(-4) + 6(4) = 4 \qquad -4 + 2(4) = 4$$
$$-20 + 24 = 4 \qquad -4 + 8 = 4$$
$$4 = 4 \qquad 4 = 4$$

Therefore, the solution is (-4, 4).

> **Review Video: Substitution and Elimination for Solving Linear Systems**
> Visit mometrix.com/academy and enter code: 958611

GRAPHICALLY

To solve a system of linear equations **graphically**, plot both equations on the same graph. The solution of the equations is the point where both lines cross. If the lines do not cross (are parallel), then there is **no solution**.

For example, consider the following system of equations:

$$y = 2x + 7$$
$$y = -x + 1$$

Since these equations are given in slope-intercept form, they are easy to graph; the y intercepts of the lines are (0, 7) and (0, 1). The respective slopes are 2 and –1, thus the graphs look like this:

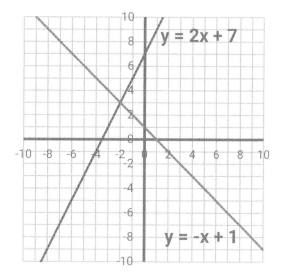

The two lines intersect at the point $(-2, 3)$, thus this is the solution to the system of equations.

Solving a system graphically is generally only practical if both coordinates of the solution are integers; otherwise the intersection will lie between gridlines on the graph and the coordinates will be difficult or impossible to determine exactly. It also helps if, as in this example, the equations are in slope-intercept form or some other form that makes them easy to graph. Otherwise, another method of solution (by substitution or elimination) is likely to be more useful.

SOLVING SYSTEMS OF EQUATIONS USING THE TRACE FEATURE

Using the **trace feature** on a calculator requires that you rewrite each equation, isolating the y-variable on one side of the equal sign. Enter both equations in the graphing calculator and plot the graphs simultaneously. Use the trace cursor to find where the two lines cross. Use the zoom feature if necessary to obtain more accurate results. Always check your answer by substituting into the original equations. The trace method is likely to be less accurate than other methods due to the resolution of graphing calculators, but is a useful tool to provide an approximate answer.

CALCULATIONS USING POINTS

Sometimes you need to perform calculations using only points on a graph as input data. Using points, you can determine what the **midpoint** and **distance** are. If you know the equation for a line you can calculate the distance between the line and the point.

To find the **midpoint** of two points (x_1, y_1) and (x_2, y_2), average the x-coordinates to get the x-coordinate of the midpoint, and average the y-coordinates to get the y-coordinate of the midpoint. The formula is: $\left(\frac{x_1+x_2}{2}, \frac{y_1+y_2}{2}\right)$.

The **distance** between two points is the same as the length of the hypotenuse of a right triangle with the two given points as endpoints, and the two sides of the right triangle parallel to the x-axis and y-axis, respectively. The length of the segment parallel to the x-axis is the difference between the x-coordinates of the two points. The length of the segment parallel to the y-axis is the difference between the y-coordinates of the two points. Use the Pythagorean theorem $a^2 + b^2 = c^2$ or $c = \sqrt{a^2 + b^2}$ to find the distance. The formula is $d = \sqrt{(x_2 - x_1)^2 + (y_2 - y_1)^2}$.

When a line is in the format $Ax + By + C = 0$, where A, B, and C are coefficients, you can use a point (x_1, y_1) not on the line and apply the formula $d = \frac{|Ax_1 + By_1 + C|}{\sqrt{A^2 + B^2}}$ to find the distance between the line and the point (x_1, y_1).

> **Review Video: Calculations Using Points on a Graph**
> Visit mometrix.com/academy and enter code: 883228

PRACTICE

P1. Solve the following systems of equations:

(a) $\quad 3x + 4y = 9$
$\quad\quad -12x + 7y = 10$

(b) $-3x + 2y = -1$
$\quad\quad 4x - 5y = 6$

P2. Find the distance and midpoint between points $(2, 4)$ and $(8, 6)$.

PRACTICE SOLUTIONS

P1. (a) If we multiply the first equation by 4, we can eliminate the x terms:

$$12x + 16y = 36$$
$$-12x + 7y = 10$$

Add the equations together and solve for y:

$$23y = 46$$
$$y = 2$$

Plug the value for y back in to either of the original equations and solve for x:

$$3x + 4(2) = 9$$
$$x = \frac{9-8}{3} = \frac{1}{3}$$

The solution is $\left(\frac{1}{3}, 2\right)$

(b) Solving the first equation for y:

$$-3x + 2y = -1$$
$$2y = 3x - 1$$
$$y = \frac{3x-1}{2}$$

Substitute this expression in place of y in the second equation, and solve for x:

$$4x - 5\left(\frac{3x-1}{2}\right) = 6$$
$$4x - \frac{15x}{2} + \frac{5}{2} = 6$$
$$8x - 15x + 5 = 12$$
$$-7x = 7$$
$$x = -1$$

Plug the value for x back in to either of the original equations and solve for y:

$$-3(-1) + 2y = -1$$
$$3 + 2y = -1$$
$$2y = -4$$
$$y = -2$$

The solution is $(-1, -2)$

P2. Use the formulas for distance and midpoint:

$$\text{Distance} = \sqrt{(x_2 - x_1)^2 + (y_2 - y_1)^2}$$
$$= \sqrt{(8-2)^2 + (6-4)^2}$$
$$= \sqrt{(6)^2 + (2)^2}$$
$$= \sqrt{36 + 4}$$
$$= \sqrt{40} \text{ or } 2\sqrt{10}$$

$$\text{Midpoint} = \left(\frac{x_1 + x_2}{2}, \frac{y_1 + y_2}{2}\right)$$
$$= \left(\frac{2+8}{2}, \frac{4+6}{2}\right)$$
$$= \left(\frac{10}{2}, \frac{10}{2}\right)$$
$$= (5,5)$$

POLYNOMIAL ALGEBRA

POLYNOMIALS

Polynomials are made up of monomials and polynomials. A **monomial** is a single constant, variable, or product of constants and variables, such as 7, x, $2x$, or x^3y. There will never be addition or subtraction symbols in a monomial. Like monomials have like variables, but they may have different coefficients. **Polynomials** are algebraic expressions which use addition and subtraction to combine two or more monomials. Two terms make a **binomial**, three terms make a **trinomial**, etc. The **degree of a monomial** is the sum of the exponents of the variables. The **degree of a polynomial** is the highest degree of any individual term.

> **Review Video: Polynomials**
> Visit mometrix.com/academy and enter code: 305005

SIMPLIFYING POLYNOMIALS

Simplifying polynomials requires combining like terms. The like terms in a polynomial expression are those that have the same variable raised to the same power. It is often helpful to connect the like terms with arrows or lines in order to separate them from the other monomials. Once you have determined the like terms, you can rearrange the polynomial by placing them together. Remember to include the sign that is in front of each term. Once the like terms are placed together, you can apply each operation and simplify. When adding and subtracting polynomials, only add and subtract the **coefficient**, or the number part; the variable and exponent stay the same.

> **Review Video: Adding and Subtracting Polynomials**
> Visit mometrix.com/academy and enter code: 124088

THE FOIL METHOD

In general, multiplying polynomials is done by multiplying each term in one polynomial by each term in the other and adding the results. In the specific case for multiplying binomials, there is useful acronym, FOIL, that can help you make sure to cover each combination of terms. The **FOIL method** for $(Ax + By)(Cx + Dy)$ would be:

F	Multiply the *first* terms of each binomial	$(\overset{first}{Ax} + By)(\overset{first}{Cx} + Dy)$	ACx^2
O	Multiply the *outer* terms	$(\overset{outer}{Ax} + By)(Cx + \overset{outer}{Dy})$	$ADxy$
I	Multiply the *inner* terms	$(Ax + \overset{inner}{By})(\overset{inner}{Cx} + Dy)$	$BCxy$
L	Multiply the *last* terms of each binomial	$(Ax + \overset{last}{By})(Cx + \overset{last}{Dy})$	BDy^2

Then add up the result of each and combine like terms: $ACx^2 + (AD + BC)xy + BDy^2$.

For example, using the FOIL method on binomials $(x + 2)$ and $(x - 3)$:

First: $(\boxed{x} + 2)(\boxed{x} + (-3)) \rightarrow (x)(x) = x^2$
Outer: $(\boxed{x} + 2)(x + \boxed{(-3)}) \rightarrow (x)(-3) = -3x$
Inner: $(x + \boxed{2})(\boxed{x} + (-3)) \rightarrow (2)(x) = 2x$
Last: $(x + \boxed{2})(x + \boxed{(-3)}) \rightarrow (2)(-3) = -6$

This results in: $(x^2) + (-3x) + (2x) + (-6)$

Combine like terms: $x^2 + (-3 + 2)x + (-6) = x^2 - x - 6$

> **Review Video: Multiplying Terms Using the FOIL Method**
> Visit mometrix.com/academy and enter code: 854792

DIVIDING POLYNOMIALS

Use long division to divide a polynomial by either a monomial or another polynomial of equal or lesser degree.

When **dividing by a monomial**, divide each term of the polynomial by the monomial.

When **dividing by a polynomial**, begin by arranging the terms of each polynomial in order of one variable. You may arrange in ascending or descending order, but be consistent with both polynomials. To get the first term of the quotient, divide the first term of the dividend by the first term of the divisor. Multiply the first term of the quotient by the entire divisor and subtract that product from the dividend. Repeat for the second and successive terms until you either get a remainder of zero or a remainder whose degree is less than the degree of the divisor. If the quotient has a remainder, write the answer as a mixed expression in the form:

$$\text{quotient} + \frac{\text{remainder}}{\text{divisor}}$$

For example, we can evaluate the following expression in the same way as long division:

$$\frac{x^3 - 3x^2 - 2x + 5}{x - 5}$$

$$\begin{array}{r}
x^2 + 2x + 8 \\
x - 5 \overline{\smash{)}\, x^3 - 3x^2 - 2x + 5} \\
\underline{x^3 - 5x^2} \\
2x^2 - 2x \\
\underline{2x^2 - 10x} \\
8x + 5 \\
\underline{8x + 40} \\
45
\end{array}$$

$$\frac{x^3 - 3x^2 - 2x + 5}{x - 5} = x^2 + 2x + 8 + \frac{45}{x - 5}$$

When **factoring** a polynomial, first check for a common monomial factor, that is look to see if each coefficient has a common factor or if each term has an x in it. If the factor is a trinomial but not a perfect trinomial square, look for a factorable form, such as one of these:

$$x^2 + (a + b)x + ab = (x + a)(x + b)$$
$$(ac)x^2 + (ad + bc)x + bd = (ax + b)(cx + d)$$

For factors with four terms, look for groups to factor. Once you have found the factors, write the original polynomial as the product of all the factors. Make sure all of the polynomial factors are prime. Monomial factors may be *prime* or *composite*. Check your work by multiplying the factors to make sure you get the original polynomial.

Below are patterns of some special products to remember to help make factoring easier:

- Perfect trinomial squares: $x^2 + 2xy + y^2 = (x + y)^2$ or $x^2 - 2xy + y^2 = (x - y)^2$
- Difference between two squares: $x^2 - y^2 = (x + y)(x - y)$
- Sum of two cubes: $x^3 + y^3 = (x + y)(x^2 - xy + y^2)$
  - Note: the second factor is *not* the same as a perfect trinomial square, so do not try to factor it further.
- Difference between two cubes: $x^3 - y^3 = (x - y)(x^2 + xy + y^2)$
  - Again, the second factor is *not* the same as a perfect trinomial square.
- Perfect cubes: $x^3 + 3x^2y + 3xy^2 + y^3 = (x + y)^3$ and $x^3 - 3x^2y + 3xy^2 - y^3 = (x - y)^3$

RATIONAL EXPRESSIONS

Rational expressions are fractions with polynomials in both the numerator and the denominator; the value of the polynomial in the denominator cannot be equal to zero. Be sure to keep track of values that make the denominator of the original expression zero as the final result inherits the same restrictions. For example, a denominator of $x - 3$ indicates that the expression is not defined when $x = 3$ and as such, regardless of any operations done to the expression, it remains undefined there.

To **add or subtract** rational expressions, first find the common denominator, then rewrite each fraction as an equivalent fraction with the common denominator. Finally, add or subtract the numerators to get the numerator of the answer, and keep the common denominator as the denominator of the answer.

When **multiplying** rational expressions factor each polynomial and cancel like factors (a factor which appears in both the numerator and the denominator). Then, multiply all remaining factors in the numerator to get the numerator of the product, and multiply the remaining factors in the denominator to get the denominator of the product. Remember: cancel entire factors, not individual terms.

To **divide** rational expressions, take the reciprocal of the divisor (the rational expression you are dividing by) and multiply by the dividend.

> **Review Video: Rational Expressions**
> Visit mometrix.com/academy and enter code: 415183

SIMPLIFYING RATIONAL EXPRESSIONS

To simplify a rational expression, factor the numerator and denominator completely. Factors that are the same and appear in the numerator and denominator have a ratio of 1. For example, look at the following expression:

$$\frac{x-1}{1-x^2}$$

The denominator, $(1-x^2)$, is a difference of squares. It can be factored as $(1-x)(1+x)$. The factor $1-x$ and the numerator $x-1$ are opposites and have a ratio of -1. Rewrite the numerator as $-1(1-x)$. So, the rational expression can be simplified as follows:

$$\frac{x-1}{1-x^2} = \frac{-1(1-x)}{(1-x)(1+x)} = \frac{-1}{1+x}$$

Note that since the original expression is only defined for $x \neq \{-1, 1\}$, the simplified expression has the same restrictions.

> **Review Video: Reducing Rational Expressions**
> Visit mometrix.com/academy and enter code: 788868

PRACTICE

P1. Expand the following polynomials:

(a) $(x+3)(x-7)(2x)$

(b) $(x+2)^2(x-2)^2$

(c) $(x^2+5x+5)(3x-1)$

P2. Evaluate the following rational expressions:

(a) $\frac{x^3-2x^2-5x+6}{3x+6}$

(b) $\frac{x^2+4x+4}{4-x^2}$

Practice Solutions

P1. (a) Apply the FOIL method and the distributive property of multiplication:

$$(x+3)(x-7)(2x) = (x^2 - 7x + 3x - 21)(2x)$$
$$= (x^2 - 4x - 21)(2x)$$
$$= 2x^3 - 8x^2 - 42x$$

(b) Note the difference of squares form:

$$(x+2)^2(x-2)^2 = (x+2)(x+2)(x-2)(x-2)$$
$$= [(x+2)(x-2)][(x+2)(x-2)]$$
$$= (x^2 - 4)(x^2 - 4)$$
$$= x^4 - 8x^2 + 16$$

(c) Multiply each pair of monomials and combine like terms:

$$(x^2 + 5x + 5)(3x - 1) = 3x^3 + 15x^2 + 15x - x^2 - 5x - 5$$
$$= 3x^3 + 14x^2 + 10x - 5$$

P2. (a) Rather than trying to factor the fourth-degree polynomial, we can use long division:

$$\frac{x^3 - 2x^2 - 5x + 6}{3x + 6} = \frac{x^3 - 2x^2 - 5x + 6}{3(x+2)}$$

$$\begin{array}{r}
x^2 - 4x + 3 \\
x+2 \overline{\smash{)}\, x^3 - 2x^2 - 5x + 6} \\
\underline{x^3 + 2x^2} \\
-4x^2 - 5x \\
\underline{-4x^2 - 8x} \\
3x + 6 \\
\underline{3x + 6} \\
0
\end{array}$$

$$\frac{x^3 - 2x^2 - 5x + 6}{3(x+2)} = \frac{x^2 - 4x + 3}{3}$$

Note that since the original expression is only defined for $x \neq \{-2\}$, the simplified expression has the same restrictions.

(b) The denominator, $(4 - x^2)$, is a difference of squares. It can be factored as $(2-x)(2+x)$. The numerator, $(x^2 + 4x + 4)$, is a perfect square. It can be factored as $(x+2)(x+2)$. So, the rational expression can be simplified as follows:

$$\frac{x^2 + 4x + 4}{4 - x^2} = \frac{(x+2)(x+2)}{(2-x)(2+x)} = \frac{(x+2)}{(2-x)}$$

Note that since the original expression is only defined for $x \neq \{-2, 2\}$, the simplified expression has the same restrictions.

QUADRATICS
SOLVING QUADRATIC EQUATIONS

Quadratic equations are a special set of trinomials of the form $y = ax^2 + bx + c$ that occur commonly in math and real-world applications. The **roots** of a quadratic equation are the solutions that satisfy the equation when $y = 0$; in other words, where the graph touches the x-axis. There are several ways to determine these solutions including using the quadratic formula, factoring, completing the square, and graphing the function.

> **Review Video: Changing Constants in Graphs of Functions: Quadratic Equations**
> Visit mometrix.com/academy and enter code: 476276

QUADRATIC FORMULA

The **quadratic formula** is used to solve quadratic equations when other methods are more difficult. To use the quadratic formula to solve a quadratic equation, begin by rewriting the equation in standard form $ax^2 + bx + c = 0$, where a, b, and c are coefficients. Once you have identified the values of the coefficients, substitute those values into the quadratic formula

$$x = \frac{-b \pm \sqrt{b^2 - 4ac}}{2a}$$

Evaluate the equation and simplify the expression. Again, check each root by substituting into the original equation. In the quadratic formula, the portion of the formula under the radical ($b^2 - 4ac$) is called the **discriminant**. If the discriminant is zero, there is only one root: $-\frac{b}{2a}$. If the discriminant is positive, there are two different real roots. If the discriminant is negative, there are no real roots, you will instead find complex roots. Often these solutions don't make sense in context and are ignored.

> **Review Video: Using the Quadratic Formula**
> Visit mometrix.com/academy and enter code: 163102

FACTORING

To solve a quadratic equation by factoring, begin by rewriting the equation in standard form, $x^2 + bx + c = 0$. Remember that the goal of factoring is to find numbers f and g such that $(x + f)(x + g) = x^2 + (f + g)x + fg$, in other words $(f + g) = b$ and $fg = c$. This can be a really useful method when b and c are integers. Determine the factors of c and look for pairs that could sum to b.

For example, consider finding the roots of $x^2 + 6x - 16 = 0$. The factors of -16 include, -4 and 4, -8 and 2, -2 and 8, -1 and 16, and 1 and -16. The factors that sum to 6 are -2 and 8. Write these factors as the product of two binomials, $0 = (x - 2)(x + 8)$. Finally, since these binomials multiply together to equal zero, set them each equal to zero and solve each for x. This results in $x - 2 = 0$, which simplifies to $x = 2$ and $x + 8 = 0$, which simplifies to $x = -8$. Therefore, the roots of the equation are 2 and -8.

> **Review Video: Factoring Quadratic Equations**
> Visit mometrix.com/academy and enter code: 336566

COMPLETING THE SQUARE

One way to find the roots of a quadratic equation is to find a way to manipulate it such that it follows the form of a perfect square ($x^2 + 2px + p^2$) by adding and subtracting a constant. This process is called **completing the square**. In other words, if you are given a quadratic that is not a perfect square, $x^2 + bx + c = 0$, you can find a constant d that could be added in to make it a perfect square:

$$x^2 + bx + c + (d - d) = 0; \text{ \{Let } b = 2p \text{ and } c + d = p^2\}$$
$$\text{then: } x^2 + 2px + p^2 - d = 0 \text{ and } d = \frac{b^2}{4} - c$$

Once you have completed the square you can find the roots of the resulting equation:

$$x^2 + 2px + p^2 - d = 0$$
$$(x + p)^2 = d$$
$$x + p = \pm\sqrt{d}$$
$$x = -p \pm \sqrt{d}$$

It is worth noting that substituting the original expressions into this solution gives the same result as the quadratic formula where $a = 1$:

$$x = -p \pm \sqrt{d} = -\frac{b}{2} \pm \sqrt{\frac{b^2}{4} - c} = -\frac{b}{2} \pm \frac{\sqrt{b^2 - 4c}}{2} = \frac{-b \pm \sqrt{b^2 - 4c}}{2}$$

Completing the square can be seen as arranging block representations of each of the terms to be as close to a square as possible and then filling in the gaps. For example, consider the quadratic expression $x^2 + 6x + 2$:

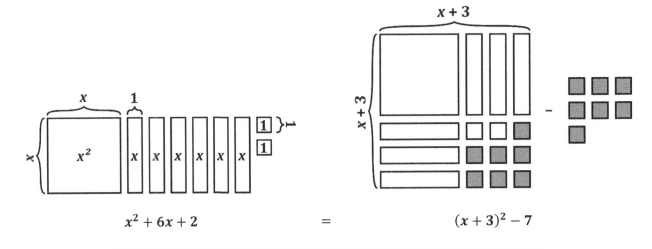

$$x^2 + 6x + 2 \quad = \quad (x + 3)^2 - 7$$

> **Review Video: Completing the Square**
> Visit mometrix.com/academy and enter code: 982479

USING GIVEN ROOTS TO FIND QUADRATIC EQUATION

One way to find the roots of a quadratic equation is to factor the equation and use the **zero product property**, setting each factor of the equation equal to zero to find the corresponding root. We can use this technique in reverse to find an equation given its roots. Each root corresponds to a linear equation which in turn corresponds to a factor of the quadratic equation.

For example, we can find a quadratic equation whose roots are $x = 2$ and $x = -1$. The root $x = 2$ corresponds to the equation $x - 2 = 0$, and the root $x = -1$ corresponds to the equation $x + 1 = 0$.

These two equations correspond to the factors $(x - 2)$ and $(x + 1)$, from which we can derive the equation $(x - 2)(x + 1) = 0$, or $x^2 - x - 2 = 0$.

Any integer multiple of this entire equation will also yield the same roots, as the integer will simply cancel out when the equation is factored. For example, $2x^2 - 2x - 4 = 0$ factors as $2(x - 2)(x + 1) = 0$.

SOLVING A SYSTEM OF EQUATIONS CONSISTING OF A LINEAR EQUATION AND A QUADRATIC EQUATION

ALGEBRAICALLY

Generally, the simplest way to solve a system of equations consisting of a linear equation and a quadratic equation algebraically is through the method of substitution. One possible strategy is to solve the linear equation for y and then substitute that expression into the quadratic equation. After expansion and combining like terms, this will result in a new quadratic equation for x which, like all quadratic equations, may have zero, one, or two solutions. Plugging each solution for x back into one of the original equations will then produce the corresponding value of y.

For example, consider the following system of equations:

$$x + y = 1$$
$$y = (x + 3)^2 - 2$$

We can solve the linear equation for y to yield $y = -x + 1$. Substituting this expression into the quadratic equation produces $-x + 1 = (x + 3)^2 - 2$. We can simplify this equation:

$$-x + 1 = (x + 3)^2 - 2$$
$$-x + 1 = x^2 + 6x + 9 - 2$$
$$-x + 1 = x^2 + 6x + 7$$
$$0 = x^2 + 7x + 6$$

This quadratic equation can be factored as $(x + 1)(x + 6) = 0$. It therefore has two solutions: $x_1 = -1$ and $x_2 = -6$. Plugging each of these back into the original linear equation yields $y_1 = -x_1 + 1 = -(-1) + 1 = 2$ and $y_2 = -x_2 + 1 = -(-6) + 1 = 7$. Thus, this system of equations has two solutions, $(-1, 2)$ and $(-6, 7)$.

It may help to check your work by putting each x and y value back into the original equations and verifying that they do provide a solution.

GRAPHICALLY

To solve a system of equations consisting of a linear equation and a quadratic equation graphically, plot both equations on the same graph. The linear equation will of course produce a straight line, while the quadratic equation will produce a parabola. These two graphs will intersect at zero, one, or two points; each point of intersection is a solution of the system.

For example, consider the following system of equations:

$$y = -2x + 2$$
$$y = -2x^2 + 4x + 2$$

The linear equation describes a line with a y-intercept of $(0, 2)$ and a slope of -2.

To graph the quadratic equation, we can first find the vertex of the parabola: the x-coordinate of the vertex is $h = -\frac{b}{2a} = -\frac{4}{2(-2)} = 1$, and the y coordinate is $k = -2(1)^2 + 4(1) + 2 = 4$. Thus, the vertex lies at $(1, 4)$. To get a feel for the rest of the parabola, we can plug in a few more values of x to find more points; by putting in $x = 2$ and $x = 3$ in the quadratic equation, we find that the points $(2, 2)$ and $(3, -4)$ lie on the parabola; by symmetry thus do $(0, 2)$ and $(-1, -4)$. We can now plot both equations:

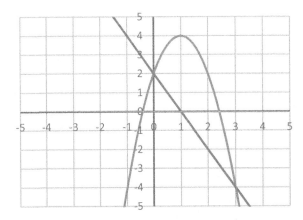

These two curves intersect at the points $(0, 2)$ and $(3, -4)$, thus these are the solutions of the equation.

Review Video: Solving a System of Equations Consisting of a Linear Equation and Quadratic Equations
Visit mometrix.com/academy and enter code: 194870

PRACTICE

P1. Find the roots of $y = 2x^2 + 8x + 4$.

P2. Find a quadratic equation with roots $x = 4$ and $x = -6$.

PRACTICE SOLUTIONS

P1. First, substitute 0 in for y in the quadratic equation: $0 = 2x^2 + 8x + 4$

Next, try to factor the quadratic equation. Since $a \neq 1$, list the factors of ac, or 8:

$$(1, 8), (-1, -8), (2, 4), (-2, -4)$$

Look for the factors of ac that add up to b, or 8. Since none do, the equation cannot be factored with whole numbers. Substitute the values of a, b, and c into the quadratic formula, $x = \frac{-b \pm \sqrt{b^2 - 4ac}}{2a}$:

$$x = \frac{-8 \pm \sqrt{8^2 - 4(2)(4)}}{2(2)}$$

Use the order of operations to simplify:

$$x = \frac{-8 \pm \sqrt{64 - 32}}{4}$$
$$x = \frac{-8 \pm \sqrt{32}}{4}$$

Reduce and simplify:

$$x = \frac{-8 \pm \sqrt{(16)(2)}}{4}$$
$$x = \frac{-8 \pm 4\sqrt{2}}{4}$$
$$x = -2 \pm \sqrt{2}$$
$$x = \left(-2 + \sqrt{2}\right) \text{ and } \left(-2 - \sqrt{2}\right)$$

P2. The root $x = 4$ corresponds to the equation $x - 4 = 0$, and the root $x = -6$ corresponds to the equation $x + 6 = 0$. These two equations correspond to the factors $(x - 4)$ and $(x + 6)$, from which we can derive the equation $(x - 4)(x + 6) = 0$, or $x^2 + 2x - 24 = 0$.

BASIC FUNCTIONS

FUNCTION AND RELATION

When expressing functional relationships, the **variables** x and y are typically used. These values are often written as the **coordinates** (x, y). The x-value is the independent variable and the y-value is the dependent variable. A **relation** is a set of data in which there is not a unique y-value for each x-value in the dataset. This means that there can be two of the same x-values assigned to different y-values. A relation is simply a relationship between the x and y-values in each coordinate but does not apply to the relationship between the values of x and y in the data set. A **function** is a relation where one quantity depends on the other. For example, the amount of money that you make depends on the number of hours that you work. In a function, each x-value in the data set has one unique y-value because the y-value depends on the x-value.

FUNCTIONS

A function has exactly one value of **output variable** (dependent variable) for each value of the **input variable** (independent variable). The set of all values for the input variable (here assumed to be x) is the domain of the function, and the set of all corresponding values of output variable (here assumed to be y) is the range of the function. When looking at a graph of an equation, the easiest way to determine if the equation is a function or not is to conduct the vertical line test. If a vertical line drawn through any value of x crosses the graph in more than one place, the equation is not a function.

FINDING THE DOMAIN AND RANGE OF A FUNCTION

The **domain** of a function $f(x)$ is the set of all input values for which the function is defined. The **range** of a function $f(x)$ is the set of all possible output values of the function—that is, of every possible value of $f(x)$, for any value of x in the function's domain. For a function expressed in a table, every input-output pair is given explicitly. To find the domain, we just list all the x values and to find the range, we just list all the values of $f(x)$. Consider the following example:

x	-1	4	2	1	0	3	8	6
$f(x)$	3	0	3	–1	–1	2	4	6

In this case, the domain would be {-1, 4, 2, 1, 0, 3, 8, 6}, or, putting them in ascending order, {-1, 0, 1, 2, 3, 4, 6, 8}. (Putting the values in ascending order isn't strictly necessary, but generally makes the set easier to read.) The range would be {3, 0, 3, –1, –1, 2, 4, 6}. Note that some of these values appear more than once. This is entirely permissible for a function; while each value of x must be matched to a unique value of $f(x)$, the converse is not true. We don't need to list each value more than once, so eliminating duplicates, the range is {3, 0, –1, 2, 4, 6}, or, putting them in ascending order, {–1, 0, 2, 3, 4, 6}.

Note that by definition of a function, no input value can be matched to more than one output value. It is good to double check to make sure that the data given follows this and is therefore actually a function.

> **Review Video: How to Find Domain and Range**
> Visit mometrix.com/academy and enter code: 778133

DETERMINING A FUNCTION

You can determine whether an equation is a **function** by substituting different values into the equation for x. These values are called input values. All possible input values are referred to as the **domain**. The result of substituting these values into the equation is called the output, or **range**. You can display and organize these numbers in a data table. A **data table** contains the values for x and y, which you can also list as coordinates. In order for a function to exist, the table cannot contain any repeating x-values that correspond with different y-values. If each x-coordinate has a unique y-coordinate, the table contains a function. However, there can be repeating y-values that correspond with different x-values. An example of this is when the function contains an exponent. For example, if $x^2 = y$, $2^2 = 4$, and $(-2)^2 = 4$.

> **Review Video: Definition of a Function**
> Visit mometrix.com/academy and enter code: 784611

WRITING A FUNCTION RULE USING A TABLE

If given a set of data, place the corresponding x and y-values into a table and analyze the relationship between them. Consider what you can do to each x-value to obtain the corresponding y-value. Try adding or subtracting different numbers to and from x and then try multiplying or dividing different numbers to and from x. If none of these **operations** give you the y-value, try combining the operations. Once you find a rule that works for one pair, make sure to try it with each additional set of ordered pairs in the table. If the same operation or combination of operations satisfies each set of coordinates, then the table contains a function. The rule is then used to write the equation of the function in "$y =$" form.

DIRECT AND INVERSE VARIATIONS OF VARIABLES

Variables that vary directly are those that either both increase at the same rate or both decrease at the same rate. For example, in the functions $y = kx$ or $y = kx^n$, where k and n are positive, the value of y increases as the value of x increases and decreases as the value of x decreases.

Variables that vary inversely are those where one increases while the other decreases. For example, in the functions $y = \frac{k}{x}$ or $y = \frac{k}{x^n}$ where k and n are positive, the value of y increases as the value of x decreases and decreases as the value of x increases.

In both cases, k is the constant of variation.

PROPERTIES OF FUNCTIONS

There are many different ways to classify functions based on their structure or behavior. Important features of functions include:

- **End behavior**: the behavior of the function at extreme values ($f(x)$ as $x \to \pm\infty$)
- **y-intercept**: the value of the function at $f(0)$
- **Roots**: the values of x where the function equals zero ($f(x) = 0$)
- **Extrema**: minimum or maximum values of the function or where the function changes direction ($f(x) \geq k$ or $f(x) \leq k$)

CLASSIFICATION OF FUNCTIONS

An **invertible function** is defined as a function, $f(x)$, for which there is another function, $f^{-1}(x)$, such that $f^{-1}(f(x)) = x$. For example, if $f(x) = 3x - 2$ the inverse function, $f^{-1}(x)$, can be found:

$$x = 3(f^{-1}(x)) - 2$$
$$\frac{x+2}{3} = f^{-1}(x)$$

$$f^{-1}(f(x)) = \frac{3x - 2 + 2}{3}$$
$$= \frac{3x}{3}$$
$$= x$$

Note that $f^{-1}(x)$ is a valid function over all values of x.

In a **one-to-one function**, each value of x has exactly one value for y on the coordinate plane (this is the definition of a function) and each value of y has exactly one value for x. While the vertical line test will determine if a graph is that of a function, the horizontal line test will determine if a function is a one-to-one function. If a horizontal line drawn at any value of y intersects the graph in more than one place, the graph is not that of a one-to-one function. Do not make the mistake of using the horizontal line test exclusively in determining if a graph is that of a one-to-one function. A one-to-one function must pass both the vertical line test and the horizontal line test. As such, one-to-one functions are invertible functions.

A **many-to-one function** is a function whereby the relation is a function, but the inverse of the function is not a function. In other words, each element in the domain is mapped to one and only one element in the range. However, one or more elements in the range may be mapped to the same element in the domain. A graph of a many-to-one function would pass the vertical line test, but not the horizontal line test. This is why many-to-one functions are not invertible.

A **monotone function** is a function whose graph either constantly increases or constantly decreases. Examples include the functions $f(x) = x$, $f(x) = -x$, or $f(x) = x^3$.

An **even function** has a graph that is symmetric with respect to the y-axis and satisfies the equation $f(x) = f(-x)$. Examples include the functions $f(x) = x^2$ and $f(x) = ax^n$, where a is any real number and n is a positive even integer.

An **odd function** has a graph that is symmetric with respect to the origin and satisfies the equation $f(x) = -f(-x)$. Examples include the functions $f(x) = x^3$ and $f(x) = ax^n$, where a is any real number and n is a positive odd integer.

Constant functions are given by the equation $f(x) = b$, where b is a real number. There is no independent variable present in the equation, so the function has a constant value for all x. The graph of a constant function is a horizontal line of slope 0 that is positioned b units from the x-axis. If b is positive, the line is above the x-axis; if b is negative, the line is below the x-axis.

Identity functions are identified by the equation $f(x) = x$, where every value of the function is equal to its corresponding value of x. The only zero is the point $(0, 0)$. The graph is a line with slope of 1.

In **linear functions**, the value of the function changes in direct proportion to x. The rate of change, represented by the slope on its graph, is constant throughout. The standard form of a linear equation is $ax + cy = d$, where a, c, and d are real numbers. As a function, this equation is commonly in the form $y = mx + b$ or $f(x) = mx + b$ where $m = -\frac{a}{c}$ and $b = \frac{d}{c}$. This is known as the slope-intercept form, because the coefficients give the slope of the graphed function (m) and its y-intercept (b). Solve the equation $mx + b = 0$ for x to get $x = -\frac{b}{m}$, which is the only zero of the function. The domain and range are both the set of all real numbers.

Algebraic functions are those that exclusively use polynomials and roots. These would include polynomial functions, rational functions, square root functions, and all combinations of these functions, such as polynomials as the radicand. These combinations may be joined by addition, subtraction, multiplication, or division, but may not include variables as exponents.

> **Review Video: Common Functions**
> Visit mometrix.com/academy and enter code: 629798
>
> **Review Video: Even and Odd Functions**
> Visit mometrix.com/academy and enter code: 278985

ABSOLUTE VALUE FUNCTIONS

An **absolute value function** is in the format $f(x) = |ax + b|$. Like other functions, the domain is the set of all real numbers. However, because absolute value indicates positive numbers, the range is limited to positive real numbers. To find the zero of an absolute value function, set the portion inside the absolute value sign equal to zero and solve for x. An absolute value function is also known as a piecewise function because it must be solved in pieces—one for if the value inside the absolute value sign is positive, and one for if the value is negative. The function can be expressed as

$$f(x) = \begin{cases} ax + b \text{ if } ax + b \geq 0 \\ -(ax + b) \text{ if } ax + b < 0 \end{cases}$$

This will allow for an accurate statement of the range. The graph of an example absolute value function, $f(x) = |2x - 1|$, is below:

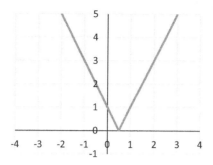

PIECEWISE FUNCTIONS

A **piecewise function** is a function that has different definitions on two or more different intervals. The following, for instance, is one example of a piecewise-defined function:

$$f(x) = \begin{cases} x^2, & x < 0 \\ x, & 0 \leq x \leq 2 \\ (x-2)^2, & x > 2 \end{cases}$$

To graph this function, we'd simply graph each part separately in the appropriate domain. The final graph would look like this:

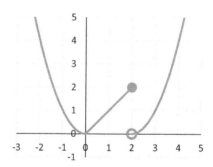

Note the filled and hollow dots at the discontinuity at $x = 2$. This is important to show which side of the graph that point corresponds to. Because $f(x) = x$ on the closed interval $0 \leq x \leq 2$, $f(2) = 2$. The point $(2, 2)$ is therefore marked with a filled circle, and the point $(2, 0)$, which is the endpoint of the rightmost $(x - 2)^2$ part of the graph but *not actually part of the function*, is marked with a hollow dot to indicate this.

> **Review Video: Piecewise Functions**
> Visit mometrix.com/academy and enter code: 707921

QUADRATIC FUNCTIONS

A **quadratic function** is a function in the form $y = ax^2 + bx + c$, where a does not equal 0. While a linear function forms a line, a quadratic function forms a **parabola**, which is a u-shaped figure that either opens upward or downward. A parabola that opens upward is said to be a **positive quadratic function** and a parabola that opens downward is said to be a **negative quadratic function**. The shape of a parabola can differ, depending on the values of a, b, and c. All parabolas contain a **vertex**, which is the highest possible point, the **maximum**, or the lowest possible point, the **minimum**. This is the point where the graph begins moving in the opposite direction. A quadratic function can have zero, one, or two solutions, and therefore, zero, one, or two *x*-intercepts. Recall that the *x*-intercepts are referred to as the zeros, or roots, of a function. A quadratic function will have only one *y*-intercept. Understanding the basic components of a quadratic function can give you an idea of the shape of its graph.

> **Review Video: Solutions of a Quadratic Equation on a Graph**
> Visit mometrix.com/academy and enter code: 328231

Example graph of a positive quadratic function, $x^2 + 2x - 3$:

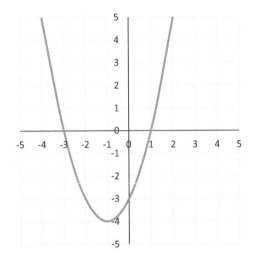

POLYNOMIAL FUNCTIONS

A **polynomial function** is a function with multiple terms and multiple powers of *x*, such as:

$$f(x) = a_n x^n + a_{n-1} x^{n-1} + a_{n-2} x^{n-2} + \cdots + a_1 x + a_0$$

where *n* is a non-negative integer that is the highest exponent in the polynomial and $a_n \neq 0$. The domain of a polynomial function is the set of all real numbers. If the greatest exponent in the polynomial is even, the polynomial is said to be of even degree and the range is the set of real numbers that satisfy the function. If the greatest exponent in the polynomial is odd, the polynomial is said to be odd and the range, like the domain, is the set of all real numbers.

> **Review Video: Simplifying Rational Polynomial Functions**
> Visit mometrix.com/academy and enter code: 351038

RATIONAL FUNCTIONS

A **rational function** is a function that can be constructed as a ratio of two polynomial expressions: $f(x) = \frac{p(x)}{q(x)}$, where $p(x)$ and $q(x)$ are both polynomial expressions and $q(x) \neq 0$. The domain is the set of all real numbers, except any values for which $q(x) = 0$. The range is the set of real numbers that satisfies the function when the domain is applied. When you graph a rational function, you will have vertical asymptotes wherever $q(x) = 0$. If the polynomial in the numerator is of lesser degree than the polynomial in the denominator, the *x*-axis will also be a horizontal asymptote. If the numerator and denominator have equal degrees, there will be a horizontal asymptote not on the *x*-axis. If the degree of the numerator is exactly one greater than the degree of the denominator, the graph will have an oblique, or diagonal, asymptote. The asymptote will be along the line $y = $

$\frac{p_n}{q_{n-1}}x + \frac{p_{n-1}}{q_{n-1}}$, where p_n and q_{n-1} are the coefficients of the highest degree terms in their respective polynomials.

SQUARE ROOT FUNCTIONS

A **square root function** is a function that contains a radical and is in the format $f(x) = \sqrt{ax + b}$. The domain is the set of all real numbers that yields a positive radicand or a radicand equal to zero. Because square root values are assumed to be positive unless otherwise identified, the range is all real numbers from zero to infinity. To find the zero of a square root function, set the radicand equal to zero and solve for x. The graph of a square root function is always to the right of the zero and always above the x-axis.

Example graph of a square root function, $f(x) = \sqrt{2x + 1}$:

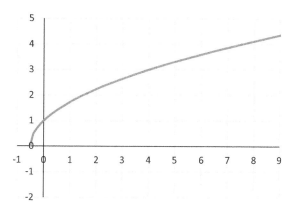

RELATIVE MAXIMUM AND RELATIVE MINIMUM

A **relative maximum** of a function is a point where the function has a higher value than any other point that is near it. In other words, a relative maximum is a point (x, y). Let's say that we choose an acceptable small interval around x. Then, $f(x) > f(c)$ for any other point within the interval (c).

A relative minimum is just the opposite. This is a point where the function has a lower value than any other point that is near it. In other words, a point (x, y). Let's say that we choose an acceptable small interval around x. Then, $f(x) < f(c)$ for any other point within the interval (c).

A function may have many relative maxima* and relative minima*. However, it may have none. A linear function like $y = x$ has no relative maxima or minima. Now, $y = \sin(x)$ has an unending amount of relative maxima and minima.

*Note that 'maxima' is plural for maximum. Also, 'minima' is plural for minimum.

FINDING A RELATIVE MAXIMUM OR MINIMUM FROM A GRAPH

At a relative maximum, the graph goes from increasing to decreasing. This makes a "peak" on the graph. Also, at a relative minimum, the graph goes from decreasing to increasing. This makes a "trough". On the graph below, the points A and C are relative maxima. The point B is a relative minimum.

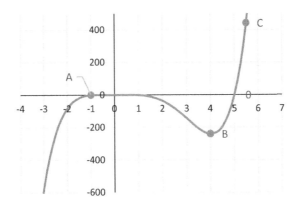

Note that point A is a relative maximum. However, this is not an absolute maximum. Also, this function has a higher value at point C. Now, point B is a relative minimum. However, this is not an absolute minimum. Also, the function has a lower value at the left and right ends of the graph than at point B. Point C is a relative and an absolute maximum. The reason is that at no place on the graph is there a function that has a higher value than at point C.

PERIODIC FUNCTIONS

A function is **periodic** if there is a repetition of the same shape. In other words, a periodic function is unchanged if it is moved some distance left or right on the graph. The distance that it has to be moved is called the function's **period** (P). A function $f(x)$ is periodic if $f(x + P) = f(x)$ for all x. Note that if this is true for P, then it's also true for all multiples of P. However, the function's period is known as the smallest possible value of P that the relation holds.

SYMMETRICAL FUNCTIONS

A function is **symmetrical** if it does not change with certain kinds of transformations. There are many kinds of transformations and symmetries. For functions, the type of transformation that is considered is reflection. Two important pieces are reflections through the y-axis and reflections through the origin on a coordinate plane.

If the mirror image (i.e., reflection) of a function is the same through the y-axis, then the function is symmetrical. This can be written as $f(x) = f(-x)$. This function is known to be **even**. A function can be symmetrical with reflection through the origin. The function needs to stay the same when each point is reflected to the other side of the origin. This can be written as $f(x) = -f(-x)$. This function is known to be **odd**.

A periodic function is also symmetrical. This may not be with reflection. However, this can be done with **translation**. The function is unchanged when translated (i.e., moved) horizontally by a distance that is equal to the function's period.

FUNCTION END BEHAVIOR

A function's **end behavior** is its tendency or activity at the extreme right and left sides of the graph. In other words, this is what happens to the function as x moves towards positive or negative ∞. There are three main possibilities.

First, $f(x)$ increases without limit (i.e., $f(x)$ goes to infinity). Second, $f(x)$ decreases without limit (i.e., $f(x)$ goes to negative infinity). Third, $f(x)$ tends toward some finite value (i.e., a horizontal asymptote). The behavior may be different at the two sides. For example, while $f(x) = x^2$ goes to ∞ on both sides, $g(x) = x^3$ goes to ∞ on the right side and to $-\infty$ on the left. Also, $h(x) = e^{-x}$ goes to ∞ on the left and approaches the horizontal asymptote $y = 0$ on the right.

PRACTICE

P1. Martin needs a 20% medicine solution. The pharmacy has a 5% solution and a 30% solution. He needs 50 mL of the solution. If the pharmacist must mix the two solutions, how many milliliters of 5% solution and 30% solution should be used?

P2. Describe two different strategies for solving the following problem:

> Kevin can mow the yard in 4 hours. Mandy can mow the same yard in 5 hours. If they work together, how long will it take them to mow the yard?

P3. A car, traveling at 65 miles per hour, leaves Flagstaff and heads east on I-40. Another car, traveling at 75 miles per hour, leaves Flagstaff 2 hours later, from the same starting point and also heads east on I-40. Determine how many hours it will take the second car to catch the first car by:

(a) Using a table.

(b) Using algebra.

PRACTICE SOLUTIONS

P1. To solve this problem, a table may be created to represent the variables, percentages, and total amount of solution. Such a table is shown below:

	mL solution	% medicine	Total mL medicine
5% solution	x	0.05	$0.05x$
30% solution	y	0.30	$0.30y$
Mixture	$x + y = 50$	0.20	$(0.20)(50) = 10$

The variable x may be rewritten as $50 - y$, so the equation $0.05(50 - y) + 0.30y = 10$ may be written and solved for y. Doing so gives $y = 30$. So, 30 mL of 30% solution are needed. Evaluating the expression, $50 - y$ for an x-value of 20, shows that 20 mL of 5% solution are needed.

P2. Two possible strategies both involve the use of rational equations to solve. The first strategy involves representing the fractional part of the yard mowed by each person in one hour and setting this sum equal to the ratio of 1 to the total time needed. The appropriate equation is $1/4 + 1/5 = 1/t$, which simplifies as $9/20 = 1/t$, and finally as $t = 20/9$. So the time it will take them to mow the yard, when working together, is a little more than 2.2 hours.

A second strategy involves representing the time needed for each person as two fractions and setting the sum equal to 1 (representing 1 yard). The appropriate equation is $t/4 + t/5 = 1$, which simplifies as $9t/20 = 1$, and finally as $t = 20/9$. This strategy also shows the total time to be a little more than 2.2 hours.

P3. (a) One strategy might involve creating a table of values for the number of hours and distances for each car. The table may be examined to find the same distance traveled and the corresponding number of hours taken. Such a table is shown below:

Car A		Car B	
x (hours)	y (distance)	x (hours)	y (distance)
0	0	0	
1	65	1	
2	130	2	0
3	195	3	75
4	260	4	150
5	325	5	225
6	390	6	300
7	455	7	375
8	520	8	450
9	585	9	525
10	650	10	600
11	715	11	675
12	780	12	750
13	845	13	825
14	910	14	900
15	975	15	975

The table shows that after 15 hours, the distance traveled is the same. Thus, the second car catches up with the first car after a distance of 975 miles and 15 hours.

(b) A second strategy might involve setting up and solving an algebraic equation. This situation may be modeled as $65x = 75(x - 2)$. This equation sets the distances traveled by each car equal to one another. Solving for x gives $x = 15$. Thus, once again, the second car will catch up with the first car after 15 hours.

GED Math Practice Test #1

Question 1 is based on the following figure:

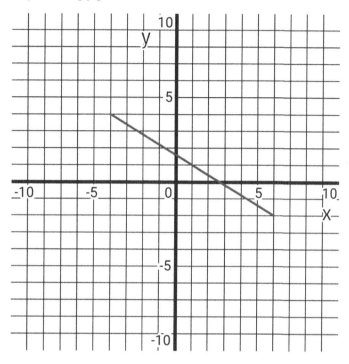

1. For each coordinate pair listed below, consider a line connecting the two coordinates. Which coordinate pairs represent a line that will intersect the line segment in the above figure? (Select all that apply.)

   a. (-8, 5) and (5, 5)
   b. (-3, 2) and (1, -1)
   c. (-1, 1) and (3, 5)
   d. (0, -4) and (5, -6)
   e. (7, 3) and (-1, 5)
   f. (4, 2) and (0, -2)

Question 2 is based on the following figure:

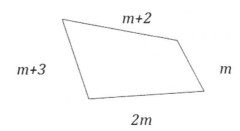

2. The figure shows an irregular quadrilateral and the lengths of its sides. Which of the following equations best shows the perimeter of the quadrilateral?
   a. $m^4 + 5$
   b. $2m^4 + 5$
   c. $4m + 5$
   d. $5m + 5$

3. If $a = -6$ and $b = 7$, then $4a(3b + 5) + 2b = ?$
   a. 638
   b. -610
   c. 624
   d. 610

4. Which of the following expressions represents the ratio of the area of a circle to its circumference?
   a. πr^2
   b. $\dfrac{\pi r^2}{2\pi}$
   c. $\dfrac{2\pi r}{r^2}$
   d. $\dfrac{r}{2}$

5. Mrs. Patterson's classroom has sixteen empty chairs. All the chairs are filled when every student is present. If 2/5 of the students are absent, how many students make up her entire class?
   a. 40
   b. 32
   c. 24
   d. 16

6. Jamie had $6.50 in his wallet when he left home. He spent $4.25 on drinks and $2.00 on a magazine. Later, his friend repaid him $2.50 that he had borrowed the previous day. How much money does Jamie have in his wallet now?
   a. $12.25
   b. $14.25
   c. $3.25
   d. $2.75

Question 7 is based on the following table:

Metric - English Equivalents	
1 meter	1.094 yard
2.54 centimeter	1 inch
1 kilogram	2.205 pound
1 liter	1.06 quart

7. A building is 19 meters tall. What is its height in inches?
   a. 254
   b. 1094
   c. 4826
   d. 748

8. Rachel needs to buy extra items for her restaurant. She went to the store and spent $24.15 on vegetables. She bought 2 lbs of onions, 3 lbs of carrots, and $1\frac{1}{2}$ lbs of mushrooms. The onions cost $3.69 per lb, and the carrots cost $ 4.29 per lb. So, what is the price per pound of mushrooms?
   a. $2.60
   b. $2.25
   c. $2.80
   d. $3.10

Question 9 is based on the following figure:

9. In the figure, A, B, and C are points on the number line. Also, O is the origin. What is the ratio of the distance *BC* to distance *AB*?
   a. 3:5
   b. 8:5
   c. 8:11
   d. 3:11

10. Jesse invests $7,000 in a certificate of deposit that pays interest at the rate of 7.5% annually. How much interest (in dollars) does Jesse gain from this investment during the first year that he holds the certificate?

11. In an election in Kimball County, Candidate A gained 36,800 votes. His opponent, Candidate B, had 32,100 votes. 2,100 votes went to write-in candidates. What percentage of the vote went to Candidate A?
   a. 51.8%
   b. 53.4%
   c. 45.2%
   d. 46.8%

12. Francine can ride 16 miles on her bicycle in 45 minutes. At this speed, how many minutes would it take Francine to ride 60 miles?

Question 13 is based upon the following figure:

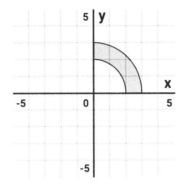

13. Marcus draws a plan for a hot tub in his backyard. He wants to put a concrete path around the tub. So, he starts with one area of the pool to find out how much material he needs. Now, the inner circle has a radius of two units. The outer circle has a radius of three units. What is the area of the shaded part?

Questions 14– 16 are based on the following table. This gives the closing prices of a number of stocks traded on the New York Stock Exchange:

Stock	Price per Share	Shares Traded
Microsoft	$45.14	89,440,000
Oracle	$19.11	12,415,000
Apple Computer	$16.90	17,953,000
Cisco Systems	$3.50	73,019,000
Garmin	$29.30	53,225,000

14. David bought 200 shares of Oracle stock yesterday and sold it today. His profit was $22.00. At what price did he buy the stock yesterday?
   a. $18.89
   b. $19.00
   c. $19.06
   d. $18.96

15. Lynn buys a package of stocks that has 100 shares each of Microsoft and Apple. Also, the package has 200 shares of Garmin at the closing prices from the table. What is the average price per share that she pays for these stocks?

16. James decides to invest $4500 in Cisco Systems stock and buys it at the price shown in the table. At what price should he sell it to have a profit of 10%?

17. Erica started work today at 7:00AM and worked until 4:30 PM. She earns $12 per hour for her regular shift which is 8 hours. Also, she works 50% more per hour for overtime. How much did Erica make today?

Question 18 is based upon the following diagram:

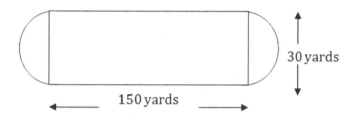

18. A company is building a track for a local high school. There are two straight sections and two semi-circular turns. Given the dimensions, which of the following most closely measures the perimeter of the entire track?
   a. 300 yards
   b. 180 yards
   c. 360 yards
   d. 395 yards

19. Elijah drove 45 miles to his job in an hour and ten minutes in the morning. On the way home, traffic was bad. So, the same trip took an hour and a half. What was his average speed in miles per hour for the round trip?
   a. 30
   b. 45
   c. $33\frac{3}{4}$
   d. $32\frac{1}{2}$

20. The distance traveled by a moving object is found with the formula: *d = rt*, where *r* is the rate of travel (speed) and *t* is the time of travel. A major league pitcher throws a fastball at a speed of 125 ft/sec. The distance from the pitching rubber to home plate is 60.5 feet. How long, in seconds, does it take a fastball to travel this distance? Write your answer to the nearest hundredth of a second.

21. Lauren had $80 in her savings account. When she received her paycheck, she put some money in her savings account. This brought the balance up to $120. By what percentage did the total amount in her account increase by putting this amount in her savings account?
   a. 50%
   b. 40%
   c. 35%
   d. 80%

Question 22 is based on the following diagram:

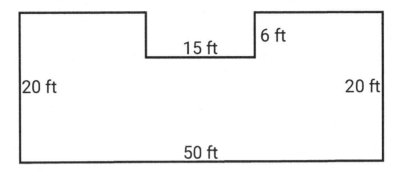

22. What is the area of the figure shown above? Give your answer in square feet.

23. Which of the following is a solution to the inequality $4x - 12 < 4$?
    a. 7
    b. 6
    c. 5
    d. 3

24. Mark is leaving a job site and moving equipment to Phoenix which is located 210 miles north. He drives the first ten miles in 12 minutes. If he continues at the same rate, how long will it take him to reach his destination?
    a. 3 hours 15 minutes
    b. 4 hours 12 minutes
    c. 3 hours 45 minutes
    d. 4 hours 20 minutes

25. An airplane leaves Atlanta at 2 PM and flies north at 250 miles per hour. A second airplane leaves Atlanta 30 minutes later and flies north at 280 miles per hour. At what time will the second airplane overtake the first?
    a. 6:00 PM
    b. 6:20 PM
    c. 6:40 PM
    d. 6:50 PM

Question 26 is based on the following diagram:

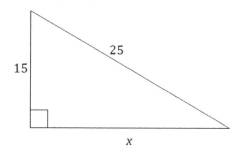

26. Find the length of the side labeled *x*. The triangle is a right triangle.
    a. 18
    b. 20
    c. 22
    d. 24

27. A company has been asked to design a building for an athletic event. The building is in the shape of a square pyramid. The pyramid has a height of 481 ft, and the length of each side of the base is 756 ft. What is the volume of the pyramid?
    a. $1.21 \times 10^5 \text{ ft}^3$
    b. $4.85 \times 10^5 \text{ ft.}^3$
    c. $9.16 \times 10^7 \text{ ft.}^3$
    d. $2.75 \times 10^8 \text{ ft.}^3$

28. If $x + y > 0$ when $x > y$, which of the following cannot be true?
    a. $x = 3$ and $y = 0$
    b. $x = 6$ and $y = -1$
    c. $x = -3$ and $y = 0$
    d. $x = 3$ and $y = -3$

29. Which of the following expressions is equal to $x^3 x^5$?
    a. $2x^8$
    b. x^{15}
    c. x^2
    d. x^8

30. If $\frac{12}{x} = \frac{30}{6}$, what is the value of *x*?
    a. 3.6
    b. 2.4
    c. 3.0
    d. 2.0

31. Which of the following could be a graph of the function $y = \frac{1}{x}$?

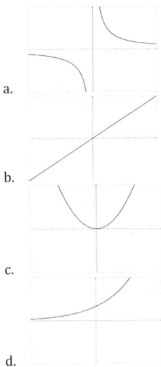

a.

b.

c.

d.

Question 32 is based on the following figure:

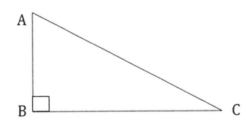

32. △ABC is a right triangle, and ∠ACB=30°. What is the measure of ∠BAC?
   a. 40°
   b. 50°
   c. 60°
   d. 45°

Question 33 is based on the following table:

Hours	1	2	3
Cost	$3.60	$7.20	$10.80

33. The table shows the cost of renting a bicycle for 1, 2, or 3 hours. Which of the following equations best represents the data? Let C stand for the cost and h stand for the time of the rental.

　a. $C = 3.60h$
　b. $C = h + 3.60$
　c. $C = 3.60h + 10.80$
　d. $C = \frac{10.80}{h}$

34. Which of the following statements is true?
　a. Perpendicular lines have opposite slopes
　b. Perpendicular lines have the same slopes
　c. Perpendicular lines have reciprocal slopes
　d. Perpendicular lines have opposite reciprocal slopes

35. There are 64 squares on a checkerboard. Bobby puts one penny on the first square, two on the second square, four on the third, eight on the fourth. He continues to double the number of coins at each square until he has covered all 64 squares. How many coins must he place on the last square?
　a. 2^{64}
　b. $2^{64} - 1$
　c. 2^{63}
　d. $2^{63} + 1$

36. Carrie wants to decorate her party with bundles of balloons containing three balloons each. Balloons are available in 4 different colors. There must be three different colors in each bundle. How many different kinds of bundles can she make?
　a. 18
　b. 12
　c. 4
　d. 6

Question 37 is based on the following figure:

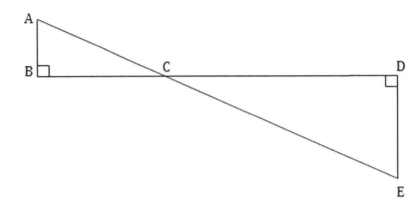

37. In the figure above, segment BC is 4 units long. Segment CD is 8 units long. Segment DE is 6 units long. What is the length of segment AC?

   a. 7 units
   b. 5 units
   c. 3 units
   d. 2.5 units

38. The expressions $y = -3x + 6$ and $y = 2x - 4$ represent straight lines. Find the coordinates of the point at which they intersect.

39. In a game of chance, 3 dice are thrown at the same time. What is the probability that all three will land with a 6?

   a. 1 in 6
   b. 1 in 18
   c. 1 in 216
   d. 1 in 30

40. Rafael has a business selling computers. He buys computers from the manufacturer for $450 each and sells them for $800. Each month, he must also pay fixed costs of $3000 for rent and utilities for his store. If he sells n computers in a month, which of the following equations can be used to find his profit?

   a. $P = n(800 - 450)$
   b. $P = n(800 - 450 - 3000)$
   c. $P = 3000\, n(800 - 450)$
   d. $P = n(800 - 450) - 3000$

41. Put the following numbers in order from the least to greatest $2^3, 4^2, 6^0, 9, 10^1$.

   a. $2^3, 4^2, 6^0, 9, 10^1$
   b. $6^0, 9, 10^1, 2^3, 4^2$
   c. $10^1, 2^3, 6^0, 9, 4^2$
   d. $6^0, 2^3, 9, 10^1, 4^2$

Questions 42-43 are based on the following chart:

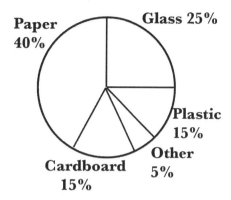

42. The Charleston Recycling Company collects 50,000 tons of recyclable material every month. The chart shows the kinds of materials that are collected by the company's five trucks. What is the second most common material that is recycled?

   a. Cardboard
   b. Glass
   c. Paper
   d. Plastic

43. About how much paper is recycled every month?

   a. 40,000 tons
   b. 50,000 tons
   c. 15,000 tons
   d. 20,000 tons

44. Dorothy is half her sister's age. Dorothy will be three fourths of her sister's age in 20 years. What is Dorothy's current age?

   a. 10
   b. 15
   c. 20
   d. 25

45. Chan receives a bonus from his job. He pays 30% in taxes, gives 30% to charity, and uses another 25% to pay off an old debt. He has $600 remaining from his bonus. What was the total amount of Chan's bonus?

Question 46 is based on the following diagram:

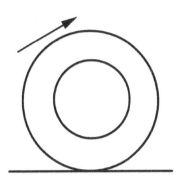

46. A tire on a car rotates at 500 RPM (revolutions per minute) when the car is traveling at 50 km/hr (kilometers per hour). What is the circumference of the tire? Give your answer in meters.

   a. $\frac{50,000}{2\pi}$
   b. $\frac{50,000}{60 \times 2\pi}$
   c. $\frac{50,000}{60}$
   d. $\frac{10}{6}$

47. A farmer installed a new grain silo on his property for the fall harvest. The silo is in the shape of a cylinder with a diameter of 8 m and a height of 24 m. How much grain will the farmer be able to store in the silo?

   a. 402.1 m³
   b. 1,206.4 m³
   c. 1,608.5 m³
   d. 4,825.5 m³

48. Which of the following expressions is equivalent to $(a+b)(a-b)$?

   a. $a^2 - b^2$
   b. $(a+b)^2$
   c. $(a-b)^2$
   d. $ab(a-b)$

Questions 49 and 50 are based upon the following table:

Kyle bats third in the batting order for the Badgers baseball team. The table shows the number of hits that Kyle had in the 7 consecutive games played during one week in July.

Day of Week	Number of Hits
Monday	1
Tuesday	2
Wednesday	3
Thursday	1
Friday	1
Saturday	4
Sunday	2

49. What is the mode of the numbers in the distribution shown in the table?
- a. 1
- b. 2
- c. 3
- d. 4

50. What is the mean of the numbers in the distribution shown in the table?
- a. 1
- b. 2
- c. 3
- d. 4

Answer Key and Explanations for Test #1

1. C and F: The other coordinates make lines that do not intersect the line in the figure.

2. D: The perimeter (P) of the quadrilateral is simply the sum of its sides:

$$P = m + (m+2) + (m+3) + 2m$$

Put together like terms by adding the variables (m terms) together. Then, add the constants. This gives you: $P = 5m + 5$.

3. B: Substitute the given values for the variables into the expression:

$$4 \times -6(3 \times 7 + 5) + 2 \times 7$$

Using order of operations, find the expression in the parentheses first. Remember that first you must multiply 3 by 7. Then, add 5 to follow the order of operations

$= 4 \times -6(21 + 5) + 2 \times 7$ Next add the values in the parenthesis
$= 4 \times -6(26) + 2 \times 7$ Simplify by multiplying the numbers outside the parenthesis
$= -24(26) + 14$ Multiply -24 by 26
$= -624 + 14$ Add
$= -610$ Final answer

4. D: The area of the circle is πr^2. The circumference is $2\pi r$. First, take the ratio of these two expressions: Ratio=$\frac{\pi r^2}{2\pi r}$. Then, reduce it to: $\frac{r}{2}$.

5. A: There are 16 empty chairs. This gives 2/5 of the total enrollment. So, the full class must be:

$$\text{Class} = 5/2 \times 16 = 40 \text{ students}$$

Another option is to use proportions:

$$\frac{2}{5} = \frac{16}{x}$$

First, cross multiply to get: $2x = 80$. Then, divide each side by 2 to solve for x. So, $x = 40$ students

6. D: Jamie had $2.75 in his wallet. To solve this problem, you subtract $4.25 and $2.00 from the first sum of $6.50. So, you are left with $0.25. Then, you add $2.50. So, you come to the final answer of $2.75.

7. D: There are two ways to solve this problem. First, you can convert meters to centimeters. Then, use the conversion factor in the table to convert centimeters to inches. Second, use the table to convert meters to yards. Then, convert to inches.

For the first way, remember that there are 100 centimeters in a meter (*centi* means "hundredth"). So, 19 m = 1900 cm = $\left(\frac{1900}{2.54}\right)$ = 748 inches.

In the second way to solve the problem, remember that there are 36 inches in a yard.

So, $19 \text{ m} \times 1.094 \frac{\text{yd}}{\text{m}} = 20.786 \text{ yd} \times 36 \frac{\text{inches}}{\text{yd}} = 748$ inches.

Often, proportions are used for conversions. After converting meters to centimeters, you set up proportions to solve for an unknown variable, x.

$$\frac{1900 \text{ cm}}{x \text{ in}} = \frac{2.54 \text{ cm}}{1 \text{ in}}$$

Cross multiply to get: $1900 = 2.54x$. Then, divide each side by 2.54 to solve for x. So, $x = 748$

8. A: You know the price for each pound of onions and carrots. So, start by finding the total cost of the onions and carrots. This will equal $(2 \times \$3.69) + (3 \times \$4.29) = \$20.25$. Next, this sum is subtracted from the total cost of the vegetables. This is done to find the cost of the mushrooms: $\$24.15 - \$20.25 = \$3.90$. Finally, the cost of the mushrooms is divided by the quantity (lbs) to find the cost per pound:

$$\text{Cost per pound lb} = \frac{\$3.90}{1.5} = \$2.60$$

9. D: The figure is a number line. So, the distance from point A to point B will be the difference of B − A. This is $5 - (-6) = 11$. Also, the distance from point B to point C will be the difference of C − B. This is $8 - 5 = 3$. So, the ratio BC:AB will be 3:11.

10. The correct answer is $525. In the first year that he holds the certificate, Jesse's income will be equal to 7.5% of the principal that he has invested which was $7,000. Remember the formula: $I = Prt$ where I is interest, P is principal, r is rate (given as a decimal) and t is time (in years). So, $I = \$7,000 \times 0.75 \times 1$. This equals $525.

11. A: Candidate A's vote ratio is the number of votes that he obtained divided by the total number of votes cast. Then, multiply that decimal by 100 to convert the decimal into a percentage. Now, Candidate A's vote is: $\frac{36800}{36800+32100+2100} \times 100$. So, you have a percentage of 51.8%

12. The correct answer is 168.75 minutes. First, find the time that is needed to ride 1 mile.

This is equal to 45 / 16 or 2.8125 minutes. Next, multiply this by the total number of miles to be ridden, or 60, to have the final answer. When you put all of this together, you have:

$$\text{Time} = \frac{45}{16} \times 60 = 168.75 \text{ minutes}$$

Another way is to use proportions. To begin set up your proportions:

$$\frac{16 \text{ miles}}{45 \text{ min}} = \frac{60 \text{ miles}}{x \text{ min}}$$

Then, cross multiply to get: $16x = 2700$. Now, divide each side by 16. So, you have $x = 168.75$ minutes

13. The area is 3.93 square units. Note that the shaded area is one fourth of the difference between the areas of the inner and outer circles. The formula for finding the area of a circle is:

$A = \pi r^2$. The radius (r) of the outer circle is 3. So, you have $A_{out} = \pi \times 3^2$, or 9π. The radius of the inner circle is $A_{in} = \pi \times 2^2$, or 4π. So, one fourth of the difference between the areas is: $\frac{1}{4}(9\pi - 4\pi)$ Then, factor out π. So, you have: $\frac{1}{4}\pi(9-4) = \frac{5\pi}{4} \cong 3.93$

14. B: $19.00 per share. Divide David's total profit of $22.00 by the number of shares he purchased (200) to find David's profit per share:

$P = \$22.00 \div 200 = \$0.11$ per share. So, the price he paid was 11¢ lower than the closing price given in the table. The table shows that Oracle closed at $19.11 per share today. So, the price David paid was $19.11 - \$0.11 = \$19.00$ per share.

15. The correct answer is $30.16 per share. To find this weighted average, you multiply the number of shares purchased per stock by the stock price. Then, add these totals together and divide by the total number of shares. Lynn bought 100 shares of Microsoft at $45.14, 100 shares of Apple Computer at $16.90, and 200 shares of Garmin at $29.30. So, the total amount that she spent was:

$$\text{Total} = (100 \times \$45.14) + (100 \times \$16.90) + (200 \times \$29.30) = \$12064$$

She gained a total of 400 shares of stock. So, the average cost per share is:

$$\text{Avg} = \frac{\text{Total}}{\text{shares}} = \frac{\$12064}{400} = \$30.16$$

16. The correct answer is $3.85. To make a profit of 10%, James must sell the stock at a price that is 10% higher than what he paid for it. So, he must sell it at 110% of the purchase price. He buys the stock at $3.50 per share. So, he must sell it at a price (P) as follows:

$$P = \frac{110 \times \$3.50}{100} = \$3.85$$

17. The correct answer is $123. To calculate this, first find the total number of hours worked. From 7AM until noon is 5 hours. From noon until 4:30 PM is 4.5 hours. So, the total number of hours worked is: $5 + 4.5 = 9.5$ hours. Next, find the number of hours paid at the overtime rate. This is $9.5 - 8 = 1.5$ hours. The overtime pay rate is 50% greater than the regular rate of $12 per hour or $1.5 \times \$12 = \$18$ per hour. Finally, calculate the amount of pay at each rate, regular and overtime. Then, add these together to find the total pay: Total $= (8 \times \$12) + (1.5 \times \$18) = \$123$

18. D: First, add the two straight 150-yard portions. Also, note that the distance for the two semi-circles put together is the circumference of a circle. The radius (r) of that circle is half of the dimension given as the width of the track. In other words, it is 15 yards. Now, use the formula for the circumference of a circle: $2\pi r$. Then, add it to the length of the two straight portions of the track. So, you have: Length $= (2\pi \times 15) + (2 \times 150) \cong 394.25$. Choice D is the closest to this calculated answer.

19. C: First, find the total distance of the round trip. This is twice the 45 miles of the one-way trip to work in the morning. So, that equals 90 miles. Then, find the total amount of time that Elijah spent on his round trip by converting his travel times into minutes. One hour and ten minutes equals 70 minutes, and one and a half hours equals 90 minutes. So, Elijah's total travel time was $70 + 90 = 160$ minutes. Elijah's average speed can now be found in miles per minute:

$$\text{Speed} = \frac{90 \text{ miles}}{160 \text{ min}} = 0.5625 \text{ miles per minute}$$

Finally, to convert this average speed into miles per hour, you need to multiply by 60. The reason is that there are 60 minutes in an hour:

$$\text{Avg. Speed(mph)} = 60 \times 0.5625 = 33.75 \text{ miles per hour}$$

20. The correct answer is 0.48 seconds. Modify the relationship given in the question to solve for the time. You know that the distance is the product of the rate and time: $d = rt$. To change the relationship for this problem, you need to put time (t) by itself. So, this will look like:
$t = \frac{d}{r} = \frac{60.5 \text{ft}}{125 \text{ ft/sec}} = 0.484$ sec. When you round to the nearest hundredth of a second, you have the answer of 0.48 seconds.

21. A: The rate of increase equals the change in the account balance divided by the original amount: $80. Multiply that decimal by 100 to know the percentage of increase. So, to find the change in the balance, subtract the original amount from the new balance: Change = $120 − $80 = $40 Now, you can find the percentage of increase: Percent $= \frac{\$40}{\$80} \times 100 = 50\%$

22. The correct answer is 910 square feet. The answer is found by computing the area of the large rectangle and the area of the rectangular cutout. Then, the area of the cutout is subtracted from the larger rectangle. The area of the rectangle is the product of its length and width, $A_{rect} = 20 \times 50 = 1000$ square feet. The cutout is a rectangle as well. So, its area is computed in the same way: $A_{cutout} = 6 \times 15 = 90$ square feet. Then, subtracting gives you the answer: Area $= A_{rect} - A_{cutout} = 1000 - 90 = 910$ square feet.

23. D: Begin as you would with a regular equation: $4x - 12 > 4$.

$$4x - 12 + 12 > 4 + 12 \quad \text{Add 12 to each side}$$
$$4x/4 > 16/4 \quad \text{Divide each side by 4}$$
$$x > 4 \quad \text{Final result}$$

Note that the direction of the inequality does not change. The reason is that the division was by a positive 4. Only choice D follows the condition that it needs to be less than 4.

24. B: The rate, miles per minute, is constant. So, this can be solved by setting up a proportion: $\frac{\text{miles}}{\text{min}} = \frac{10}{12} = \frac{210}{x}$. Now, solve for time: $t = \frac{210 \times 12}{10} = 252$ minutes. Finally, convert to hours by dividing this total by 60. The reason is that there are 60 minutes in an hour:

$$t = 252/60 = 4 \text{ hours and } 12 \text{ minutes}$$

Note: When dividing 252 by 60, you get a decimal answer of 4.2 hours. However, the answers are given in a different unit of measurement. 4.2 hours is not the same as 4 hours and 2 minutes. In order to find the number of minutes, the decimal (0.2) has to be converted into minutes. To convert, multiply 0.2 by 60 which becomes 12 minutes.

25. C: Define the variable t as the passed time (in hours) from the time the first airplane takes off. Then, at any time the distance traveled by the first plane is $d_1 = 250t$. The second plane takes off 30 minutes later. So, at any time the distance that it has traveled is $d_2 = 280(t - 0.5)$. The units used for the half hour should remain in hours, not minutes, and they must be negative since the second plane left after the first plane. This plane will overtake the first when the two distances are equal: $d_1 = d_2$ or $250t = 280(t - 30)$.

Result	Next Step
$250t = 280(t - 0.5)$	Use the distributive property
$250t = (280 \times t) - (280 \times 0.5)$	Simplify the parentheses
$250t = 280t - 140$	Add 140 to each side
$250t + 140 = 280t - 140 + 140$	Subtract $250t$ from each side
$250t - 250t + 140 = 280t - 250t$	Divide both sides by 30
$140/30 = 30t/30$	Final result
$4\frac{2}{3} = t$	

This gives the value of t in hours. So, you have the found an elapsed time of 4 hours and 40 minutes. The first plane left at 2 PM. So, 4 hours and 40 minutes later is 6:40 PM.

26. B: The figure is a right triangle. So, the Pythagorean Theorem can be used. The side that is 25 units long is the hypotenuse. Its square will equal the sum of the squares of the other two sides. That is $25^2 = 15^2 + x^2$. Solve for x^2 by subtracting 15^2 from each side of this equation. Then, take the square root to find x.

$$x = \sqrt{25^2 - 15^2} = \sqrt{625 - 225} = \sqrt{400} = 20$$

27. C: The formula for the volume of a pyramid is $V = \frac{1}{3}BH$, where B is the area of the base and H is the height of the pyramid. The base is a square with a length of 756 ft on each side. So, the area of the base is $A = s^2 = (756 \text{ ft})^2 = 571,536 \text{ ft}^2$. With a base of $571,536 \text{ ft}^2$ and a height of 481 ft, the volume of the pyramid is $V = \frac{1}{3}(571,536 \text{ ft}^2)(481 \text{ ft}) = 9.16 \times 10^7 \text{ft}^3$.

28. D: First, test each expression to see which follows the condition $x > y$. This condition is met for all the answer choices except choice C. Next, test the remaining choices to see which follows the inequality $x + y > 0$. It can be seen that this inequality holds for choice A and choice B. However, this does not hold for choice D. The reason is that $x + y = 3 + (-3) = 3 - 3 = 0$. In this case, the sum $x + y$ is not greater than 0.

29. D: To multiply two powers that have the same base, you need to add their exponents. So, $x^3 x^5 = x^{3+5} = x^8$. Also note that $x^3 = x \times x \times x$ and $x^5 = x \times x \times x \times x \times x$. So, the expression equals $(x \times x \times x) \times (x \times x \times x \times x \times x) = x^8$.

30. B: Take the cross product of the numerators and denominators from either side for this proportion.

$$\frac{12}{x} = \frac{30}{6}$$

Cross multiply to get: $30x = 72$. Then, divide each side by 30. So, you are left with $x = 2.4$

31. A: This is a typical plot of an inverse variation where the product of the dependent and independent variables, x and y, is always equal to the same value. In this case, the product is always equal to 1. So, the plot is in the first and third quadrants of the coordinate plane. As x increases and goes to infinity, y decreases and goes to zero while keeping the constant product. In contrast, choice

B is a linear plot for an equation of the form $y = x$. Choice C is a quadratic plot for the equation $y = x^2$. Choice D is an exponential plot for the equation $y = 2x$.

32. C: The internal angles of a triangle always add up to 180°. Since $\triangle ABC$ is a right triangle, then $\angle ABC = 90°$ and $\angle ACB$ is given as 30°. The middle letter is for the vertex. By using the triangle addition theorem, the answer must be: $\angle BAC = 180 - (90 + 30)$. This equals 60°.

33. A: This equation is a linear relationship that has a slope of 3.60 and passes through the origin. The table shows that for each hour of rental, the cost increases by $3.60. This matches with the slope of the equation. Of course, if the bicycle is not rented at all (0 hours), there will be no charge ($0). If plotted on the Cartesian plane, the line would have a y intercept of 0. Choice A is the only one that follows these requirements.

34. D: The slopes of perpendicular lines are reciprocals and have the opposite sign. In the figure below, Line A has a slope of -1/2, and Line B has a slope of 2.

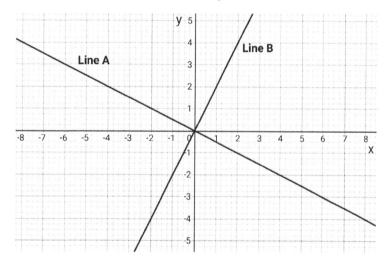

35. C: This table shows the numbers of coins added to the first few squares and the equivalent powers of 2:

Square	1	2	3	4
Coins	1	2	4	8
Power of 2	2^0	2^1	2^2	2^3

In this series, the number of coins on each is the consecutive powers of 2. The reason is that the number doubles with each consecutive square. However, the series of powers begins with 0 for the first square. For the 64th square, the number of coins will be 2^{63}.

36. C: There are four different colors. So, one color must be held back from each balloon bundle. So, there is one color set for each excluded color or four in all.

When the order of the individual parts is not important, this is called a combination. The number of combinations of n objects taken k at a time is given by $C = \frac{n!}{(n-k)!k!}$. The ! notation is for a *factorial* product where $n! = 1 \times 2 \times 3 \times ... \times (n-1) \times n$. In this case, $n = 4$ colors, and $k = 3$ balloons per bundle. Then, substitute into the equation above and simplify:

$$C = \frac{4!}{(4-3)! \times 3!} = \frac{1 \times 2 \times 3 \times 4}{(1)(1 \times 2 \times 3)} = 4$$

37. B: The two right triangles are similar because they share a pair of vertical angles. Vertical angles are always congruent (e.g., angle ACB and angle DCE). Obviously, both right angles (e.g., angle B and angle D) are congruent. So, angles A and E are congruent because of the triangular sum theorem.

With similar triangles, corresponding sides will be proportional. Segment BC is $\frac{1}{2}$ the length of segment CD. So, AC will be $\frac{1}{2}$ the length of CE. The length of CE can be computed from the Pythagorean theorem. The reason is that it is the hypotenuse of a right triangle, and the lengths of the other two sides are known: $CE = \sqrt{6^2 + 8^2} = \sqrt{100} = 10$.

The length of segment AC will be $\frac{1}{2}$ of this value or 5 units.

38. The correct answer is (2,0). To come to this answer, set the two expressions to be equal and solve for the variable x. This is the substitution method since we are substituting the expression for y:

$-3x + 6 = 2x - 4$	Gather like terms on each side of the equation and isolate the variable
$10 = 5x$	Divide each side by 5
$2 = x$	x value

Now, substitute this value of x into either of the original equations to find the y coordinate

$$y = -3x + 6 = -6 + 6 = 0$$

39. C: For each die there is a 1 in 6 chance that a 6 will be on top. The reason is that the die has 6 sides. The probability that a 6 will show for each die is not affected by the results from another roll of the die. In other words, these probabilities are independent. So, the overall probability of throwing 3 sixes is the product of the individual probabilities: $P = \frac{1}{6} \times \frac{1}{6} \times \frac{1}{6} = \frac{1}{6^3} = \frac{1}{216}$

40. D: Rafael's profit on each computer is the difference between the price he pays and the price he charges his customer: $800-$450. If he sells n computers in a month, his total profit will be n times this difference: $n(800 - 450)$. However, it is necessary to subtract his fixed costs of $3000 from $n(800 - 450)$ to find his final profit per month.

41. D: When a number is raised to a power, you multiply the number by itself by the number of times of the power. For example, $2^3 = 2 \times 2 \times 2 = 8$. A number raised to the power of 0 is always equal to 1. So, 6^0 is the smallest number shown. Similarly, for the other numbers:

$$9^1 = 9;\ 10^1 = 10;\ 4^2 = 4 \times 4 = 16$$

Since $1 < 8 < 9 < 10 < 16$, we can write the order as $6^0, 2^3, 9, 10^1, 4^2$.

42. B: This pie chart shows the relative amounts of each variable as a slice of the whole circle. The larger variables have larger slices. Also, the percentage of each variable (e.g., recycled material) is shown next to each slice. In this chart, paper is the most common recycled material (i.e., the largest variable). This is 40% of the total. The next largest is glass at 25% of the total. All of the other materials stand for smaller portions of the total.

43. D: The chart indicates that 40% of the total recycled material is paper. Since 50,000 tons of material are recycled every month, the total amount of paper will be 40% of 50,000 tons, or $\frac{40}{100} \times 50{,}000 = 20{,}000$ tons.

44. A: Let D represent Dorothy's age, and S her is sister's age. Since she is half her sister's age today, we have, $D = \frac{S}{2}$ or $S = 2D$. In twenty years, her age will be $D + 20$ years. Her sister's age will be $S + 20$ years. At that time, Dorothy will be $\frac{3}{4}$ of her sister's age. So, $D + 20 = \frac{3 \times (S+20)}{4}$ Substituting $2D$ for S in this equation gives

$$D + 20 = \frac{3(2D + 20)}{4}$$
$$D + 20 = \frac{6D + 60}{4}$$

Use the distributive property and reduce.

$$D + 20 = \frac{3}{2}D + 15$$

Gather like terms and simplify:

$$20 - 15 = \frac{3}{2}D - D$$
$$5 = \frac{D}{2}$$
$$10 = D$$

Therefore, Dorothy is ten years old today. Her sister is twenty years old. In twenty years, Dorothy will be 30 years old, and her sister will be 40.

45. The correct answer is $4000. Chan has paid out a total of $30\% + 30\% + 25\% = 85\%$ of his bonus for the items in the question. So, the $600 is the remaining 15%. To find out his total bonus, solve $\frac{100}{15} \times 600 = \$4000$.

46. D: It is not necessary to use the circle formula to solve the problem. Note that 50 km/hr matches with 50,000 meters per hour. You have the car's revolutions per minute, and the answer must be given in meters. So, the speed must be converted to meters per minute. This matches with a speed of $\frac{50{,}000}{60}$ meters per minute. The reason is that there are 60 minutes in an hour. In any given minute, the car travels at $\frac{50{,}000}{60}$ meters/min. The tires rotate 500 times around. So, this is 500 times its circumference. This matches with $\frac{50{,}000}{60 \times 500} = \frac{10}{6}$ meters per revolution. This is the circumference of the tire.

47. B: The volume of the cylinder is the amount of grain that the farmer will be able to store in the silo. The formula for the volume of a cylinder is $V = \pi r^2 h$, where r is the radius and h is the height. The cylinder has a diameter of 8 m. So, the radius is half of the diameter or 4 m. The height is 24 m. So, your equation becomes $V = \pi (4\text{ m})^2 (24\text{ m}) = 1{,}206.4\text{ m}^3$.

48. A: Find the product using the FOIL method. As a result, $(a+b)(a-b) = a^2 + ba - ab - b^2$. Since ab is equal to ba, the middle terms cancel each other. This leaves you with $a^2 - b^2$.

49. A: The mode is the number that appears most often in a set of data. If no item appears most often, then the data set has no mode. In this case, Kyle had one hit for a total of three times. There were two times that he had two hits. Also, on one day, he had three hits. Then, on another day, he had four hits. One hit happened the most times. So, the mode of the data set is 1.

50. B: The mean, or average, is the sum of the numbers in a data set. Then, the sum is divided by the total number of items. This data set has seven items (i.e., one for each day of the week). The total number of hits that Kyle had during the week is the sum of the numbers in the right-hand column. The sum is 14. So, to find the average: Mean $= \frac{14}{7} = 2$.

GED Math Practice Test #2

1. If $10x + 2 = 7$, what is the value of $2x$?
   a. 0.5
   b. -0.5
   c. 1
   d. 5

2. A long distance runner does a first lap around a track in exactly 50 seconds. As she tires, each subsequent lap takes 20% longer than the previous one. How long does she take to run 3 laps?
   a. 180 seconds
   b. 182 seconds
   c. 160 seconds
   d. 72 seconds

3. A number N is multiplied by 3. The result is the same as when N is divided by 3. What is the value of N?
   a. 1
   b. 0
   c. -1
   d. 3

4. Which of the following equations satisfies the five sets of numbers shown in the following table?

y	-4	31	4	68	12
x	-2	3	0	4	2

   a. $y = 2x^2 + 7$
   b. $y = x^3 + 4$
   c. $y = 2x$
   d. $y = 3x + 1$

5. John buys 100 shares of stock at $100 per share. The price goes up by 10% and he sells 50 shares. Then, prices drop by 10% and he sells his remaining 50 shares. How much did he get for the last 50?
   a. $5000
   b. $5500
   c. $4900
   d. $4950

6. The sides of a triangle are equal to integral numbers of units. Two sides are 4 and 6 units long, respectively; what is the minimum value for the triangle's perimeter?
   a. 10 units
   b. 11 units
   c. 12 units
   d. 13 units

141

7. Herbert plans to use the earnings from his lemonade stand according to the table below, for the first month of operations. If he buys $70 worth of lemons, how much profit does he take home?

Lemons	35%
Sugar	20%
Cups	25%
Stand improvements	5%
Profits	15%

a. $15
b. $20
c. $30
d. $35.50

8. A teacher has 3 hours to grade all the papers submitted by the 35 students in her class. She gets through the first 5 papers in 30 minutes. How much faster does she have to work to grade the remaining papers in the allotted time?

a. 10%
b. 15%
c. 20%
d. 25%

9. A sailor judges the distance to a lighthouse by holding a ruler at arm's length and measuring the apparent height of the lighthouse. He knows that the lighthouse is actually 60 feet tall. If it appears to be 3 inches tall when the ruler is held 2 feet from his eye, how far away is it?

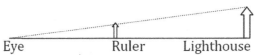

a. 60 feet
b. 120 feet
c. 240 feet
d. 480 feet

10. If $x^2 - 4 = 45$, then x could be equal to

a. 9
b. 5
c. 3
d. -7

11. What is the value of the product of the first two prime numbers that are larger than 10 divided by the largest prime number smaller than 30?

12. Determine the volume of a rectangular box with a length of 5 inches, a height of 7 inches, and a width of 9 inches.

a. 445.095 in³
b. 315 in³
c. 45 in³
d. 35 in³

13. What is the greatest integer value of y for which $5y - 20 < 0$?
    a. 5
    b. 4
    c. 3
    d. 2

14. A commuter survey counts the people riding in cars on a highway in the morning. Each car contains only one man, only one woman, or both one man and one woman. Out of 25 cars, 13 contain a woman and 20 contain a man. How many contain both a man and a woman?

15. Which equation is represented by the graph shown below?

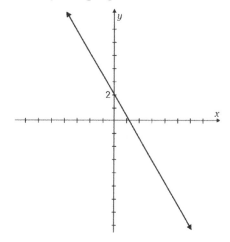

   a. $y = \frac{5}{3}x + 2$
   b. $y = -\frac{5}{3}x - 2$
   c. $y = -\frac{5}{3}x + 2$
   d. $y = \frac{5}{3}x - 2$

16. If x is a negative integer and $5 < |x - 3| < 7$, what is the value of $|x|$?

17. The right circular cylinder shown in the figure below has a height of 10 units and a radius of 1 unit. Points O and P are the centers of the top and bottom surfaces, respectively. A slice is cut from the cylinder as shown, so that the angle at the top, O, is 60 degrees, and the angle at the bottom, P, is 60 degrees. What is the volume of the slice?

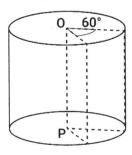

   a. 31.4 units^3
   b. 5.23 units^3
   c. 10.47 units^3
   d. 7.85 units^3

18. For the number set {7, 12, 5, 16, 23, 44, 18, 9, Z}, which of the following values could be equal to Z if Z is the median of the set?
   a. 14
   b. 11
   c. 12
   d. 17

19. If Q is divisible by 2 and 7, which of the following is also divisible by 2 and 7?
   a. $Q + 2$
   b. $Q + 7$
   c. $Q + 28$
   d. $Q + 9$

20. There are 400 fish in a tank. 150 are blue, 150 are red, and the remainder are brown. Tranh dips a net into the tank and pulls out one fish. The probability of pulling out any single fish is the same. What is the probability, as a percentage, that the fish he pulls out is brown?

21. If $a = 3$ and $b = -2$, what is the value of $a^2 + 3ab - b^2$?
   a. 5
   b. -13
   c. -4
   d. 13

22. Jack and Kevin play in a basketball game. If the ratio of points scored by Jack to points scored by Kevin is 4 to 3, which of the following could NOT be the total number of points scored by the two boys?
   a. 7
   b. 14
   c. 16
   d. 28

23. Factor the following expression: $x^2 + x - 12$
    a. $(x-2)(x+6)$
    b. $(x+6)(x-2)$
    c. $(x-4)(x+3)$
    d. $(x+4)(x-3)$

24. Five less than three times a number is equal to 58. What is the number?

25. The average of six numbers is 4. If the average of two of those numbers is 2, what is the average of the other four numbers?
    a. 5
    b. 6
    c. 7
    d. 8

26. In a rectangular x, y coordinate system, what is the intersection of two lines formed by the equations $y = 2x + 3$ and $y = x - 5$?
    a. (5, 3)
    b. (8, 13)
    c. (-4, 13)
    d. (-8, -13)

27. A function $f(x)$ is defined by $f(x) = 2x^2 + 7$. What is the value of $2f(x) - 3$?
    a. $4x^2 + 11$
    b. $4x^4 + 11$
    c. $x^2 + 11$
    d. $4x^2 + 14$

28. The two shortest sides of a right triangle are 6 and 8 units long, respectively. What is the length of the perimeter?
    a. 10 units
    b. 18 units
    c. 24 units
    d. 14 units

29. If p and n are positive consecutive integers such that $p > n$, and $p + n = 15$, what is the value of n?
    a. 5
    b. 6
    c. 7
    d. 8

30. What is the area of a square inscribed in a circle of radius r?
    a. $2r^2$
    b. $2r^3$
    c. $2\pi r$
    d. $4r^2$

31. Forty students in a class take a test that is graded on a scale of 1 to 10. The histogram in the figure shows the grade distribution, with the x-axis representing the grades and the y-axis representing the number of students obtaining each grade. If the mean, median, and modal values are represented by *n*, *p*, and *q*, respectively, which of the following is true?

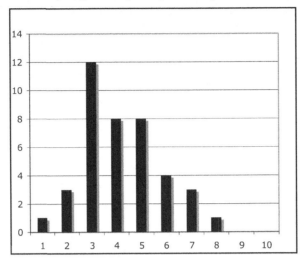

   a. $n > p > q$
   b. $n > q > p$
   c. $q > p > n$
   d. $p > q > n$

32. If x and y are positive integers, which of the following expressions is equivalent to $(xy)^{7y} - (xy)^y$?

   a. $(xy)^{6y}$
   b. $(xy)^{7y-1}$
   c. $(xy)^y[(xy)^7 - 1]$
   d. $(xy)^y[(xy)^{6y} - 1]$

33. The average of 3 numbers x, y, and z is 23. The average of three numbers a, b, and c is also 23. What is the average of all six numbers a, b, c, x, y, and z?

   a. 11.5
   b. 23
   c. 34.5
   d. 46

34. In the system of equations below, what is the value of $2x + y$?

   $2x + y + 7a = 50$
   $2x + y + 5a = 40$

35. If $(6a)x^2 = 30$, then ax^2

   a. 6
   b. 5
   c. 30
   d. $\frac{\sqrt{30}}{6}$

36. In a game played with toothpicks, players A and B take turns removing toothpicks from a row on a table. At each turn, each player must remove 1, 2, or 3 toothpicks from the row. The object is to force the other player to remove the last toothpick. If there are 6 toothpicks in the row, which of the following moves ensures a win?
   a. Remove 1
   b. Remove 2
   c. Remove 3
   d. Remove 1 or 2

37. Determine the perimeter of a rectangle with a length of 5 inches and a height of 7 inches.

38. A water sprinkler covers a circular area with a radius of 6 feet. If the water pressure is increased so that the radius increases to 8 feet, by approximately how much is the area covered by the water increased?
   a. 4 square feet
   b. 36 square feet
   c. 64 square feet
   d. 88 square feet

39. The graph below, not drawn to scale, shows a straight line passing through the origin. Point P_1 has the (x, y) coordinates (-5, -3). What is the x-coordinate of point P_2 if its y-coordinate is 3?

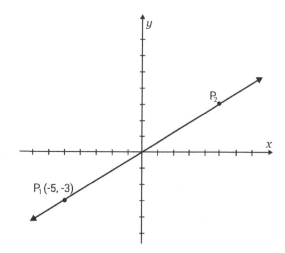

   a. 0.8
   b. 1
   c. 5
   d. 3

40. What is the area of an isosceles triangle inscribed in a circle of radius r if the base of the triangle is the diameter of the circle?
   a. r^2
   b. $2r^2$
   c. πr^2
   d. $2\pi r$

41. A regular deck of cards has 52 cards. What is the probability of drawing three aces in a row?

   a. 1 in 52
   b. 1 in 156
   c. 1 in 5525
   d. 1 in 132600

42. If $ax^2 + by = 0$, which of the following must be true?

   a. $ax^2 = by$
   b. $ax^2 = \sqrt{by}$
   c. $ax = b\sqrt{y}$
   d. $ax^2 = -by$

43. In the graph shown below, what is the slope of a line through the origin that will intercept the line $y = f(x)$ at a point where $y = 2$?

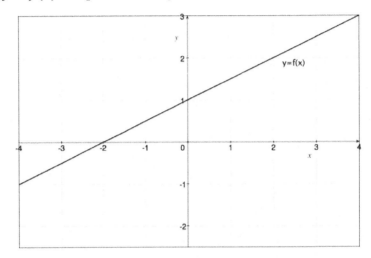

44. Equal numbers of dimes and pennies are placed in a single row on a table. Which of the following must be true?

   a. Every dime will be next to a penny.
   b. If there are two dimes at one end of the row, two pennies must be next to one another.
   c. If there is a dime at one end of the row, there must be a penny at the other end.
   d. If there are two pennies together anywhere in the row, there must be dimes at both ends.

45. A satellite in a circular orbit rotates around Earth every 120 minutes. If Earth's radius is 4,000 miles at sea level, and the satellite's orbit is 400 miles above sea level, approximately what distance does the satellite travel in 40 minutes?

   a. 9,210 miles
   b. 4,400 miles
   c. 4,120 miles
   d. 8,000 miles

46. Which of the following equations best describes the straight line in the graph below? Note that a and b are non-zero constants.

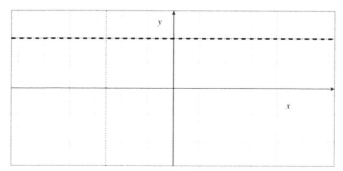

a. $y = x$
b. $x = a$
c. $y = ax + b$
d. $y = b$

47. Order the figures by increasing area:

Figure A, which is a circle with a diameter of 9 inches
Figure B, which is a circle with a radius of 5 inches
Figure C, which is a square with a side length of 7 inches

a. $B < C < A$
b. $B < A < C$
c. $C < B < A$
d. $C < A < B$

Questions 48 and 49 use the following information:

A ticket agency finds that demand for tickets for a concert in a 25,000-seat stadium falls if the price is raised. The number of tickets sold, N, varies with the dollar price, p, according to the relationship $N = 25000 - 0.1p^2$.

48. What is the lowest price at which they will sell no tickets at all?

a. $10
b. $25
c. $50
d. $500

49. No matter how many tickets are sold, the cost of putting on a concert is $500,000. Which of the following equations can be used to calculate the profit Q made for any ticket price?

a. $Q = 25{,}000p - 0.1p^3$
b. $Q = 25{,}000p - 0.1p^3 - 500{,}000$
c. $Q = 25{,}000p - 0.1p^3 - 500{,}000p$
d. $Q = p(25{,}000 - 0.1p) - 500{,}000$

50. In the system of equations below, what is the value of y?

$x^2 + y^2 = 24$
$2x^2 + 3y^2 = 52$

Answer Key and Explanations for Test #2

1. C: To determine this, you must solve the given equation for x. Since $10x + 2 = 7$, we have $x = \frac{7-2}{10} = \frac{5}{10} = 0.5$, and $2x = 1$. Alternately, $10x = 5$; divide both sides by 5 to get $2x = 1$.

2. B: If the first lap takes 50 seconds, the second one takes 20% more, or $T_2 = 1.2 \times T_1 = 1.2 \times 50 = 60$ seconds, where T_1 and T_2 are the times required for the first and second laps, respectively. Similarly, $T_3 = 1.2 \times T_2 = 1.2 \times 60 = 72$ seconds, the time required for the third lap. Add the times for the three laps: $50 + 60 + 72 = 182$.

3. B: Zero is the only number that gives the same result when multiplied or divided by a factor. In each case, the answer is zero.

4. B: The easiest pair to test is the third: $y = 4$ and $x = 0$. Substitute these values in each of the given equations and evaluate: $y = x^3 + 4$ becomes $4 = 0 + 4$

5. D: The stock first increased by 10%, that is, by $10 (10% of $100) to $110 per share. Then, the price decreased by $11 (10% of $110) so that the sale price was $110 - $11 = $99 per share, and the sale price for 50 shares was $99 \times \$50 = \$4950$.

6. D: The sides of a triangle must all be greater than zero. The sum of the lengths of the two shorter sides must be greater than the length of the third side. Since we are looking for the minimum value of the perimeter, assume the longer of the two given sides, which is 6, is the longest side of the triangle. Then the third side must be greater than $6 - 4 = 2$. Since we are told the sides are all integral numbers, the last side must be 3 units in length. Thus, the minimum length for the perimeter is $4 + 6 + 3 = 13$ units.

7. C: If $70, the amount used to buy more lemons, represents 35% of Herbert's earnings, then 1% corresponds to $\frac{\$70}{35} = \$2$, and 15% corresponds to $\$2 \times 15 = \$30$.

8. C: She has been working at the rate of 10 papers per hour. She has 30 papers remaining and must grade them in the 2.5 hours that she has left, which corresponds to a rate of 12 papers per hour. $\frac{12}{10} = 120\%$ of her previous rate, or 20% faster.

9. D: The ratio of the ruler's height to the distance from eye to ruler, which is the tangent of the angle subtended at the eye by the ruler's height, must be the same as the ratio of the lighthouse's height to its distance, which is the tangent of the same angle. Since 3 inches is ¼ foot, we have $\frac{1/4}{2} = \frac{60}{D}$, and solving for D gives $D = \frac{2 \times 60}{1/4} = 4 \times 120 = 480$ feet.

10. D: $x^2 = 49$. When you take the square root of a number, the answer is the positive and negative values of the root. Therefore, $x = 7$ and $x = -7$. Only -7 is an answer choice.

11. The correct answer is 4.93. When gridding an answer that does not come out evenly, you must either enter the entire fraction, or as many decimal places as the answer field allows. The first two prime numbers larger than 10 are 11 and 13, and their product is 143. The largest prime number smaller than 30 is 29. The fraction will not fit in the answer field, so you must convert it to a decimal and round to the appropriate number of places: $\frac{143}{29} = 4.93$.

12. B: The volume of a rectangular box can be determined using the formula $V = l \times w \times h$. This means that the volume of a rectangular box can be determined by multiplying the length of the base of the box by the width of the box and multiplying that product by the height of the box. Therefore, the volume of the box described in this question is equal to $5 \times 7 \times 9$, or 315 in^3.

13. C: If $5y - 20 < 0$, then $5y < 20$ and $y < 4$. Since y must be an integer, the answer must be 3, the largest integer that is less than 4. Choice B is wrong because, in this case, $5y - 20 = 0$, which is not less than 0.

14. The correct answer is 8. The total $20 + 13 = 33$, but only 25 cars have been scored. Therefore $33 - 25$, or 8 cars must have had both a man and a woman inside.

15. C: The line in the graph has a negative slope and a positive y-axis intercept, so the factor multiplying the variable x, or the slope, must be negative, and the constant, or y-intercept, must be positive.

16. The correct answer is 3. By definition, $x - 3 = 6$ and $x - 3 = -6$. Since x is defined as a negative integer, solve $x - 3 = 6 \Rightarrow x = -3$. The question asks for $|x|$, therefore $|x| = 3$.

17. B: The total volume of the cylinder is given by $V = h\pi r^2 = 10\pi \times 1 = 31.4$, when $\pi = 3.14$. Since the slice is a straight, 60-degree slice, its volume is one sixth of this ($\frac{60}{360} = \frac{1}{6}$), or 5.23.

18. A: The median of a set of numbers is one for which the set contains an equal number of greater and lesser values. Besides Z, there are 8 numbers in the set, so that 4 must be greater and 4 lesser than Z. The 4 smallest values are 5, 7, 9, and 12. The 4 largest are 16, 18, 23, and 44. So Z must fall between 12 and 16.

19. C: If Q is divisible by both 7 and 2, it must be a multiple of 14, which is the least common multiple of both 2 and 7. Therefore, if one adds another multiple of 14 to Q, it will also be divisible by both 2 and 7. Of the choices given, only 28 is a multiple of 14.

20. The correct answer is 25. Three quarters of the fish, or 300, are red or blue, leaving only 100, or 25% brown fish. Since the probability of pulling out any single fish is the same, he has a 25% chance of getting a brown fish.

21. B: Substitute the given values for a and b and perform the required operations:

$$a^2 + 3ab - b^2 = 3^2 + 3(3)(-2) - (-2)^2$$
$$= 9 - 18 - 4$$
$$= -13$$

22. C: Every possible combination of scores is a multiple of 7, since the two terms of the ratio have a sum of seven. 16 is not divisible by 7.

23. D: Recall that the general form of a quadratic expression is $ax^2 + bx + c$. A great way to factor quadratic expression like this, where $a = 1$ and all the answer choices are integer factors, would be to consider the factors of the last term, c. Specifically, any two factors of c that would add to b. Essentially: $f_1 \times f_2 = -12$ and $f_1 + f_2 = 1$. We can check the factors of -12:

f_1	f_2	$f_1 + f_2$
12	-1	11
6	-2	4
4	-3	1
3	-4	-1
2	-6	-4
1	-12	-11

From this it is clear that the only option that works is 4 and -3.

24. The correct answer is 21. The sentence in the question is translates to $3x - 5 = 58$. Thus:

$$x = \frac{58 + 5}{3} = 21$$

25. A: A set of six numbers with an average of 4 must have a collective sum of 24. The two numbers that average 2 will add up to 4, so the remaining numbers must add up to 20. The average of these four numbers can be calculated: $20/4 = 5$.

26. D: At the point of intersection, the y-coordinates are equal on both lines so that $2x + 3 = x - 5$. Solving for x, we have $x = -8$. Then, evaluating y with either equation yields $y = 2(-8) + 3 = -16 + 3 = -13$ or $y = -8 - 5 = -13$.

27. A: Evaluate as follows: $2f(x) - 3 = 2(2x^2 + 7) - 3 = 4x^2 + 14 - 3 = 4x^2 + 11$.

28. C: The hypotenuse must be the longest side of a right triangle, so it must be the lengths of the other two sides that are given as 6 and 8 units. Calculate the length of the hypotenuse, H, from the Pythagorean Theorem: $H^2 = S_1^2 + S_2^2 = 6^2 + 8^2 = 36 + 64 = 100$, which yields $H = 10$ and the perimeter equals $10 + 6 + 8 = 24$.

29. C: This can be solved as two equations with two unknowns. Since the integers are consecutive with $p > n$, we have $p - n = 1$, so that $p = 1 + n$. Substituting this value into $p + n = 15$ gives $1 + 2n = 15$, or $n = \frac{14}{2} = 7$.

30. A: The square is one whose diagonal corresponds to the diameter of the circle. This allows calculation of the side a by the Pythagorean Theorem, where the diameter is $d = 2r$: $d^2 = 4r^2 = a^2 + a^2$. Thus, $4r^2 = 2a^2$, and the area of the square $a^2 = 2r^2$.

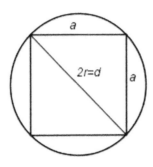

31. A: The mean, or average of the distribution can be computed by multiplying each grade by the number of students obtaining it, summing, and dividing by the total number of students. Here, $n = 4.2$. The median is the value for which an equal number of students have received higher or lower grades. Here, $p = 4$. The mode is the most frequently obtained grade, and here, $q = 3$. Therefore, $n > p > q$.

32. D: Remember that when you multiply like bases, you add the exponents, and when you divide like bases, you subtract the exponents. $(xy)^{7y} - (xy)^y = (xy)^y[(xy)^{7y-y} - 1] = (xy)^y[(xy)^{6y} - 1]$

33. B: If the averages are equal, then we have $\frac{x+y+z}{3} = \frac{a+b+c}{3}$, so that it must be true that $(x + y + z) = (a + b + c)$. Therefore, the average of all six numbers is $\frac{(x+y+z)+(a+b+c)}{6} = \frac{2(x+y+z)}{6} = \frac{(x+y+z)}{3} = 23$.

34. The correct answer is 15. Subtracting the second equation from the first, we have $2x + y + 7a - 2x - y - 5a = 50 - 40$, which simplifies to $2a = 10$, or $a = 5$. Substitute this value into either of the original equations. The first equation yields $2x + y + 35 = 50$, so that $2x + y = 15$. The second equation gives the same answer: $2x + y + 25 = 40 \Rightarrow 2x + y = 15$.

35. B: $(6a)x^2$ is equivalent to $6 \times ax^2$, so that ax^2 is simply 1/6th of this, or $\frac{30}{6} = 5$.

36. A: Since a player cannot remove fewer than 1 or more than 3 toothpicks per turn, it follows that leaving 2, 3 or 4 toothpicks in a row allows a winning response, and that leaving 5 toothpicks forces the next player to leave 2, 3, or 4.

37. The correct answer may be gridded as 24 in. The perimeter of a rectangle can be determined by using the formula $P = 2 \times (Side\ 1 + Side\ 2)$. This means that the perimeter of a rectangle can be determined by adding the length of the base of the rectangle to the height of the rectangle and multiplying by 2. Therefore, the perimeter of the rectangle described in this question is equal to $2 \times (5\ inches + 7\ inches)$, or 24 inches.

38. D: The circular area covered by the sprinkler is πr^2, so the difference is obtained as $\pi \times 8^2 - \pi \times 6^2 = \pi(64 - 36) = 28\pi = 87.92$.

39. C: Since the line is straight, the slope is the same throughout. Thus, if 5 y-units are traversed in going from $x = -3$ to $x = 0$ (where y increases from -5 to 0, to reach the origin), then 5 y-units will be traversed in going from $x = 0$ to $x = 3$.

40. A: The area of a triangle equals half the product of base times height. Since the base passes through the center, we have $base = 2r$ and $height = r$, so that the area A is $A = \frac{r \times 2r}{2} = r^2$.

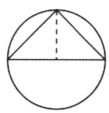

41. C: The probability of getting three aces in a row is the product of the probabilities for each draw. For the first ace, that is 4 in 52, since there are 4 aces in a deck of 52 cards. For the second, it is 3 in 51, since 3 aces and 51 cards remain; and for the third, it is 2 in 50. So, the overall probability, P, is $P = \frac{4}{52} \times \frac{3}{51} \times \frac{2}{50} = \frac{24}{132600} = \frac{1}{5525}$.

42. D: This answer is obtained by moving the second term to the right of the equality and changing its sign.

43. The correct answer is 1. At $y = 2$, we see that $x = 2$ for the plotted line. The equation for a straight line is of the form $y = ax + b$, where a is the slope and b is the y-intercept at $x = 0$. If the new line passes through the origin, then $b = 0$, and the slope a must be 1 for y to equal 2 when x equals 2.

44. B: Since there are equal numbers of each coin in the row, if two of one type are next to each other, two of the other type must also be next to each other someplace within the row, or else at each end of the row. Since the two dimes take up one end of the row, the two pennies must be together.

45. A: The radius, R, of the satellite's orbit is the sum of Earth's radius plus the satellite's orbital altitude, or $R = 4400$ miles. The circumference of the circular orbit is therefore $C = 2\pi r = 2\pi(4400) = 8800\pi$ miles. Since 40 minutes is one third of the satellite's 120-minute orbital time, it traverses one third of this distance in that time. So, the distance, $D = \frac{40}{120} \times 2\pi \times 4400 = 9210.66$ miles, using 3.14 for π.

46. D: The line in the graph has a constant value of y, one that does not change regardless of the value of x. This is a special case of the equation for the straight line, $y = mx + b$, for which $m = 0$.

47. D: Find the area of each figure. The area of a square is $A = s^2$, so the area of figure C is 7^2 or 49 in^2 The area of a circle can be determined by using the formula $A = \pi \times r^2$. Also, note that the radius of a circle is equal to half of the circle's diameter. This means that the radius of figure A is 4.5 inches and the radius of figure B, which is stated within the question, is 5 inches. Therefore, the area of figure A is equal to 3.14×4.5^2 or 63.585 in^2 and the area of figure B is equal to 3.14×5^2 or 78.5 in^2. In order, 49 in^2 < 63.585 in^2 < 78.5 in^2, so $C < A < B$.

48. D: When no tickets are sold, $N = 0$, and $0 = 25000 - 0.1p^2$, so that $0.1p^2 = 25000$, and $p^2 = \frac{25000}{0.1} = 250,000 = 2500 \times 100 = 50^2 \times 10^2$, so that $p = 50 \times 10 = 500$.

49. B: Remember that profit = (tickets sold) × (price) − cost. The number of tickets sold is given by the equation $N = 25000 - 0.1p^2$. Multiplying this expression by price, p, gives $25,000p - 0.1p^3$, and subtracting cost gives $Q = 25,000p - 0.1p^3 - 500,000$.

50. The correct answer is 2. Rearranging the first equation gives $x^2 = 24 - y^2$. Now, substituting this value into the second equation gives $2(24 - y^2) + 3y^2 = 52 \Rightarrow 48 - 2y^2 + 3y^2 = 52$. Rearranging once again gives $y^2 = 4$, or $y \pm 2$. The grid does not allow for negative numbers, so grid in 2.

GED Math Practice Test #3

1. What is the next-highest prime number after 67?
   a. 68
   b. 69
   c. 71
   d. 73

2. Dean's Department Store reduces the price of a $30 shirt by 20%, but later raises it again by 20% of the sale price. What is the final price of the shirt?
   a. $24.40
   b. $32
   c. $30
   d. $28.80

3. How many 3-inch segments can a 4.5-yard line be divided into?
   a. 15
   b. 45
   c. 54
   d. 64

4. Sheila, Janice, and Karen, working together at the same rate, can complete a job in 3 1/3 days. Working at the same rate, how much of the job could Janice and Karen do in one day?
   a. 1/5
   b. 1/4
   c. 1/3
   d. 1/9

5. Of the following expressions, which is equal to $6\sqrt{10}$?
   a. 36
   b. $\sqrt{600}$
   c. $\sqrt{360}$
   d. $10\sqrt{6}$

6. A box of laundry detergent contains 16.5 oz of product. What is the maximum number of loads that can be washed if each load requires a minimum of ¾ oz of detergent?
   a. 10
   b. 50
   c. 22
   d. 18

7. There are n musicians in a marching band. All play either a drum or a brass instrument. If p represents the fraction of musicians playing drums, how many play a brass instrument?
   a. $pn - 1$
   b. $(p - 1)n$
   c. $(p + 1)n$
   d. $(1 - p)n$

8. Given the triangle shown in the figure, what is the length of the side A?

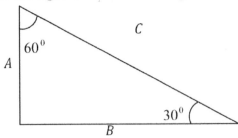

   a. $C/2$
   b. $B/2$
   c. $(B+C)/2$
   d. $2B$

9. A bullet travels at 5×10^6 feet per hour. If it strikes its target in 2×10^{-4} hours, how far has it traveled?

   a. 50 feet
   b. 100 feet
   c. 1000 feet
   d. 200 feet

10. If $3a + 5b = 98$ and $a = 11$, what is the value of $a + b$?

11. If the two lines $2x + y = 0$ and $y = 3$ are plotted on a typical xy-coordinate grid, at which point will they intersect?

   a. $(-1.5, 3)$
   b. $(1.5, 3)$
   c. $(-1.5, 0)$
   d. $(4, 1)$

12. Which of the following equations describes a line that is parallel to the x-axis?

   a. $y = 3$
   b. $y = 2x$
   c. $(x + y) = 0$
   d. $y = -3x$

13. How many identical cubes, each with edges of 3 inches, can fit in a box measuring 15 inches by 9 inches by 6 inches?

14. A blouse normally sells for $138, but is on sale for 25% off. What is the cost of the blouse?

   a. $67
   b. $103.50
   c. $113
   d. $125

15. $|7-5| - |5-7| =$
    a. 0
    b. 4
    c. 2
    d. -2

16. The rectangle below has an area of 245 inches^2. What is the length of the longest side of the rectangle?

17. What is the average of $\frac{7}{5}$ and 1.4?
    a. 5.4
    b. 1.4
    c. 2.4
    d. 7.4

18. What is the surface area, in square inches, of a cube if the length of one side is 3 inches?
    a. 9
    b. 27
    c. 54
    d. 21

19. If it took Lex from 10:00a.m. to 11:45a.m. to walk 14 blocks, what was his average speed in blocks per hour?

20. Which of the following values is closest to the diameter of a circle with an area of 314 square inches?
    a. 20 inches
    b. 10 inches
    c. 100 inches
    d. 31.4 inches

21. The following table shows the distance from a point to a moving car at various times.

d	Distance	50	70	110
t	Time	2	3	5

If the speed of the car is constant, which of the following equations describes the distance from the point to the car?
    a. $d = 25t$
    b. $d = 35t$
    c. $d = 55t$
    d. $d = 20t + 10$

22. The average of 4, 7, 9 and x is 9. What is the value of x?

23. A circle has a perimeter of 35 feet. What is its diameter?
   a. 11.14 feet
   b. 6.28 feet
   c. 5.57 feet
   d. 3.5 feet

24. A jar contains pennies and nickels. The ratio of nickels to pennies is 6:2. What percentage of the coins are pennies?

25. What is the sum of the largest prime factor of 42 and the smallest prime factor of 42?

26. $4^6 \div 2^8 =$
   a. 2
   b. 8
   c. 16
   d. 32

27. If $a = 4, b = 3,$ and $c = 1$, then $\frac{a(b-c)}{b(a+b+c)} =$
   a. 4/13
   b. 1/3
   c. 1/4
   d. 1/6

28. What is 20% of $\frac{12}{5}$, expressed as a percentage?
   a. 48%
   b. 65%
   c. 72%
   d. 76%

29. Which number equals 2^{-3}?
   a. 1/2
   b. 1/4
   c. 1/8
   d. 1/16

30. The flower shop puts all flowers in bouquets of 12. If the shop has 137 flowers, how many are left over when there aren't enough to make a full bouquet?

Questions 31-33 are based upon the following diagram of a circle, where O is the center and OA and OC are radii:

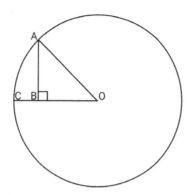

31. If the length of segment AB = x, and the length of segment OB = y, which of the following expressions describes the radius of the circle?

 a. $x + y$
 b. $x^2 + y^2$
 c. $y + 4$
 d. $\sqrt{x^2 + y^2}$

32. If the length of segment AB equals that of segment OB, what is the angle AOC?

 a. 45 degrees
 b. Same as angle BAO
 c. Same as angle ABO
 d. A and B are true but not C

33. Which of the following must be true?

 a. OA = OC
 b. OB = BC
 c. OB = OC
 d. AB = OC

34. What fractional part of an hour is 400 seconds?

 a. 1/6
 b. 1/7
 c. 1/8
 d. 1/9

35. Larry gave 1/4 of his Halloween candy to his little sister Eva and 1/5 to his mom. What percentage of his Halloween candy did Larry have left?

36. A straight line with slope +4 is plotted on a standard Cartesian (xy) coordinate system so that it intersects the y-axis at a value of $y = 1$. Which of the following points will the line pass through?

 a. (2, 9)
 b. (0, -1)
 c. (0, 0)
 d. (4, 1)

37. A crane raises one end of a 3300 lb steel beam. The other end rests upon the ground. If the crane supports 30% of the beam's weight, how many pounds does it support?

   a. 330 lbs
   b. 990 lbs
   c. 700 lbs
   d. 1100 lbs

38. Two angles of a triangle measure 15° and 70°, respectively. What is the size of the third angle?

   a. 90 degrees
   b. 80 degrees
   c. 75 degrees
   d. 95 degrees

39. If 24 people tried to climb a mountain and 6 people completed the climb, what percentage of people didn't climb the mountain?

40. The triangle shown in the figure has angles A, B, and C, and sides a, b, and c. If $a = 14$ cm, $b = 12$ cm, and $\angle B = 35$ degrees, what is $\angle A$?

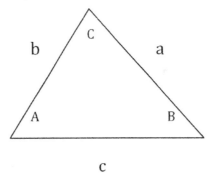

   a. 35 degrees
   b. 42 degrees
   c. 64 degrees
   d. 18 degrees

41. A metal rod used in manufacturing must be as close as possible to 15 inches in length. The tolerance of the length, L, in inches, is specified by the inequality $|L - 15| \leq 0.01$. What is the minimum length permissible for the rod?

   a. 14.9 inches
   b. 14.99 inches
   c. 15.01 inches
   d. 15.1 inches

42. Two numbers are said to be reciprocals of one another if their product equals 1. Which of the following represents the reciprocal of the variable x?

   a. $x - 1$
   b. $\frac{1}{x}$
   c. $-x$
   d. $1 - x$

43. A taxi service charges $5.50 for the first 1/5 of a mile, $1.50 for each additional 1/5 of a mile, and 20¢ per minute of waiting time. Joan took a cab from her place to a flower shop 8 miles away, where she bought a bouquet, then another 3.6 miles to her mother's place. The driver had to wait 9 minutes while she bought the bouquet. What was the fare?
   a. $20
   b. $120.20
   c. $92.80
   d. $91

44. Which of the following expressions is equivalent to the equation $3x^2 + 4x - 15$?
   a. $(x-3)(x+5)$
   b. $(x+5)(3+x^2)$
   c. $x(3x^2 + 4 - 15)$
   d. $(x+3)(3x-5)$

45. It takes Roxana 1 hour and 30 minutes to ride her bike on the uphill trip to the park at an average speed of 4 miles per hour. If she comes home on the same route at an average speed of 5 miles per hour, how long in minutes does the return trip take?
   a. 52
   b. 62
   c. 72
   d. 82

Use the following information to answer questions 46-47:

An MP3 player is set to play songs at random from the fifteen songs it contains in memory. Any song can be played at any time, even if it is repeated. There are 5 songs by Band A, 3 songs by Band B, 2 by Band C, and 5 by Band D.

46. If the player has just played two songs in a row by Band D, what is the probability that the next song will also be by Band D?
   a. 1 in 5
   b. 1 in 3
   c. 1 in 9
   d. 1 in 27

47. What is the probability that the next two songs will both be by Band B?
   a. 1 in 25
   b. 1 in 3
   c. 1 in 5
   d. 1 in 9

48. Which of the following expressions is equivalent to $3\left(\frac{6x-3}{3}\right) - 3(9x + 9)$?
   a. $-3(7x + 10)$
   b. $-3x + 6$
   c. $(x+3)(x-3)$
   d. $3x^2 - 9$

49. A circle is inscribed within a square, as shown. What is the difference between the area of the square and that of the circle, where *r* is the radius of the circle?

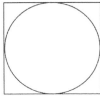

- a. 2π
- b. $\frac{4}{3}\pi r^3$
- c. $r^2(4-\pi)$
- d. $2\pi r$

50. A two-digit number is chosen at random. What is the probability that the chosen number is a multiple of 7?

- a. 13/90
- b. 1/9
- c. 11/90
- d. 2/15

Answer Key and Explanations for Test #3

1. C: Prime numbers are those that are only evenly divisible by one and themselves.

2. D: Multiply 30 by 0.2 and subtract this from the original price of the shirt to find the sale price: $24. Then multiply 24 by 0.2 and add the product to the sale price to find the final price.

3. C: For this problem there are 3 inches in each segment, 12 inches in a foot, and 3 feet in a yard. Set up a conversion problem and simplify:

$$4.5 \text{ yd} \times \frac{3 \text{ ft}}{1 \text{ yd}} \times \frac{12 \text{ in}}{1 \text{ ft}} \times \frac{1 \text{ segment}}{3 \text{ in}} = 4.5 \times 12 \text{ segments} = 54 \text{ segments}$$

4. A: If it takes 3 people 3 1/3 days to do the job, then it would take one person 10 days: $3 \times 3\frac{1}{3} = 10$. Thus, it would take 2 people 5 days, and one day of work for two people would complete 1/5 of the job.

5. C: Since $360 = 36 \times 10$ and $36 = 6^2$, $\sqrt{360} = \sqrt{6^2 \times 10} = 6\sqrt{10}$.

6. C: Recall that dividing by a fraction is the same as multiplying by its reciprocal: $16.5 \times \frac{4}{3} = 22$.

7. D: The fraction of those playing drums plus the fraction of those playing a brass instrument must total 1. So the number that play drums is pn, and the number playing brass must be $(1-p)n$.

8. A: This is a right triangle, since the two angles shown add up to 90 degrees, and the remaining angle must therefore be 90 degrees. For a right triangle, the length of a side is related to the hypotenuse by the sine of the opposite angle. Thus $A = C \sin(30°)$ and since the sine of a 30-degree angle is 0.5, $A = C/2$.

9. C: Distance is the product of velocity and time:

$$(5 \times 10^6)\frac{\text{feet}}{\text{hr}} \times (2 \times 10^{-4}) \text{ hr} = (5 \times 2) \times (10^6 \times 10^{-4})$$
$$= 10 \times 10^{6-4}$$
$$= 10^{1+2}$$
$$= 10^3$$
$$= 1000 \text{ feet}$$

10. 24: First solve for b. If $3a + 5b = 98$ and $a = 11$:

$$3(11) + 5b = 98$$
$$33 + 5b = 98$$
$$5b = 65$$
$$b = 13$$

Therefore, $a + b = 11 + 13 = 24$.

11. A: Since the second line, $y = 3$, is a vertical, the intersection must occur at a point where $y = 3$. If $x = -1.5$, the equation describing the line is satisfied: $2 \times (-1.5) + 3 = 0$

12. A: For the line to be parallel to the x-axis, the slope must be 0. This condition is met if y has a constant value.

13. 30: The answer is found by dividing the volume of the box by the volume of the cube:

$$\frac{V_{box}}{V_{cube}} = \frac{(15 \text{ in}) \times (9 \text{ in}) \times (6 \text{ in})}{(3 \text{ in}) \times (3 \text{ in}) \times (3 \text{ in})} = \frac{810 \text{ in}^3}{27 \text{ in}^3} = 30$$

14. B: 25% off is equivalent to $\frac{25}{100} \times \$138 = \$34.50$, so the sale price becomes:

$$\$138 - \$34.50 = \$103.50$$

15. A: The vertical operators indicate absolute values, which are always positive. Thus, $|7 - 5| = 2$, and $|7 - 5|=|-2|=2$, and $2 - 2 = 0$.

16. 35: A rectangle's area is length times width. Here, length is $5x$ and width is x so:

$$245 \text{ in}^2 = x \times 5x$$
$$245 \text{ in}^2 = 5x^2$$
$$49 \text{ in}^2 = x^2$$
$$7 \text{ in} = x$$

Therefore, the longest side is $5 \times 7 \text{ in} = 35 \text{ in}$.

17. B: The value of the fraction $\frac{7}{5}$ can be evaluated by dividing 7 by 5, which yields 1.4. The average of 1.4 and 1.4 is $\frac{1.4+1.4}{2} = 1.4$.

18. C: The surface of a cube is obtained by multiplying the area of each face by 6, since there are 6 faces. The area of each face is the square of the length of one edge:

$$A = 6 \times 3^2 = 6 \times 9 = 54$$

19. 8: Remember that rate is distance divided by time. The distance is 14 and time is 1 hour and 45 minutes, or $1\frac{3}{4}$ hr, or $\frac{7}{4}$ hr.

$$\frac{14 \text{ blocks}}{\frac{7}{4} \text{ hr}} = 14 \times \frac{4}{7} = 8 \frac{\text{blocks}}{\text{hr}}$$

20. A: The area A of a circle is given by $A = \pi \times r^2$, where r is the radius. Since π is approximately 3.14, we can solve for $r = \sqrt{\frac{A}{\pi}} = \sqrt{\frac{314 \text{ inches}^2}{3.14}} = \sqrt{100 \text{ inches}^2} = 10$ inches. Now, the diameter d is twice the radius, or 2×10 inches $= 20$ inches.

21. D: Inspection of the data shows that the distance traveled by the car during any 1-unit interval (velocity) is 20 units. However, the first data point shows that the car is 50 units from the point of origin at time 2, so it had a 10-unit head start before time measurement began.

22. 16: To solve this problem, first set up the equation, then multiply both sides by four, and solve:

$$\frac{4+7+9+x}{4} = 9$$
$$20 + x = 36$$
$$x = 16$$

23. A: The perimeter of a circle is given by $2\pi r$, where r is the radius. We solve for $r = \frac{35}{2\pi} = 5.57$, and double this value to obtain the diameter $d = 11.14$ feet.

24. 25: If the ratio of pennies to nickels is 2:6, the ratio of the pennies to the combined coins is 2:2+6, or 2:8. This is ¼ or, expressed as a percentage, 25%.

25. 9: The largest prime factor of 42 is 7 and the smallest is 2. The sum of the two is 9.

26. C: Since 4 is the same as 2^2, $4^6 = 2^{12}$. When dividing exponents with the same base, simply subtract the exponent in the denominator from the exponent in the numerator.

$$2^{12} \div 2^8 = 2^{12-8} = 2^4 = 16$$

27. B: Substitute the given values and solve. Resolve the parenthetical operations first.

$$\frac{a(b-c)}{b(a+b+c)} = \frac{4(3-1)}{3(4+3+1)}$$
$$= \frac{4(2)}{3(8)}$$
$$= \frac{8}{3(8)}$$
$$= \frac{1}{3}$$

28. A: Convert 20% to the fraction 1/5, then multiply by 12/5. The resulting fraction, 12/25, must have both numerator and denominator multiplied by 4 to become a percentage.

29. C: The expression 2^{-3} is equivalent to $\frac{1}{2^3}$, and since $2^3 = 8$, it is equivalent to 1/8.

30. 5: Use long division to determine how many times 12 goes into 137 (11 times) and see what remains. There is a remainder of 5.

31. D: The radius r of this circle is the line OA. Since B is a right angle, OA is the hypotenuse and by the Pythagorean theorem, $r^2 = x^2 + y^2$ so that $r = \sqrt{x^2 + y^2}$.

32. D: If segment AB equals segment OB, then the tangent of the angle AOB must be 1 (tan AOB) = $\frac{AB}{OB}$ = 1, which is the tangent of a 45-degree angle. Further, since AOB is a right triangle with angle ABO = 90 degrees, and since the sum of the angles in a triangle must equal 180 degrees, angle BAO must also be 45 degrees (45+45+90=180).

33. A: Since both OA and OC are radii of the same circle, they must be equal.

34. D: Each hour has 60 minutes, and each of those minutes has 60 seconds. Expressed in seconds, then, an hour is $60 \times 60 = 3600$. $400/3600 = 1/9$.

35. 55: First, determine how much Larry gave away:

$$\frac{1}{4} + \frac{1}{5} = \frac{5}{20} + \frac{4}{20} = \frac{9}{20}$$

He had 11/20 left:

$$\frac{11}{20} = \frac{55}{100} = 55\%$$

36. A: As defined, the line will be described by the equation $y = 4x + 1$. Check each of the options:

$$9 = 4 \times 2 + 1$$
$$-1 \neq 4 \times 0 + 1$$
$$0 \neq 4 \times 0 + 1$$
$$1 \neq 4 \times 4 + 1$$

37. B: It is helpful to recall that percentages can be converted to decimals: 30% of 3300 is 0.3×3300 lbs $= 990$ lbs

38. D: The sum of angles in a triangle equals 180 degrees. Therefore, solve for the remaining angle as $180 - (15 + 70) = 95$ degrees.

39. 75: Of the 24 people that set out to climb, only 6 made it to the top so 18 people did not complete the climb. 18/24=3/4=75%.

40. B: This answer may be determined using the Law of Sines, which relates the sides of a triangle and their opposing angles as follows:

$$\frac{a}{\sin A} = \frac{b}{\sin B} = \frac{c}{\sin C}$$

Thus, we have $\sin A = a \times \frac{\sin B}{b} = 14 \times \frac{\sin(35)}{12} = 14 \times \frac{0.57}{12} = 0.67$, and

$$\sin^{-1}(0.67) = 42 \text{ degrees}$$

41. B: The inequality specifies that the difference between L and 15 inches must be less or equal to 0.01. Note that $|14.99 - 15| = |-0.01| = 0.01$, which is equal to the specified tolerance and therefore meets the condition.

42. B: The product of x and $\frac{1}{x}$ is $\frac{1}{x} \times x = \frac{x}{x} = 1$.

43. C: The total distance traveled was 8 mi + 3.6 mi = 11.6 mi. The first 1/5 of a mile is charged at the higher rate. Since 1/5 = 0.2, the remainder of the trip is 11.4 miles. Now multiply this amount by 5 to determine the number of 1/5 of a mile increments covered. Thus, the fare for the distance traveled is computed as $\$5.50 + 5\frac{\text{fifths}}{\text{mi}} \times 11.4$ mi $\times \$1.50 = \$91$. The charge for waiting time is added next, which is simply $9 \times 20¢ = 180¢ = \$1.80$. Finally, add the two charges, $\$91 + \$1.80 = \$92.80$.

44. D: Each term of each expression in parentheses must be multiplied by each term in the other:

$$(x-3)(x+5) = x^2 - 3x + 5x - 15 = x^2 + 2x - 15 \neq 3x^2 + 4x - 15$$
$$(x+5)(3+x^2) = 3x + 15 + x^3 + 5x^2 \neq 3x^2 + 4x - 15$$
$$x(3x + 4 - 15) = 3x^2 + 4x - 15x = 3x^2 - 11x \neq 3x^2 + 4x - 15$$
$$(x+3)(3x-5) = 3x^2 + 9x - 5x - 15 = 3x^2 + 4x - 15$$

45. C: Recall that $distance = rate \times time$. Here, Roxana's rate was 4 mph, and her time was 1.5 hours. Distance, therefore, is 6 miles. To determine how long it took Roxana to return, we solve the formula for time:

$$6 \text{ miles} = 5 \text{ mph} \times time$$
$$time = 1\frac{1}{5} \text{ hours} = 72 \text{ minutes}$$

46. B: The probability of playing a song by any band is proportional to the number of songs by that band over the total number of songs, or $\frac{5}{15} = \frac{1}{3}$ for Band D. The probability of playing any particular song is not affected by what has been played previously, since the choice is random.

47. A: Since 3 of the 15 songs are by Band B, the probability that any one song will be by that band is $\frac{3}{15} = \frac{1}{5}$. The probability that two successive events will occur is the product of the probabilities for any one event or, in this case $\frac{1}{5} \times \frac{1}{5} = \frac{1}{25}$.

48. A: From the starting expression, compute:

$$3\left(\frac{6x-3}{3}\right) - 3(9x+9) = 3(2x-1) - 27x - 27$$
$$= 6x - 3 - 27x - 27$$
$$= -21x - 30$$
$$= -3(7x + 10)$$

49. C: The side of the square is equal to the diameter of the circle, or twice the radius, that is, $2r$. The area of the square is this quantity squared, or $4r^2$. The area of the circle is, πr^2. Subtracting gives the difference between the two areas, $\Delta A = 4r^2 - \pi r^2 = r^2(4 - \pi)$.

50. A: There are 90 two-digit numbers (all integers from, and including, 10 to, and including, 99). Of those, there are 13 multiples of 7: 14, 21, 28, 35, 42, 49, 56, 63, 70, 77, 84, 91, 98.

How to Overcome Test Anxiety

Just the thought of taking a test is enough to make most people a little nervous. A test is an important event that can have a long-term impact on your future, so it's important to take it seriously and it's natural to feel anxious about performing well. But just because anxiety is normal, that doesn't mean that it's helpful in test taking, or that you should simply accept it as part of your life. Anxiety can have a variety of effects. These effects can be mild, like making you feel slightly nervous, or severe, like blocking your ability to focus or remember even a simple detail.

If you experience test anxiety—whether severe or mild—it's important to know how to beat it. To discover this, first you need to understand what causes test anxiety.

Causes of Test Anxiety

While we often think of anxiety as an uncontrollable emotional state, it can actually be caused by simple, practical things. One of the most common causes of test anxiety is that a person does not feel adequately prepared for their test. This feeling can be the result of many different issues such as poor study habits or lack of organization, but the most common culprit is time management. Starting to study too late, failing to organize your study time to cover all of the material, or being distracted while you study will mean that you're not well prepared for the test. This may lead to cramming the night before, which will cause you to be physically and mentally exhausted for the test. Poor time management also contributes to feelings of stress, fear, and hopelessness as you realize you are not well prepared but don't know what to do about it.

Other times, test anxiety is not related to your preparation for the test but comes from unresolved fear. This may be a past failure on a test, or poor performance on tests in general. It may come from comparing yourself to others who seem to be performing better or from the stress of living up to expectations. Anxiety may be driven by fears of the future—how failure on this test would affect your educational and career goals. These fears are often completely irrational, but they can still negatively impact your test performance.

> **Review Video: 3 Reasons You Have Test Anxiety**
> Visit mometrix.com/academy and enter code: 428468

Elements of Test Anxiety

As mentioned earlier, test anxiety is considered to be an emotional state, but it has physical and mental components as well. Sometimes you may not even realize that you are suffering from test anxiety until you notice the physical symptoms. These can include trembling hands, rapid heartbeat, sweating, nausea, and tense muscles. Extreme anxiety may lead to fainting or vomiting. Obviously, any of these symptoms can have a negative impact on testing. It is important to recognize them as soon as they begin to occur so that you can address the problem before it damages your performance.

> **Review Video: 3 Ways to Tell You Have Test Anxiety**
> Visit mometrix.com/academy and enter code: 927847

The mental components of test anxiety include trouble focusing and inability to remember learned information. During a test, your mind is on high alert, which can help you recall information and stay focused for an extended period of time. However, anxiety interferes with your mind's natural processes, causing you to blank out, even on the questions you know well. The strain of testing during anxiety makes it difficult to stay focused, especially on a test that may take several hours. Extreme anxiety can take a huge mental toll, making it difficult not only to recall test information but even to understand the test questions or pull your thoughts together.

> **Review Video: How Test Anxiety Affects Memory**
> Visit mometrix.com/academy and enter code: 609003

Effects of Test Anxiety

Test anxiety is like a disease—if left untreated, it will get progressively worse. Anxiety leads to poor performance, and this reinforces the feelings of fear and failure, which in turn lead to poor performances on subsequent tests. It can grow from a mild nervousness to a crippling condition. If allowed to progress, test anxiety can have a big impact on your schooling, and consequently on your future.

Test anxiety can spread to other parts of your life. Anxiety on tests can become anxiety in any stressful situation, and blanking on a test can turn into panicking in a job situation. But fortunately, you don't have to let anxiety rule your testing and determine your grades. There are a number of relatively simple steps you can take to move past anxiety and function normally on a test and in the rest of life.

> **Review Video: How Test Anxiety Impacts Your Grades**
> Visit mometrix.com/academy and enter code: 939819

Physical Steps for Beating Test Anxiety

While test anxiety is a serious problem, the good news is that it can be overcome. It doesn't have to control your ability to think and remember information. While it may take time, you can begin taking steps today to beat anxiety.

Just as your first hint that you may be struggling with anxiety comes from the physical symptoms, the first step to treating it is also physical. Rest is crucial for having a clear, strong mind. If you are tired, it is much easier to give in to anxiety. But if you establish good sleep habits, your body and mind will be ready to perform optimally, without the strain of exhaustion. Additionally, sleeping well helps you to retain information better, so you're more likely to recall the answers when you see the test questions.

Getting good sleep means more than going to bed on time. It's important to allow your brain time to relax. Take study breaks from time to time so it doesn't get overworked, and don't study right before bed. Take time to rest your mind before trying to rest your body, or you may find it difficult to fall asleep.

> **Review Video: The Importance of Sleep for Your Brain**
> Visit mometrix.com/academy and enter code: 319338

Along with sleep, other aspects of physical health are important in preparing for a test. Good nutrition is vital for good brain function. Sugary foods and drinks may give a burst of energy but this burst is followed by a crash, both physically and emotionally. Instead, fuel your body with protein and vitamin-rich foods.

Also, drink plenty of water. Dehydration can lead to headaches and exhaustion, especially if your brain is already under stress from the rigors of the test. Particularly if your test is a long one, drink water during the breaks. And if possible, take an energy-boosting snack to eat between sections.

> **Review Video: How Diet Can Affect your Mood**
> Visit mometrix.com/academy and enter code: 624317

Along with sleep and diet, a third important part of physical health is exercise. Maintaining a steady workout schedule is helpful, but even taking 5-minute study breaks to walk can help get your blood pumping faster and clear your head. Exercise also releases endorphins, which contribute to a positive feeling and can help combat test anxiety.

When you nurture your physical health, you are also contributing to your mental health. If your body is healthy, your mind is much more likely to be healthy as well. So take time to rest, nourish your body with healthy food and water, and get moving as much as possible. Taking these physical steps will make you stronger and more able to take the mental steps necessary to overcome test anxiety.

Mental Steps for Beating Test Anxiety

Working on the mental side of test anxiety can be more challenging, but as with the physical side, there are clear steps you can take to overcome it. As mentioned earlier, test anxiety often stems from lack of preparation, so the obvious solution is to prepare for the test. Effective studying may be the most important weapon you have for beating test anxiety, but you can and should employ several other mental tools to combat fear.

First, boost your confidence by reminding yourself of past success—tests or projects that you aced. If you're putting as much effort into preparing for this test as you did for those, there's no reason you should expect to fail here. Work hard to prepare; then trust your preparation.

Second, surround yourself with encouraging people. It can be helpful to find a study group, but be sure that the people you're around will encourage a positive attitude. If you spend time with others who are anxious or cynical, this will only contribute to your own anxiety. Look for others who are motivated to study hard from a desire to succeed, not from a fear of failure.

Third, reward yourself. A test is physically and mentally tiring, even without anxiety, and it can be helpful to have something to look forward to. Plan an activity following the test, regardless of the outcome, such as going to a movie or getting ice cream.

When you are taking the test, if you find yourself beginning to feel anxious, remind yourself that you know the material. Visualize successfully completing the test. Then take a few deep, relaxing breaths and return to it. Work through the questions carefully but with confidence, knowing that you are capable of succeeding.

Developing a healthy mental approach to test taking will also aid in other areas of life. Test anxiety affects more than just the actual test—it can be damaging to your mental health and even contribute to depression. It's important to beat test anxiety before it becomes a problem for more than testing.

> **Review Video: Test Anxiety and Depression**
> Visit mometrix.com/academy and enter code: 904704

Study Strategy

Being prepared for the test is necessary to combat anxiety, but what does being prepared look like? You may study for hours on end and still not feel prepared. What you need is a strategy for test prep. The next few pages outline our recommended steps to help you plan out and conquer the challenge of preparation.

STEP 1: SCOPE OUT THE TEST

Learn everything you can about the format (multiple choice, essay, etc.) and what will be on the test. Gather any study materials, course outlines, or sample exams that may be available. Not only will this help you to prepare, but knowing what to expect can help to alleviate test anxiety.

STEP 2: MAP OUT THE MATERIAL

Look through the textbook or study guide and make note of how many chapters or sections it has. Then divide these over the time you have. For example, if a book has 15 chapters and you have five days to study, you need to cover three chapters each day. Even better, if you have the time, leave an extra day at the end for overall review after you have gone through the material in depth.

If time is limited, you may need to prioritize the material. Look through it and make note of which sections you think you already have a good grasp on, and which need review. While you are studying, skim quickly through the familiar sections and take more time on the challenging parts. Write out your plan so you don't get lost as you go. Having a written plan also helps you feel more in control of the study, so anxiety is less likely to arise from feeling overwhelmed at the amount to cover.

STEP 3: GATHER YOUR TOOLS

Decide what study method works best for you. Do you prefer to highlight in the book as you study and then go back over the highlighted portions? Or do you type out notes of the important information? Or is it helpful to make flashcards that you can carry with you? Assemble the pens, index cards, highlighters, post-it notes, and any other materials you may need so you won't be distracted by getting up to find things while you study.

If you're having a hard time retaining the information or organizing your notes, experiment with different methods. For example, try color-coding by subject with colored pens, highlighters, or post-it notes. If you learn better by hearing, try recording yourself reading your notes so you can listen while in the car, working out, or simply sitting at your desk. Ask a friend to quiz you from your flashcards, or try teaching someone the material to solidify it in your mind.

STEP 4: CREATE YOUR ENVIRONMENT

It's important to avoid distractions while you study. This includes both the obvious distractions like visitors and the subtle distractions like an uncomfortable chair (or a too-comfortable couch that makes you want to fall asleep). Set up the best study environment possible: good lighting and a comfortable work area. If background music helps you focus, you may want to turn it on, but otherwise keep the room quiet. If you are using a computer to take notes, be sure you don't have any other windows open, especially applications like social media, games, or anything else that could distract you. Silence your phone and turn off notifications. Be sure to keep water close by so you stay hydrated while you study (but avoid unhealthy drinks and snacks).

Also, take into account the best time of day to study. Are you freshest first thing in the morning? Try to set aside some time then to work through the material. Is your mind clearer in the afternoon or evening? Schedule your study session then. Another method is to study at the same time of day that you will take the test, so that your brain gets used to working on the material at that time and will be ready to focus at test time.

STEP 5: STUDY!

Once you have done all the study preparation, it's time to settle into the actual studying. Sit down, take a few moments to settle your mind so you can focus, and begin to follow your study plan. Don't give in to distractions or let yourself procrastinate. This is your time to prepare so you'll be ready to fearlessly approach the test. Make the most of the time and stay focused.

Of course, you don't want to burn out. If you study too long you may find that you're not retaining the information very well. Take regular study breaks. For example, taking five minutes out of every hour to walk briskly, breathing deeply and swinging your arms, can help your mind stay fresh.

As you get to the end of each chapter or section, it's a good idea to do a quick review. Remind yourself of what you learned and work on any difficult parts. When you feel that you've mastered the material, move on to the next part. At the end of your study session, briefly skim through your notes again.

But while review is helpful, cramming last minute is NOT. If at all possible, work ahead so that you won't need to fit all your study into the last day. Cramming overloads your brain with more information than it can process and retain, and your tired mind may struggle to recall even previously learned information when it is overwhelmed with last-minute study. Also, the urgent nature of cramming and the stress placed on your brain contribute to anxiety. You'll be more likely to go to the test feeling unprepared and having trouble thinking clearly.

So, don't cram, and don't stay up late before the test, even just to review your notes at a leisurely pace. Your brain needs rest more than it needs to go over the information again. In fact, plan to finish your studies by noon or early afternoon the day before the test. Give your brain the rest of the day to relax or focus on other things, and get a good night's sleep. Then you will be fresh for the test and better able to recall what you've studied.

STEP 6: TAKE A PRACTICE TEST

Many courses offer sample tests, either online or in the study materials. This is an excellent resource to check whether you have mastered the material, as well as to prepare for the test format and environment.

Check the test format ahead of time: the number of questions, the type (multiple choice, free response, etc.), and the time limit. Then create a plan for working through them. For example, if you have 30 minutes to take a 60-question test, your limit is 30 seconds per question. Spend less time on the questions you know well so that you can take more time on the difficult ones.

If you have time to take several practice tests, take the first one open book, with no time limit. Work through the questions at your own pace and make sure you fully understand them. Gradually work up to taking a test under test conditions: sit at a desk with all study materials put away and set a timer. Pace yourself to make sure you finish the test with time to spare and go back to check your answers if you have time.

After each test, check your answers. On the questions you missed, be sure you understand why you missed them. Did you misread the question (tests can use tricky wording)? Did you forget the information? Or was it something you hadn't learned? Go back and study any shaky areas that the practice tests reveal.

Taking these tests not only helps with your grade, but also aids in combating test anxiety. If you're already used to the test conditions, you're less likely to worry about it, and working through tests until you're scoring well gives you a confidence boost. Go through the practice tests until you feel comfortable, and then you can go into the test knowing that you're ready for it.

Test Tips

On test day, you should be confident, knowing that you've prepared well and are ready to answer the questions. But aside from preparation, there are several test day strategies you can employ to maximize your performance.

First, as stated before, get a good night's sleep the night before the test (and for several nights before that, if possible). Go into the test with a fresh, alert mind rather than staying up late to study.

Try not to change too much about your normal routine on the day of the test. It's important to eat a nutritious breakfast, but if you normally don't eat breakfast at all, consider eating just a protein bar. If you're a coffee drinker, go ahead and have your normal coffee. Just make sure you time it so that the caffeine doesn't wear off right in the middle of your test. Avoid sugary beverages, and drink enough water to stay hydrated but not so much that you need a restroom break 10 minutes into the test. If your test isn't first thing in the morning, consider going for a walk or doing a light workout before the test to get your blood flowing.

Allow yourself enough time to get ready, and leave for the test with plenty of time to spare so you won't have the anxiety of scrambling to arrive in time. Another reason to be early is to select a good seat. It's helpful to sit away from doors and windows, which can be distracting. Find a good seat, get out your supplies, and settle your mind before the test begins.

When the test begins, start by going over the instructions carefully, even if you already know what to expect. Make sure you avoid any careless mistakes by following the directions.

Then begin working through the questions, pacing yourself as you've practiced. If you're not sure on an answer, don't spend too much time on it, and don't let it shake your confidence. Either skip it and come back later, or eliminate as many wrong answers as possible and guess among the remaining ones. Don't dwell on these questions as you continue—put them out of your mind and focus on what lies ahead.

Be sure to read all of the answer choices, even if you're sure the first one is the right answer. Sometimes you'll find a better one if you keep reading. But don't second-guess yourself if you do immediately know the answer. Your gut instinct is usually right. Don't let test anxiety rob you of the information you know.

If you have time at the end of the test (and if the test format allows), go back and review your answers. Be cautious about changing any, since your first instinct tends to be correct, but make sure you didn't misread any of the questions or accidentally mark the wrong answer choice. Look over any you skipped and make an educated guess.

At the end, leave the test feeling confident. You've done your best, so don't waste time worrying about your performance or wishing you could change anything. Instead, celebrate the successful completion of this test. And finally, use this test to learn how to deal with anxiety even better next time.

> **Review Video: 5 Tips to Beat Test Anxiety**
> Visit mometrix.com/academy and enter code: 570656

Important Qualification

Not all anxiety is created equal. If your test anxiety is causing major issues in your life beyond the classroom or testing center, or if you are experiencing troubling physical symptoms related to your anxiety, it may be a sign of a serious physiological or psychological condition. If this sounds like your situation, we strongly encourage you to seek professional help.

How to Overcome Your Fear of Math

Not again. You're sitting in math class, look down at your test, and immediately start to panic. Your stomach is in knots, your heart is racing, and you break out in a cold sweat. You're staring at the paper, but everything looks like it's written in a foreign language. Even though you studied, you're blanking out on how to begin solving these problems.

Does this sound familiar? If so, then you're not alone! You may be like millions of other people who experience math anxiety. Anxiety about performing well in math is a common experience for students of all ages. In this article, we'll discuss what math anxiety is, common misconceptions about learning math, and tips and strategies for overcoming math anxiety.

What Is Math Anxiety?

Psychologist Mark H. Ashcraft explains math anxiety as a feeling of tension, apprehension, or fear that interferes with math performance. Having math anxiety negatively impacts people's beliefs about themselves and what they can achieve. It hinders achievement within the math classroom and affects the successful application of mathematics in the real world.

SYMPTOMS AND SIGNS OF MATH ANXIETY

To overcome math anxiety, you must recognize its symptoms. Becoming aware of the signs of math anxiety is the first step in addressing and resolving these fears.

NEGATIVE SELF-TALK

If you have math anxiety, you've most likely said at least one of these statements to yourself:

- "I hate math."
- "I'm not good at math."
- "I'm not a math person."

The way we speak to ourselves and think about ourselves matters. Our thoughts become our words, our words become our actions, and our actions become our habits. Thinking negatively about math creates a self-fulfilling prophecy. In other words, if you take an idea as a fact, then it will come true because your behaviors will align to match it.

AVOIDANCE

Some people who are fearful or anxious about math will tend to avoid it altogether. Avoidance can manifest in the following ways:

- Lack of engagement with math content
- Not completing homework and other assignments
- Not asking for help when needed
- Skipping class
- Avoiding math-related courses and activities

Avoidance is one of the most harmful impacts of math anxiety. If you steer clear of math at all costs, then you can't set yourself up for the success you deserve.

Lack of Motivation

Students with math anxiety may experience a lack of motivation. They may struggle to find the incentive to get engaged with what they view as a frightening subject. These students are often overwhelmed, making it difficult for them to complete or even start math assignments.

Procrastination

Another symptom of math anxiety is procrastination. Students may voluntarily delay or postpone their classwork and assignments, even if they know there will be a negative consequence for doing so. Additionally, they may choose to wait until the last minute to start projects and homework, even when they know they need more time to put forth their best effort.

Physiological Reactions

Many people with a fear of math experience physiological side effects. These may include an increase in heart rate, sweatiness, shakiness, nausea, and irregular breathing. These symptoms make it difficult to focus on the math content, causing the student even more stress and fear.

Strong Emotional Responses

Math anxiety also affects people on an emotional level. Responding to math content with strong emotions such as panic, anger, or despair can be a sign of math anxiety.

Low Test Scores and Performance

Low achievement can be both a symptom and a cause of math anxiety. When someone does not take the steps needed to perform well on tests and assessments, they are less likely to pass. The more they perform poorly, the more they accept this poor performance as a fact that can't be changed.

Feeling Alone

People who experience math anxiety feel like they are the only ones struggling, even if the math they are working on is challenging to many people. Feeling isolated in what they perceive as failure can trigger tension or nervousness.

Feeling of Permanency

Math anxiety can feel very permanent. You may assume that you are naturally bad at math and always will be. Viewing math as a natural ability rather than a skill that can be learned causes people to believe that nothing will help them improve. They take their current math abilities as fact and assume that they can't be changed. As a result, they give up, stop trying to improve, and avoid engaging with math altogether.

Lack of Confidence

People with low self-confidence in math tend to feel awkward and incompetent when asked to solve a math problem. They don't feel comfortable taking chances or risks when problem-solving because they second-guess themselves and assume they are incorrect. They don't trust in their ability to learn the content and solve problems correctly.

Panic

A general sense of unexplained panic is also a sign of math anxiety. You may feel a sudden sense of fear that triggers physical reactions, even when there is no apparent reason for such a response.

CAUSES OF MATH ANXIETY

Math anxiety can start at a young age and may have one or more underlying causes. Common causes of math anxiety include the following:

THE ATTITUDE OF PARENTS OR GUARDIANS

Parents often put pressure on their children to perform well in school. Although their intentions are usually good, this pressure can lead to anxiety, especially if the student is struggling with a subject or class.

Perhaps your parents or others in your life hold negative predispositions about math based on their own experiences. For instance, if your mother once claimed she was not good at math, then you might have incorrectly interpreted this as a predisposed trait that was passed down to you.

TEACHER INFLUENCE

Students often pick up on their teachers' attitudes about the content being taught. If a teacher is happy and excited about math, students are more likely to mirror these emotions. However, if a teacher lacks enthusiasm or genuine interest, then students are more inclined to disengage.

Teachers have a responsibility to cultivate a welcoming classroom culture that is accepting of mistakes. When teachers blame students for not understanding a concept, they create a hostile classroom environment where mistakes are not tolerated. This tension increases student stress and anxiety, creating conditions that are not conducive to inquiry and learning. Instead, when teachers normalize mistakes as a natural part of the problem-solving process, they give their students the freedom to explore and grapple with the math content. In such an environment, students feel comfortable taking chances because they are not afraid of being wrong.

Students need teachers that can help when they're having problems understanding difficult concepts. In doing so, educators may need to change how they teach the content. Since different people have unique learning styles, it's the job of the teacher to adapt to the needs of each student. Additionally, teachers should encourage students to explore alternate problem-solving strategies, even if it's not the preferred method of the educator.

FEAR OF BEING WRONG

Embarrassing situations can be traumatic, especially for young children and adolescents. These experiences can stay with people through their adult lives. Those with math anxiety may experience a fear of being wrong, especially in front of a group of peers. This fear can be paralyzing, interfering with the student's concentration and ability to focus on the problem at hand.

TIMED ASSESSMENTS

Timed assessments can help improve math fluency, but they often create unnecessary pressure for students to complete an unrealistic number of problems within a specified timeframe. Many studies have shown that timed assessments often result in increased levels of anxiety, reducing a student's overall competence and ability to problem-solve.

Debunking Math Myths

There are lots of myths about math that are related to the causes and development of math-related anxiety. Although these myths have been proven to be false, many people take them as fact. Let's go over a few of the most common myths about learning math.

Myth: Men Are Better at Math Than Women

Math has a reputation for being a male-dominant subject, but this doesn't mean that men are inherently better at math than women. Many famous mathematical discoveries have been made by women. Katherine Johnson, Dame Mary Lucy Cartwright, and Marjorie Lee Brown are just a few of the many famous women mathematicians. Expecting to be good or bad at math because of your gender sets you up for stress and confusion. Math is a skill that can be learned, just like cooking or riding a bike.

Myth: There Is Only One Good Way to Solve Math Problems

There are many ways to get the correct answer when it comes to math. No two people have the same brain, so everyone takes a slightly different approach to problem-solving. Moreover, there isn't one way of problem-solving that's superior to another. Your way of working through a problem might differ from someone else's, and that is okay. Math can be a highly individualized process, so the best method for you should be the one that makes you feel the most comfortable and makes the most sense to you.

Myth: Math Requires a Good Memory

For many years, mathematics was taught through memorization. However, learning in such a way hinders the development of critical thinking and conceptual understanding. These skill sets are much more valuable than basic memorization. For instance, you might be great at memorizing mathematical formulas, but if you don't understand what they mean, then you can't apply them to different scenarios in the real world. When a student is working from memory, they are limited in the strategies available to them to problem-solve. In other words, they assume there is only one correct way to do the math, which is the method they memorized. Having a variety of problem-solving options can help students figure out which method works best for them. Additionally, it provides students with a better understanding of how and why certain mathematical strategies work. While memorization can be helpful in some instances, it is not an absolute requirement for mathematicians.

Myth: Math Is Not Creative

Math requires imagination and intuition. Contrary to popular belief, it is a highly creative field. Mathematical creativity can help in developing new ways to think about and solve problems. Many people incorrectly assume that all things are either creative or analytical. However, this black-and-white view is limiting because the field of mathematics involves both creativity and logic.

Myth: Math Isn't Supposed To Be Fun

Whoever told you that math isn't supposed to be fun is a liar. There are tons of math-based activities and games that foster friendly competition and engagement. Math is often best learned through play, and lots of mobile apps and computer games exemplify this.

Additionally, math can be an exceptionally collaborative and social experience. Studying or working through problems with a friend often makes the process a lot more fun. The excitement and satisfaction of solving a difficult problem with others is quite rewarding. Math can be fun if you look for ways to make it more collaborative and enjoyable.

MYTH: NOT EVERYONE IS CAPABLE OF LEARNING MATH

There's no such thing as a "math person." Although many people think that you're either good at math or you're not, this is simply not true. Everyone is capable of learning and applying mathematics. However, not everyone learns the same way. Since each person has a different learning style, the trick is to find the strategies and learning tools that work best for you. Some people learn best through hands-on experiences, and others find success through the use of visual aids. Others are auditory learners and learn best by hearing and listening. When people are overwhelmed or feel that math is too hard, it's often because they haven't found the learning strategy that works best for them.

MYTH: GOOD MATHEMATICIANS WORK QUICKLY AND NEVER MAKE MISTAKES

There is no prize for finishing first in math. It's not a race, and speed isn't a measure of your ability. Good mathematicians take their time to ensure their work is accurate. As you gain more experience and practice, you will naturally become faster and more confident.

Additionally, everyone makes mistakes, including good mathematicians. Mistakes are a normal part of the problem-solving process, and they're not a bad thing. The important thing is that we take the time to learn from our mistakes, understand where our misconceptions are, and move forward.

MYTH: YOU DON'T NEED MATH IN THE REAL WORLD

Our day-to-day lives are so infused with mathematical concepts that we often don't even realize when we're using math in the real world. In fact, most people tend to underestimate how much we do math in our everyday lives. It's involved in an enormous variety of daily activities such as shopping, baking, finances, and gardening, as well as in many careers, including architecture, nursing, design, and sales.

Tips and Strategies for Overcoming Math Anxiety

If your anxiety is getting in the way of your level of mathematical engagement, then there are lots of steps you can take. Check out the strategies below to start building confidence in math today.

FOCUS ON UNDERSTANDING, NOT MEMORIZATION

Don't drive yourself crazy trying to memorize every single formula or mathematical process. Instead, shift your attention to understanding concepts. Those who prioritize memorization over conceptual understanding tend to have lower achievement levels in math. Students who memorize may be able to complete some math, but they don't understand the process well enough to apply it to different situations. Memorization comes with time and practice, but it won't help alleviate math anxiety. On the other hand, conceptual understanding will give you the building blocks of knowledge you need to build up your confidence.

REPLACE NEGATIVE SELF-TALK WITH POSITIVE SELF-TALK

Start to notice how you think about yourself. Whenever you catch yourself thinking something negative, try replacing that thought with a positive affirmation. Instead of continuing the negative thought, pause to reframe the situation. For ideas on how to get started, take a look at the table below:

Instead of thinking...	Try thinking...
"I can't do this math." "I'm not a math person."	"I'm up for the challenge, and I'm training my brain in math."
"This problem is too hard."	"This problem is hard, so this might take some time and effort. I know I can do this."
"I give up."	"What strategies can help me solve this problem?"
"I made a mistake, so I'm not good at this."	"Everyone makes mistakes. Mistakes help me to grow and understand."
"I'll never be smart enough."	"I can figure this out, and I am smart enough."

PRACTICE MINDFULNESS

Practicing mindfulness and focusing on your breathing can help alleviate some of the physical symptoms of math anxiety. By taking deep breaths, you can remind your nervous system that you are not in immediate danger. Doing so will reduce your heart rate and help with any irregular breathing or shakiness. Taking the edge off of the physiological effects of anxiety will clear your mind, allowing your brain to focus its energy on problem-solving.

DO SOME MATH EVERY DAY

Think about learning math as if you were learning a foreign language. If you don't use it, you lose it. If you don't practice your math skills regularly, you'll have a harder time achieving comprehension and fluency. Set some amount of time aside each day, even if it's just for a few minutes, to practice. It might take some discipline to build a habit around this, but doing so will help increase your mathematical self-assurance.

USE ALL OF YOUR RESOURCES

Everyone has a different learning style, and there are plenty of resources out there to support all learners. When you get stuck on a math problem, think about the tools you have access to, and use them when applicable. Such resources may include flashcards, graphic organizers, study guides, interactive notebooks, and peer study groups. All of these are great tools to accommodate your individual learning style. Finding the tools and resources that work for your learning style will give you the confidence you need to succeed.

REALIZE THAT YOU AREN'T ALONE

Remind yourself that lots of other people struggle with math anxiety, including teachers, nurses, and even successful mathematicians. You aren't the only one who panics when faced with a new or challenging problem. It's probably much more common than you think. Realizing that you aren't alone in your experience can help put some distance between yourself and the emotions you feel about math. It also helps to normalize the anxiety and shift your perspective.

Ask Questions

If there's a concept you don't understand and you've tried everything you can, then it's okay to ask for help! You can always ask your teacher or professor for help. If you're not learning math in a traditional classroom, you may want to join a study group, work with a tutor, or talk to your friends. More often than not, you aren't the only one of your peers who needs clarity on a mathematical concept. Seeking understanding is a great way to increase self-confidence in math.

Remember That There's More Than One Way To Solve a Problem

Since everyone learns differently, it's best to focus on understanding a math problem with an approach that makes sense to you. If the way it's being taught is confusing to you, don't give up. Instead, work to understand the problem using a different technique. There's almost always more than one problem-solving method when it comes to math. Don't get stressed if one of them doesn't make sense to you. Instead, shift your focus to what does make sense. Chances are high that you know more than you think you do.

Visualization

Visualization is the process of creating images in your mind's eye. Picture yourself as a successful, confident mathematician. Think about how you would feel and how you would behave. What would your work area look like? How would you organize your belongings? The more you focus on something, the more likely you are to achieve it. Visualizing teaches your brain that you can achieve whatever it is that you want. Thinking about success in mathematics will lead to acting like a successful mathematician. This, in turn, leads to actual success.

Focus on the Easiest Problems First

To increase your confidence when working on a math test or assignment, try solving the easiest problems first. Doing so will remind you that you are successful in math and that you do have what it takes. This process will increase your belief in yourself, giving you the confidence you need to tackle more complex problems.

Find a Support Group

A study buddy, tutor, or peer group can go a long way in decreasing math-related anxiety. Such support systems offer lots of benefits, including a safe place to ask questions, additional practice with mathematical concepts, and an understanding of other problem-solving explanations that may work better for you. Equipping yourself with a support group is one of the fastest ways to eliminate math anxiety.

Reward Yourself for Working Hard

Recognize the amount of effort you're putting in to overcome your math anxiety. It's not an easy task, so you deserve acknowledgement. Surround yourself with people who will provide you with the positive reinforcement you deserve.

Remember, You Can Do This!

Conquering a fear of math can be challenging, but there are lots of strategies that can help you out. Your own beliefs about your mathematical capabilities can limit your potential. Working toward a growth mindset can have a tremendous impact on decreasing math-related anxiety and building confidence. By knowing the symptoms of math anxiety and recognizing common misconceptions about learning math, you can develop a plan to address your fear of math. Utilizing the strategies discussed can help you overcome this anxiety and build the confidence you need to succeed.

Tell Us Your Story

We at Mometrix would like to extend our heartfelt thanks to you for letting us be a part of your journey. It is an honor to serve people from all walks of life, people like you, who are committed to building the best future they can for themselves.

We know that each person's situation is unique. But we also know that, whether you are a young student or a mother of four, you care about working to make your own life and the lives of those around you better.

That's why we want to hear your story.

We want to know why you're taking this test. We want to know about the trials you've gone through to get here. And we want to know about the successes you've experienced after taking and passing your test.

In addition to your story, which can be an inspiration both to us and to others, we value your feedback. We want to know both what you loved about our book and what you think we can improve on.

The team at Mometrix would be absolutely thrilled to hear from you! So please, send us an email at tellusyourstory@mometrix.com or visit us at mometrix.com/tellusyourstory.php and let's stay in touch.

Made in the USA
Middletown, DE
12 January 2023